Women and Folklore

Women and Folklore

A BIBLIOGRAPHIC SURVEY

Compiled by
Francis A. de Caro

GREENWOOD PRESS
Westport, Connecticut • London, England

Library of Congress Cataloging in Publication Data

De Caro, F. A.
   Women and folklore.

   Includes index.
   1. Women—Folklore—Bibliography.   2. Folklore—
Bibliography.   I. Title.
Z5983.W65D4   1983   016.398′088042   83-12837
[GR470]
ISBN 0-313-23821-9

Copyright © 1983 by Francis A. de Caro

Library of Congress Catalog Card Number: 83-12837
ISBN 0-313-23821-9

First published in 1983

Greenwood Press
A division of Congressional Information Service, Inc.
88 Post Road West, Westport, Connecticut 06881

Printed in the United States of America

10 9 8 7 6 5 4 3 2 1

CONTENTS

ACKNOWLEDGMENTS

In compiling this bibliographic survey I have had the assistance of a number of individuals to whom I am grateful. In the early stages of the work Rosan Jordan provided many suggestions, and Susan Kalčik was especially helpful in my dealing with the section on fieldwork. They both kindly provided me access to the manuscript of their forthcoming collection of essays, *Women's Folklore, Women's Culture.* Danielle Roemer sent me an unpublished bibliographic essay. Susan Roach-Lankford and Yvonne Milspaw both gave me the benefit of their knowledge of the literature on quilting. Mary Ellen Brown provided me with some references from British sources, and Dick Bauman suggested several references also. Marta Weigle had many helpful suggestions to make, sent me copies of her *Spiders and Spinsters: Women and Mythology* in both an early draft and final stage of its development, and gave me sympathetic encouragement.

INTRODUCTION

Note: Numbers given parenthetically refer to entry numbers for citations in the bibliography.

The past decade has seen a remarkable growth in the awareness of women's contributions to society and culture and in the realization of the fact that women, whose significance in art, science, and the very functioning of society itself has commonly been ignored or misassessed, must as a group and as individuals be studied and correctly understood if we are to study and understand the human condition. The attempt to study women and their true psychological and social roles has only just begun, but it has begun with great vigor and enthusiasm. Women's studies programs have evolved at a number of universities, several very good journals have appeared in this developing field, and publishers have brought out some basic relevant volumes. This has, of course, been pioneering, catch-up activity in various fields of study, an attempt to fill in some vast gaps in our record of knowledge. For example, recent folkloristic commentators and those in the closely allied science of anthropology have been unanimous in agreeing that women by and large have been ignored in past studies of society. For example, Hammond and Jablow state:

Until recently most anthropologists saw little reason to pay special attention to women, viewing any concentration on them as a diversion from the mainstream of anthropology. In most monographs women are present merely as shadowy figures as a background for the activities of men, and only the bare bones of women's roles are described. (676: Preface [n.p.])

A similar opinion was voiced earlier by Rosaldo and Lamphere, who cast the blame on "our own culture's ideological bias in treating women as relatively invisible," which has caused anthropologists to describe "largely the activities and interests of men" (1332: pp. 1-2). Observations much the same are made by Sol Tax in his general editor's preface to Raphael:

Former anthropological reports have been lopsided; . . . females essentially have been overlooked in the ethnographic literature; . . . most ethnographies were made by males and about male activities; . . . the viewing of the world from a male vantage point has distorted our understanding and slowed our science. (1267: p. v)

Specifically in terms of folklore studies, Claire Farrer has noted that:

The general trend throughout the history of the *Journal* [*of American Folklore*] has been to rely on data from women for information about health, charms, some games, and various beliefs and customs but in other areas to use women as informants only when men informants were unavailable.

The journal was not the only one following such a course. Similar patterns appear in regional publications. . . . The trend is also evident in collections. (503: p. viii)

She adds that "when a collector had a choice between a story told by a man or as told by a woman, the man's version was chosen" (see no. 118, for example) and terms "lip service" the attention which folklorists have paid "to the importance of women's expressive behavior" (p. vii). Marta Weigle comments on and seconds Farrer's assessment, noting that women's

skills and communications must be discovered and documented if we are to comprehend and appreciate *all* human arts.

In this respect, alas, folklorists, anthropologists, mythologists, sociologists, and other students of oral tradition have been remiss in their investigations of the verbal arts both cross-culturally and within the United States. (1598: p. 2)

A standard textbook (Brunvand, 242: p. 19) notes that as an area of study "women's folklore has barely been sketched out."

These observations about the state of past studies are accurate. It must not be imagined, however, that there is no body of literature relating to women's folklore and culture. Rosaldo and Lamphere (1332: p. 1) point out that there are exceptions to the neglect anthropological science has shown women, for example, "a handful of ethnographies that take a woman's perspective." Farrer (503) and Weigle (1598) discuss contributions as well as omissions, and scholars in other fields have found a great mass of information on women, gathered in various ways and for various reasons. Not unexpectedly, one facet of the burst of intellectual inquiry into the lives and accomplishments of women has been the compilation of bibliographies. If women are to be reassessed in the light of modern, nonsexist perspectives, a great mass of information must be ordered. Bibliographies, of course, are one tool for ordering information and making it more accessible.

A number of bibliographies relating to women have been published in recent years. Many of them are quite good and useful, especially given the fact that they are incursions into uncharted territory, attempts to investigate a subject that has been neglected. Several of them, such as those dealing with women in a particular culture area, have included folklore entries, or have covered areas broad enough to encompass folkloristics as a field of study, such as Jacobs (783), a bibliography which deals with women in cultural studies. However, due to the limitations that mark even good, carefully compiled bibliographies, folklore relevant to women and women's studies has not fared particularly well at the hands of bibliographers, and much information about the folklore of and about women is not easily found even if one searches through a number of bibliographies. Jacobs, for example, lumps folklore and mythology in with literature and provides only a few basic folklore entries.

The present bibliography is intended, then, to fill the need for a reference tool which brings together knowledge about what has been published on women's folklore, folklore about women, and related topics. It contains over 1,600 entries concerned directly or indirectly with women's folklore and folklore about women, and it has no pretense to being all-inclusive. It is intended to be indicative of some of the work of the past and suggestive of possibilities for the future. Certainly there is still a body of literature to be searched for further information on folklore relevant to women, though that may at times mean "scavenging the literature for the parenthetical remarks, footnotes, and addenda" (Hammond and Jablow, 676: Preface [n.p.]). One thinks, for example, of such vast compendia of folklore data as Brand and Ellis (201), Child (309), Frazer (549), and Thompson (1516). There are also large areas that have been touched on lightly in the following bibliography, such as folk costume and wedding customs, which at least theoretically should concern men and women equally. With a few exceptions, only English-language materials have been included.

This bibliography is intended in part as a reference work for folklorists. The realization that women's folklore exists has revolutionary implications for folklore studies in many instances, raising questions about the contexts in which folklore is performed, about genres, and about what folklorists, usually male, have considered "important" and "unimportant." It is hoped, however, that this bibliography will also be of use to other students of culture who are interested in women in society, for folkloristics is very much a cross-disciplinary field and even today, decades after the initiation of university folklore programs to train specialists in this area, many persons who would identify themselves as folklorists were trained as literary scholars, or anthropologists, or historians. Folkloristics touches on a number of other fields, anthropology, linguistics, literature, history, fine arts, psychology—this list is not exhaustive—and, indeed, many key works in the study of folklore were penned primarily from the perspectives of other disciplines.

Knowledge of women and folklore may aid in the study of women in other disciplines. Take, for example, the area of "image," important in literature, sociology, history, and popular culture studies. There is a crucial need to investigate the images of women that have been projected

down through the centuries, whether we are analyzing literature, painting, advertising, or films and the broadcast media; to understand
stereotypes of women is to understand how women have been perceived
and misperceived and how perceptions have bolstered injustices and
falsehoods. As a basic means of face-to-face communication and as a
cultural universal, folklore is a fundamental source of stereotypes, of
images of women, positive and negative, which may be far more deep-
seated and pervasive than the creations of individual authors or film-
makers or advertising copywriters. Folklore projects beliefs, ideas,
attitudes; and because women, who have often been denied full access to
many of the expressive media, have always created their own folklore,
this women's folklore can also be of great value in determining women's
self-conceptions, which may not be expressed fully or at all in other
forms. As Murphy and Murphy (1129) found in their penetrating study
of the world of women in a South American tribe, women's folklore may
project an "ideology," as they termed it, quite at variance with the male
view of things.

Folkloristics also offers insights into other areas, into the study of
women as visual and plastic artists, for example. Not only have women
not had their full share of recognition as artists, but they have been
excluded from a full measure of participation in the fine arts dominated
by male practitioners. But there have been art forms dominated by
women and many of these fall within the range of folk and vernacular
forms. Quilting is one such form that has received fairly considerable
attention, but there are many other "domestic" arts as well through
which women have found aesthetic expression; and folklore, really the
only discipline that has been concerned at all with the aesthetics of
"everyday" life and of vernacular culture, has an important role to play
in the appraisal and appreciation of art forms like samplers or knitted
goods or even the various salvage forms that often may be denigrated as
"hobby" arts, yet that are forms of human expression which should not
be ignored as part of the cultural record.

Verbal art has been the principal concern of folklorists, however, at
least in the United States, and in the last few years the transmission of
verbal art increasingly has come to be viewed within the theoretical
perspective of *performance*. The verbal artists who sing folksongs or
narrate folk stories are to be seen as performers and, indeed, this perspective has served to remind folklorists that folklore consists of not just
a collection of texts but of innumerable human speech acts set in particular social contexts with particular audiences and serving particular
human needs. Thus folklore is an important form of human communication and one important facet of studies of performance, whether we
mean by that term something that fits conventional use, like what
happens on the stage of a theater, or something much broader, such as

the rules for human interaction in general, as studied, for example, by Irving Goffman (602, 603). Men and women perform differently, in different contexts under different rules and by presenting different manners; an understanding of female performance styles in the larger context of human communication is essential to a balanced understanding of human beings as performers and communicators, and women's performance of folk materials is basic to such an understanding.

Also because folklore is cross-disciplinary, a number of works not by folklorists or only indirectly relevant to folklore have been included in the bibliography to call them to the attention of students of folklore. Folklorists study not only verbal art but other aspects of human culture —customs, rituals, cooking, goddesses, music, and games, to name a few. They study many aspects of material culture, such as quilting. They study people who are folk performers, icluding facets of their lives which may have little or nothing to do directly with their being tradition bearers. This is one of the reasons, for example, why life histories have been included in this bibliography. Some are biographies of folk artists. Others provide insights into the lives of women growing up in folk societies or into women whose lives have been shaped by folklore and folklife in some significant way. (Life histories also relate, of course, to biographical oral narratives, a form of folklore, and folklorists have been interested in life histories as an extended use of oral data in the study of culture.)

A number of basic works in other fields have been included, then, partly because they are basic and folklorists who would study women need to be aware of them because folklore interconnects with these fields. Anthropology is the obvious sister discipline, but literature, psychology, history, and popular culture are also included here. In addition to listing these works, often bibliographies, because they are fundamental to related areas, an attempt has been made to call attention to aspects of these works which are of greatest relevance to folkloristics and of the most interest to folklorists. Thus relevant sections of bibliographies are mentioned (such as "Folklore and Witchcraft" in no. 1340), chapters in general anthropological works are noted (for example, "Women and Ritual" in no. 878), and ethnographies containing various kinds of folkloric data are singled out.

The present bibliographic survey consists of two main parts, an Essay Guide and the Bibliography proper. The Essay Guide discusses individually and comparatively, works listed in the bibliography. It is presented in two broad sections, "General Works on Culture," which surveys sources in a number of related fields, and "Folklore," which describes and analyzes works more specifically concerned with folklore and folklife. The Guide is further divided by types of materials and topical areas (see table of contents), and a subject index provides greater differentiation. All 1,664 citations are listed alphabetically in the Bibliography. Each entry is preceded by a code number to which the Essay Guide (and this Introduction) refer.

A recent collection of essays, Farrer (504) has been an especially important contribution in advancing the study of women and folklore, and a second, forthcoming collection (Jordan and Kalčik, 835) promises to be of considerable significance also in bringing folklore studies to a level at which it can be said that folklorists have begun to give serious and concentrated attention to the subject. It is hoped that the present bibliography will make a further contribution by giving folklorists and others a tool that will assist them to bring this study to even greater maturity.

ESSAY GUIDE

GENERAL WORKS
ON CULTURE

Of course the interests of the folklorist concerned
with women's folklore must extend to the larger questions of
women in culture and society, and there are a number of
useful and important works which deal with this broad area,
many of them recent and part of an impressive, growing body
of literature on the subject. There are number of valuable
general and specialized bibliographies, and various
collections of essays, as well as book length treatments in
the social sciences and related humanities fields.

Ballou (91) is a survey of bibliographies relating to
research on women and hence of primary importance. Rosenberg
and Bergstrom (1340) provide an extensive review of the
literature as well as an annotated bibliography which
includes a listing of other bibliographies in addition to
citations under such categories as Sex Roles, Socialization,
Life Styles, Manners and Customs, Folklore and Witchcraft,
and Women in Ethnic Minorities. Jacobs (783) is an essential
and pioneering bibliography arranged in two ways,
geographically and in terms of certain subject categories
like Women and Religion, Women and War, and Misogyny. There
is a section on Women in Literature, Mythology, and Folk
Tradition, but relatively few folklore-relevant sources are
actually listed.

Recent anthropological work relating to women has been
surveyed by Holzberg (749), Lamphere (936), Rapp (1269), and
Stack, Caulfield, Estes, Landes, Larson, Johnson, Rake, and
Shirek (1448). A similar task has been performed for
sociological literature by Huber (764) and Lopata (1001).
The history of anthropological science is probed by Fee
(507), who finds in Victorian culture studies an attempt to
counter feminist challenges to the institution of marriage.
See also Schlachter and Belli (1376), a guide to social
scientific reference literature. Haber's bibliography for
American women (664) includes such categories as Sex Roles,
Life Styles, Black Women, and Native American Women.
Stineman, Loeb, and Walton (1466) is a bibliography of
recent works relating to non-white women. Green, a
folklorist, surveys (644) the literature on Native American
women, much of it of some relevance to folklore, which she
sees as not yet "a fully developed body of literature,"
though there has been an increasingly vigorous tradition of
writing since 1960. Cardinale (274) provides a guide to
several hundred anthologies "by and about women," some of
them relevant to the study of women in culture and society,
and Williamson (1635) is a bibliography of bibliographies
and catalogues of the "new feminist scholarship." Hays (706)
is significant as a general treatment of the fear of women
in broad social context.

There are several anthropologically-oriented basic introductions to women in culture. Martin and Voorhies state the objective of their volume as follows: "This book investigates over one-half of humanity, not only from the perspective of today's diverse societies, but from the dim beginnings of the species itself [in order] to gain a clear understanding of the myriad definitions and functions of female and male behavior, and of the way societies manipulate sex to achieve efficient adaptations to their physical and social environments" (1041: p. 1). They discuss the biological aspects of sex, personality traits thought to be sex-linked by middle-class Americans (finding no correlation between sex and these traits as exhibited in behavior when the question is considered cross-culturally), and the relationship between biological sex and social gender classifications (including here some attention to folk classifications for sex). A chapter is devoted to non-human primates and one to how anthropological science has viewed women and sex roles. The last five chapters of the book treat woman as gatherer and women in horticultural, agricultural, pastoral, and industrial societies.

Friedl (558) writes in the context of controversy over sex roles and the debate over whether these roles are biologically or culturally determined (see also Tiger, 1518, and Fried, 555). She is concerned with several basic propositions about what determines sex roles, such as the subsistence technology of a society and its related organizational systems and the control of extradomestic exchange. The book is divided into two parts, one dealing with hunting and gathering societies, the other with horticultural ones; comparisons are drawn between the two, and sections are devoted to examinations of several particular "illustrative cultures." The author is very sensitive to the importance of ritual and ceremonial as symbolic statements of sex role differences.

Kessler (878) is also to be seen as "an attempt to explore the origins of present [sex] role-determination, and to offer a view of alternative relationships as they are structured in various societies past and present." Topics surveyed include biological aspects, puberty rituals, women in the context of the archaeological record, technology and economics, and social organizations. A chapter is devoted to Women and Ritual. Particularly interesting is the second half of the book, called Silhouettes, a number of chapters which draw upon life histories and ethnographies to "let women speak for themselves." Much of this material is of relevance to folklorists.

Hammond and Jablow (676) organize their work by first dealing with Women and the Family, discussing in more or less chronological order a woman's progress through life in traditional societies, then with Women and the Economy. They pay some attention to rituals and to crafts. Their first chapter is taken up with a discussion of the theory of matriarchy, "a relic of Victorian thought"; this should be of interest to folklorists, as proponents of the idea that matriarchy was once the predominant form of social organization (see Bachofen, 81; Briffault, 211; Cothran, 351; Davis, 380; Diner, 416; Hultkrantz, 770; Matossian, 1048; Pomeroy, 1240; Reed, 1274) often use myth and other folklore in the context of their arguments. Borun, McLaughlin, Oboler, Perchonock, and Sexton also discuss matriarchy briefly (182: pp. 7-9) in their attempt to mediate between extreme anthropological positions relating to women. Their short monograph presents a balanced and readable feminist introduction to how anthropology views women and to the relevance of the field to the Women's Liberation Movement. They touch on ritual, myth, and cultural ideology. Newton and Webster (1150) and Zahler (1660) survey some of the literature on matriarchy.

Several **collections of essays compiled by anthropologists** are of interest also, though, naturally, as unified wholes they are more diffuse in their approaches than the works just noted above. Raphael (1267) organizes nearly thirty essays into three sections: Reproduction (biological aspects, birth rituals, definitions of marriage, etc.); Women and Power; and Social Trends (attitudes, concepts of femininity, family customs, etc.). Folklorists will be most interested in the essays by Newton (1151), Raphael (1268), Lomax (998), and Kurian and John (928). Reiter (1286) contains an extensive bibliography in addition to eighteen essays; in this volume folklorists will be most interested in essays by Harding (684) and Silverman (1407). Other important collections of essays include Caplan and Bujra (272), Rosaldo and Lamphere (1332), Barker and Allen (99), Rohrlich-Leavitt (1324), Safilios-Rothschild (1359), an anthology of sociological essays, and Tiffany (1517), a "reader" of previously published anthropological pieces.

Gornick and Moran (623) is an eclectic assortment of writings dealing with society, psychology, mass media, stereotypes, sex roles, and other issues; see especially nos. 622, 959, 1043. Ardener (64) contains several interesting papers, with the emphasis of the volume being upon how groups of women perceive themselves and how outsiders perceive them. Among the groups considered are Gypsy women, nuns, and British diplomats' wives. A volume on women in non-Western religions put together to get away from studies which "focused quite literally on religious man," Falk and Gross (494) contains several essays on ritual and ceremonial which are listed separately and discussed below. See also nos. 1086, 1330.

There are a handful of **ethnographies** which concentrate on women's culture, such as the pioneering work by Landes (938) which treats the life cycle of Ojibwa women and provides a very full description of the lives of women in that culture. Fernea's works on Arab women (510, 511) are very personal in their approach and highly readable. Weiner's study (1608) concentrates on women and the power of women in Trobriand society. It is especially important as a corrective to the work of Malinowski, who "deemed Trobriand women unworthy of careful study" and hence did not always provide an accurate picture. Women's ceremonies and weaving are among areas discussed. Goodale (616) structures her

study of Tiwi women around women's life cycles and includes
discussion of women's roles in ceremonies; she also briefly
touches on mythology and art. Kaberry (845) worked with the
aboriginal populations of North Western Australia, and her
book on the women of this area includes discussion of
women's ceremonies and women's corroborees. Chiñas (311)
concentrates specifically on women's roles among the Isthmus
Zapotecs. Murphy and Murphy (1129) is of great interest to
folklorists and deals with questions of women's cultures and
ideology. Roper (1328) includes information on festivals,
ceremonies, and music. Strathern (1486) is concerned with
women's roles in New Guinea and gives some attention to
ritual, ceremony, myth, and songs. Siskind's ethnography of
the Sharanahua of Peru (1413) gives careful attention to
women in that group and to interaction between the sexes;
songs, games, and myths are among the folklore genres
included. Friedl (558: pp. 146-148) lists and gives brief
descriptions of fourteen case studies from the Holt,
Rinehart, and Winston series Case Studies in Cultural
Anthropology which contain materials on sex roles; several
of these also include folkloric data. See also nos. 69, 119,
130, 213, 348, 673, 782, 844, 897, 981, 1003, 1028, 1033,
1260, 1643.

For other anthropological perspectives, see nos. 63,
491, 493, 557, 588, 700, 796, 918, 958, 1044, 1185, 1331,
1367, 1378, 1495, 1569, 1600. Shanklin (1395) reviews twelve
current books dealing with women and anthropology.

For general anthropological works on marriage and
related subjects such as bridewealth and dowries, see Fox
(540), Goody and Tambiah (619), Mair (1027), and, for
extensive information on marriage and mate-selection seen
cross-culturally, Kurian (927).

In addition to ethnographies of specific groups of
women, there are a number of more **general and
bibliographic works devoted to the women of a nation or
region**. For the women of North Africa and the Middle East,
see the bibliography compiled by Al-Qazzaz (26), which
includes sections on Sex Roles, Rural Women, Ethnology, and
Ethnolinguistics; and that compiled by Raccagni (1256).
Fernea and Bezirgan (512) is an excellent anthology of
materials relevant to Middle Eastern women; included are
selections from the Koran, memoirs, short stories,
folksongs, and biographical sketches of women in traditional
and non-traditional societies. For other works relating to
Middle Eastern women see nos. 461, 592, 776, 1188. For
Jewish women see the bibliography by Cantor (268). For
Africa there is Hafkin and Bay (667), a collection of essays
concerned primarily with economic history; Paulme (1217),
also an anthology but with an extensive analytical
bibliography; Bick (154), concerned with the rights and the
power of women; and Obbo (1164) which deals with the
migration of African women to towns. Scobie (1384) is a film
maker's "safari into the private lives of African women" and
contains some data on folklore, informally observed. For
India see Dasgupta, Usha, Saxena, and Mathur (379), an
annotated bibliography which contains a number of entries of

interest to folklorists in Society and Women and Women in Art and Culture sections; Jain (787), a collection of rather general essays; no. 1346; and Misra (1093), who deals with the women of the Mughal Empire in the sixteenth to eighteenth centuries and includes discussion of a number of their activities relevant to the folklorist.

Knaster (903) is an extensive, annotated bibliography of the women of Spanish America and includes sections on Literature, Mass Media and Folklore, Magic, Religion and Ritual, and Ethnographic Monographs/Community Studies; Cabello-Argandoña, Gomez-Quiñones, and Duran (262) fills the same role for the Chicana of the United States; the compilers include a section entitled Culture and Cultural Processes and Folk Culture. An article by Stevens (1460) details the Latin ideology of marianismo, which asserts female spiritual superiority over men and which the author sees as complementing the male ideal of machismo.

Dixson (418) is a social history of women in Australia. Gale (572) is a collection of diverse essays, all originally presented at a symposium, on Australian aboriginal women. Medicine (1072) consists of a short but valuable bibliography of the role of women in American Indian groups though Bataille (111) is more recent. Also more recent and much more extensive is a bibliography compiled by a folklorist (Green, 645), though it covers a wide range of topics; see also nos. 60, 1973, 1155.

Appalachia as a region has always exercised an important influence on American folklore studies; Appalachian women are covered bibliographically by Farr (499). Gould's profusely illustrated work on the women of British Columbia (629) has an historical-biographical orientation and includes some descriptions of folklife. For Asian women see Bacon (83) and Wolf and Witke (1644). Joyce and Thomas (840) represents an early attempt to compile information on the manners of living of women in a great number of the world's cultures; Cooper (335) and Houghton (759) are similar but for more restricted areas. Patai (1214) contains a number of articles by different authors, each giving certain basic facts on the women of a particular country.

The whole question of **sex roles** is central to any discussion of women in culture, and a large body of research material in this area has built up over the years. For bibliographies of this material see Biggar (155), Friedman (562), Harper and Meeks (687), Oetzel (1166), and Spiegel (1436). Sells (1392) deals with current research. Barry, Bacon, and Child (106) deal with differences in socialization by sex in cross-cultural perspective. D'Andrade (378) reviews "some of the ways in which sex differences have been culturally institutionalized." Sex roles as conceived by Freud and Engels are compared by Ewing (492). Hoffer (739) is a study of sex roles and political power, focusing on a female paramount chief in an African society. For the relationship between religion and women's traditional sex roles see McMurray (1064).

Mulhare (1125) considers "sex as part of a cultural system" and sex roles in relation to other aspects of society, in this instance pre-Castro Cuba. Shapiro (1396) also relates sex roles to social structure, here for a South American Indian group, and includes discussion of daily activities and ritual and ceremonial occasions. For general discussion see Filene (518), who traces the evolution of American sex roles from late Victorian times, and Oakley (1162). Several folkloristic works have dealt with the study of sex roles, such as Gorfain and Glazier (621), where myth is used in a consideration of symbols as a way of understanding sex roles, McLeod and Herndon (1063), and Mills (1098). St. John (1360) is a short study of how sexual stereotyping affected the career of a woman of words, not a folk performer but a radio broadcast pioneer. See also nos. 5, 107, 173, 187, 241, 313, 412, 419, 482, 484, 532, 664, 696, 850, 886, 909, 910, 911, 912, 1067, 1068, 1081, 1132, 1194, 1209, 1275, 1309, 1340, 1391, 1392, 1527, 1568.

The **psychology of women** is also an area in which there has been considerable recent interest and re-evaluation. There are several useful bibliographies and bibliographic surveys: Javonovich, Littenberg, Maxfield, Muller, Resnick, Rosenthal, Schary, and Wortis (798), Parlee (1199), Shearman (1397), and Vaughter (1549); Jacobs (783: pp. 126-132) has a section on psychological studies. Deutsch (408), Horney (756), and Thompson (1511) are the works of an older generation of women psychologists. Klein (898) traces the development of the "ideology" of "the feminine character." Chesler (307) deals specifically with the question of women and insanity from a feminist perspective and has been widely read. See also Blum (171), a collection of essays; Miller (1084), an anthology; and nos. 984, 1105, 1489, 1633. Kessler (878) includes a chaper entitled An Anthropological View of the Psychology of Women. Weigle, a folklorist, has discussed various Jungian approaches (1593).

For bibliography on **women in historical perspective** see the following: Goodwater (618; women in antiquity), Kelly-Gadol, Engel, and Casey (870; European women), Frey, Frey, and Schneider (554; women in western Europe from antiquity to the French Revolution), and Sicherman (1401; a review of recent work in American history). See also no. 70.

For discussions of women in antiquity, see Brittain (223), Seltman (1392), and Pomeroy (1239), a social history of Greek and Roman women aimed at supplementing our knowledge of the lives of ancient men which is especially of interest to folklorists as it deals with the relevance of mythic figures. Medieval women are dealt with by Morewedge (1119); Stuard (1490), a collection or rather specialized essays; and Walker (1565). Clark (315) deals with women at work in seventeenth-century England. Boulding (186) is an ambitious "view of women through time" which takes an ethnological-social perspective.

Each essay in Bridenthal and Koonz (210) deals with women in the context of a particular historical period in Europe. Bullough and Bullough (249) trace attitudes toward women from the ancient Near East to modern America, with attention given to Islam, China, and India. Carroll (286) is an important collection of historical essays, including theoretical essays and several on women in historical writing.

Of somewhat greater direct interest to folklore is Hartman and Banner (697), a collection of essays specifically dealing with aspects of social history. For American colonial women, see nos. 132, 411, 744, 1447. DePauw, Hunt, and Schneir (406) is a profusely illustrated volume which treats the lives and life styles of American women, 1750-1815; some attention is given to folk art and broadsides. Popular magazines are the chief source for a discussion by Welter (1614) of the nineteenth century ideal of womanhood. Scott (1385) treats the culturally-defined image of the Southern lady, 1830-1930, its effect on women's behavior, the reality of Southern women's lives, and the struggle to abandon the stereotype. The world of American pioneer women on the Overland Trail is dealt with by Faragher and Stansell (496) and by Faragher (497); the latter quotes folkloric sources and both works skirt areas of folklife, though each is more significant in terms of dealing with women as a subcultural group and the different worlds of men and women. A folklorist, Stoeltje (1496), deals with the image of the frontier woman. For women in American social history see also Baxandall, Gordon, and Revesby (114), an anthology of materials drawn from histories as well as newspapers, pamphlets, and archival sources; Dickinson (415); Dingwall (417), who concentrates on sexual morality; Millstein and Bodin (1089), a collection of documents; and nos. 568, 1403, 1422. See Lavrin (950) for Latin America; MacCurtain and Ó Corráin (1014) on Ireland; and nos. 296, 570, 973, 1167, 1403, 1553.

Literary scholars, predominantly those who are feminists, have recently expended prodigious energy on studies of women writers, the images of women in literature, and related topics. For reviews of some recent trends see Kaplan (857) and Kolodny (908). Register (1276) is a "bibliographic introduction" to American feminist criticism. The image of women in literary works, related to folk conceptions and other cultural stereotypes, is probably of greatest interest to folklorists. Deegan (398) deals with how single women have been dealt with in American novels. Ferrante (513) treats the question of "woman as image" in the context of the literature of the Middle Ages.

The stereotyping "in fact and in fiction" of nineteenth-century women and the tensions between women's aspirations and social expectations in several novels is the subject of Siefert (1405). Stewart (1481) deals with British and American novels, 1877-1977, and the figure of the "artist as heroine" in these novels. Ferguson (509) is an anthology of literary works arranged in groups which reflect social stereotyping of women (such as "the old maid"), and Jones and Arthurs (814) use literary sources to suggest the image of American women in cultural-historical perspective. Cornillon (349) contains a number of essays on women's traditional and non-traditional roles in literature, theoretical essays, and an annotated bibliography, mostly of literary works. Rogers (1323) is a history of misogyny in literature. Meese (1074), folklorist as well as literary scholar, comments on how male conceptions of genre and "universality" have affected how women's literature is viewed; this is relevant to male/female aesthetics in general. Broner and Davidson (226) is a collection of essays on mothers and daughters in literature; several individual essays on folk literature are noted separately below. See also nos. 70, 178, 717, 856, 1100, 1317.

Several writers have dealt with **the images of women in popular expressive culture**, including Douglas (432) and Weibel (1580). Higashi (730) is concerned with the American silent movie heroine and sees the jazz age heroines produced by Hollywood as mirroring various social changes. Mellen (1075) and Siclier (1402) also discuss film, and the time period of each roughly complements the other, though the latter writes only of American films. The visual stereotype of the American black woman in the mass media is taken up by Jewell (803). Cole and Robinson (326) present the history of women in American cartoons.

In a broader discussion of sex, class, and culture Robinson (1317) includes chapters on images of women in popular literature and on television. For a general review of recent literature on how women have been depicted by the mass media, see Tuchman (1528). Fishburn (526) is an extensive bibliography of women in popular culture.

Pioneering studies of women in society from a feminist perspective by non-social scientists include de Beauvoir (392), Friedan (556), and Firestone (522).

For the point of view of economics, see Boserup (183) and Glazer and Waeher (598).

FOLKLORE

As early as 1899 Isabel Cushman Chamberlain had compiled a bibliography of eighty-nine items dealing with folklore relating to women (298), though no other bibliography on the subject appeared in print until Farrer and Kalcik (506) in 1973. The latter bibliography, with brief annotations, deals only with the Journal of American Folklore and was intended to supplement existing indexes to that publication, which had no listings for women. Given the pre-eminent position of the Journal in American folkloristics, Farrer and Kalcik's bibliography is extremely useful and with it one can easily survey the interest (or lack thereof) which American folklorists have taken in women over the years. Langlois (944) includes a "working bibliography," useful though the entries are not complete. In 1903 Alexander Chamberlain surveyed the role women played in performing folklore in various primitive cultures (297), but nothing similar appeared for many years.

Thiselton-Dyer produced his Folklore of Women (1510) during the first decade of this century and, despite its limitations, this book has been viewed as a basic work on women and folklore. No attempt is made in this volume, however, to discuss women's folklore. Rather, the author, relying most heavily on proverbs (but including also superstitions, rhymes, and other forms), deals with women as depicted in folklore by dividing his discussion into chapters which note how folklore seemingly treats Women's Dress, Woman's Tongue, Bad Women, Red-Haired Girls, Women and Marriage, Widows, Brides and their Maids, etc. Drawing on literary sources as well as folklore, and providing a great deal of information, the work is essentially a broad but superficial survey and is faintly misogynistic. It is most useful as a source of basic information, although, unfortunately, sources are not indicated for much of the folklore. (For an example of an early work concentrating on the folklore of women in a particular culture, see Garnett, 580.)

Since Thiselton-Dyer, the only book-length publication to appear in America dealing with women and folklore in broad perspective has been the important collection of essays edited by Farrer (504); this originally appeared in somewhat different form as an issue of the Journal of American Folklore (vol. 88, no. 347) and grew out of two sessions at the American Folklore Society's 1974 meeting in Nashville. The essays in this collection are listed and discussed individually in this Essay Guide under relevant headings. For the controversy which surrounded the first publication of these essays, see Jordan (831) and Weigle (1588). A second collection of essays dealing with women and folklore edited by Jordan and Kalčik (835) is forthcoming. This volume will be more extensive than Farrer with essays dealing with material culture, life history, prose narratives, fieldwork and other areas. These essays are also listed and discussed separately, below. Sengupta (1394) is a collection of essays on women in Indian folklore; it covers a number of regions and genres.

Dundes (450), Farrer (503), Lewis (980), and Weigle (1598) are all recent, shorter, general discussions of women's folklore and/or the folklore of women. Farrer (503) surveys some of the scholarship of the past and brings up such issues as women's genres, women's groups and their folklore, and the image of women held by a society and the relation of such images to folklore. Lewis (980) devotes attention to the feminist "attack" on folklore, mostly beliefs and sayings which inculcate sexual stereotypes, noting that feminists have actually missed much anti-female lore in their discussions; she also touches on newly created feminist folklore.

Weigle (1598), in an introduction to a "special cluster" of essays in Frontiers, concentrates on women as verbal artists. She notes that Western aesthetic categories have often caused us to misconstrue the verbal art of other cultures and that as a consequence women's genres have been ignored, misunderstood, or denigrated ("old wives' tales"). Dundes (450) sticks to American lore in a survey of "male chauvinism" in several genres, including folk speech, rhymes, and legends.

The standard bibliography of American folklore is Haywood (707), which has useful index entries under Women and under Girls; the American Characters section has entries for Annie Oakley, Frankie and Johnny, Belle Starr, Calamity Jane, and Little Audrey. Flanagan and Flanagan (528) is a more recent general bibliography of American folklore, with very short annotations; it is divided by genre, and there is no simple way to use it to find information on folklore of or about women. For American theses and dissertations on folklore through 1968, see Dundes (451); there is no index listing for women, however. A number of post-1968 dissertations appear in the present bibliography. Grider (654), a bibliography of children's folklore, contains items of relevance to women and folklore.

For recent comments on sexism in folklore scholarship, see Starr (1450). In an informal and amusing but insightful essay (13) Köngäs-Maranda reflects on women folklorists, women's genres, sexism in folklore scholarship and female folk performers.

Feminists have made various uses of folklore, have commented upon folklore, or have rewritten folklore to make it more acceptable to their standards; see nos. 460: pp. 29-46, 742, 830, 863, 980, 983, 1092, 1230, 1231, 1473.

Women's social interaction (with men and with other women both), especially in terms of verbal art and verbal strategies, has been discussed by Abrahams (4), Barrick (104), Dresser (439), Goldstein (611), Harding (685), Stoeltje (1468), Weigle (1595, 1596, 1599), and Whitehouse (1620).

Folklorists have traditionally studied small, cohesive groups, rightly or wrongly working on the premise that the members of such groups intensely share in some common experience or set of values which generate a lore. Such groups often have also been deviant groups in one sense or another.

Farrer (503: pp. xi-xii) touches on women in groups and the effect such grouping might have on folklore; and the question of **women's folk groups and women in folk groups** is an interesting one in need of careful analysis. Folklorists have done some tentative work in this direction. Anthropologists and sociologists have also looked at women's groups and, though they have not viewed them in the framework of the concept of the folk group, their work is suggestive of inherent possibilities folklorists might follow up on.

Groups of female prostitutes have, for example, been studied by folklorists and other social scientists as well. Weigle (1595) briefly and wryly notes some of the connections between prostitution and verbal art, and one recent, pioneering article on women's folklore (Johnson, 811) deals with folkloric performance and exchange in a famous Texas brothel. Winslow (1639) attempted to study the occupational superstitions of prostitutes in upstate New York. Charpenel (303) deals with the lore of calling cards used by Mexican prostitutes. Heyl, a sociologist, has studied the "house" prostitute (728), and another sociologist, Goldman (608), deals with prostitution and social life during the gold mining days of the Comstock Lode in Nevada. From an anthropological perspective Crihfield (357) has examined the "entertaining girls" of Taipei (though she concentrates on male attitudes toward them). The ethnomusicologists McLeod and Herndon (1063) deal with prostitution in their important study of female singers in Malta. Cohen (320) deals with the role a prostitute plays in the origin legend of an American folk group, the "Jackson Whites" of New Jersey. For general works on prostitution see Bullough and Elcano (250), a bibliography on the subject, and nos. 647, 721.

Communities of nuns have been the focus of several anthropological and sociological studies; see nos. 675, 732, 1366, 1632. Dressler (440) deals with the influence of nuns on the folklore of Catholic school pupils. The nightclub stripper has been studied by Boles (179). Several other women's occupational groups have been written on also. Smith (1420) has dealt with the female domestic servant in Peru, Katzman (862) with female servants in nineteenth century America. Frances R. Donovan, in two classic studies (422, 423), has explored the worlds of, respectively, the saleswoman and the school teacher. Female involvement in the whaling industry, an industry which has generated much folklore, is investigated by Rattray (1270), and another folklorist, Braddy (196), discusses women bullfighters in Mexico. Messenger has published two excellent studies (1076, 1077) of the folklore of the Irish linen industry; females outnumbered men two to one in the linen mills, and much folklore is associated with the tasks specifically performed by women. Collins (329), a study of the folklore of American hosiery mill workers, also concentrates upon a predominantly female occupational group. Skoner (1414) is an ethnographic study of nurses, and Monteiro (1112) recounts nursing folklore, mostly narratives. For nannies see Gathorne-Hardy (583: pp. 282-288 for narrative, pp. 330-336 for proverbs and sayings). No. 929 is a brief note on a superstition found among London dressmakers.

Waitresses and barmaids have been considered in two recent articles by folklorists, Bell (128) and Walle (1567); both are interested in social interactional analysis and how women "operate" in the restaurant/bar context in terms of artistic, verbal skills. Donovan's study of waitresses (421) is a classic. The absorbing, full-length study of cocktail waitresses by Spradley and Mann (1442) was influenced by the perspectives of Erving Goffman; they examine joking relationships, bar speech, the division of labor and territory, and the lives of several waitresses; they are especially conscious of the problems of a woman working in the male-dominated world of the bar. See also no. 900. Manges (1034) deals with women tavern keepers in colonial Pennsylvania (as well as women artisans and shop keepers).

Frank (541) discusses American Jewish housewives, Scott (1387) the college sorority. Mitchell (1094) treats "informal inmate social structure" in women's prisons, and Carter (287) the question of "informal culture" in a reform school for girls.

Folklorists have also traditionally studied rural groups. For rural women see Chamberlain (299), a "portrait" of the women in a village in East Anglian fen country; Hagood (668), dealing with white tenant farm women in the American South; Kitteringham (895), nineteenth-century English country girls; and Crow (365), nineteenth-century American country girls. Fussell and Fussell (571) treat the English country woman from 1500 to 1900; their work is profusely illustrated, and they give specific attention to folklife. Kahn (846) extensively quotes the words of Southern Appalachian women in examining their lives and life styles. Fischer (523), an anthology, contains information on the folklife of American pioneer women.

Two essays in Ardener (64) focus on women's groups: Okely (1169) on Gypsy women and Callan (263) on British diplomats' wives. See also nos. 33, 172, 328, 949, 1000, 1131, 1176, 1350.

Women as Folk Performers and Informants: Farrer (503) has suggested that there has been a scholarly bias against using female informants except in limited types of situations. Women have often had folklore collected from them nonetheless. The following references are offered simply as examples of studies and collections in which women were used as informants; how useful they might be in assessing women's roles as tradition bearers or women as folk performers varies considerably, however: nos. 23, 24, 38, 39, 43, 82, 102, 115, 135, 136, 137, 138, 139, 174, 185, 206, 364, 372, 373, 404, 407, 415, 426, 427, 474, 515, 578, 601, 606, 686, 688, 722, 726, 780, 781, 795, 812, 896, 965, 1004, 1021, 1071, 1115, 1175, 1202, 1203, 1204, 1207, 1223,

1233, 1244, 1263, 1271, 1272, 1273, 1294, 1297, 1430, 1431, 1432, 1458, 1488, 1496, 1512, 1513, 1531, 1611, 1636, 1637.

Given the fact that until recently folklorists have paid relatively little attention in print to their informants as performers, as oral artists, or as individuals, whatever the sex of those informants, it is noteworthy that there are several important works devoted to female folk artists. In fact, one recent work which has often been hailed as a landmark model to follow in works devoted to folklore performers, Riddle, Abrahams, and Foss (1296), is devoted to a well-known woman singer of the Ozarks, Almeda Riddle. Edited from a series of interviews Abrahams conducted with her in 1964, 1965, and 1967, the book consists of Riddle's recollections of her life and reflections on her songs, along with the texts of a number of those songs. Finnegan (521: pp. 183-187) also comments on Riddle as a performer.

A brief though classic study of a Siberian tale-teller, originally published in German in 1926 and recently translated into English, Azadovskii (77), focuses on a woman narrator, Natal'ia Osipovna Vinokurova, "among the best representatives of Russian folktale poesy." Azadovskii deals with the informant's style, her repertoire, her themes, her relation to local Siberian culture. A more recent, much more comprehensive study of a woman and her folklore repertoire is Pentikäinen (1221), a study of the Finn Marina Tokalo and her entire cultural background. In her important study of oral narration in Hungary, Linda Dégh deals at length with one female narrator, the outstanding Zsuzsánna Palkó (399: pp. 187-234 and passim), who was awarded the title Master of Folklore by the Hungarian government in 1954, and also analyzes her tales (pp. 288-325); other female narrators are discussed in less detail.

The tale repertoires, personalities, and social contexts of East European women narrators are also treated by Brill (219) and Nagy (1135). Jordan has studied in detail the life and folklore of an "average" female tradition bearer as well as the lore of other female members of the same family (829). In a shorter work (828), the same informant's use of supernatural lore in relation to her ethnic identity as a Mexican-American is discussed; much of the material for this study was drawn from an exchange of folklore between several women. Newall (1143) is a close study of the conversational narratives of a woman in relation to her class status. One of the narators in Hall (671), a volume dealing with Eskimo storytellers, is a woman; texts of her tales and an autobiography are included.

Anna Gordon Brown, "Mrs. Brown of Falkland," who as a child learned traditional songs from other women (chiefly her aunt; the family members from whom Mrs. Brown learned her songs are commented upon by Johnson, 808) and over thirty of whose ballad texts were printed in Child's great compendium (309), has been given some attention, though more as a representative of a process than as an individual. Bronson (229) is primarily concerned with her texts. Recently Buchan (246) has suggested that Mrs. Brown was a "singer of tales," that is, an oral improvisor, a suggestion disputed by Andersen and Pettitt (30); see also Fowler (536: pp. 294-331).

Richard M. Dorson's discovery of the male narrator, J.D. Suggs, is well known, but he has also written on Aunt Jane Goudreau, a narrator in Michigan's Upper Peninsula, and has published tales from her repertoire (424). Dorson also published as a group a number of tales told by Mary Richardson, an Afro-American tale-teller (425; see also no. 427: pp. 25-27 and passim).

Morris (1122) and Cromwell, Rogers, Coffin, and Bayard (359) are concerned with the song repertoires of women singers, though both consist mainly of texts. For a short bibliography of works on Aunt Molly Jackson, traditional singer and legendary labor activist, see Parsons (1208). Greenway (648) concentrates on Jackson's Robin Hood ballads and their source, but elsewhere Greenway (649: pp. 252-275) deals with her and her art in more general terms, and also with Ella May Wiggins (pp. 244-252). Green (939: pp. 77-88, 417-423, passim) also deals with Aunt Molly Jackson.

Hopkins (754) includes discussion of the upstate New York singer, Sara Cleveland. Wiggins (1623) deals with the political songs and political activities of the Georgia folk musician Fiddlin' John Carson and includes some discussion of Carson's daughter and co-performer, Moonshine Kate. Spitzer (1440) writes about Queen Ida, the most prominent female performer in Louisiana black French music. Scheub (1374) is a study of a Xhosa performer in a dramatic song-dance genre tradition. The well-known folk singer Jean Ritchie gives a very readable account of her early life and discusses her family and its music and other lore (1302). Dunn (455) discusses Ritchie.

McCarthy (1054) discusses the ballad repertoire of a female singer of Scotland, Agnes Lyle. Several other Scottish female traditional singers have been studied as well, the famous Jeannie Robertson by Gower (631), Gower and Porter (632, 633, 634), and Porter (1243), though except for the first of these, which includes an interview on her life and songs, the emphasis has been on the repertoire rather than on the singer. Mrs. Robertson's daughter, Lizzie Higgins, is also the subject of an article (Munro, 1127), and Ross (1342) and Collinson (331) have written on the repertoire and singing style of Nan MacKinnon.

The female satiric bards of ancient Ireland as mentioned in Irish heroic texts are treated in Randolph (1261) and "singing girls" in ancient Arab culture by Hanna (680). Galvin (575) concentrates on the feminist and abolitionist Sojourner Truth as a singer and woman of words. The women discussed by Lawson (952) are school lunch room workers who perform skits and related forms while on the job. Relevant to the relationship between performance and sex roles is Pocius (1237); this article discusses a Newfoundland husband and wife, both traditional singers but only he recognized as such by the community, a situation which raises questions about sex roles and social identity.

Jones and Hawes (813) resulted from intensive collecting from one female informant.

For black blues and gospel singers, some of whom are much closer to the folk idiom than others, see Albertson (16), Chilton (310), Holiday and Dufty (743), Jones (816), Moore (1117), Oliver (1173), Spitzer (1439), and Stewart-Baxter (1464). For country music: Malone and McCulloh (1032) includes a chapter on Loretta Lynn, and Dew (409) is devoted entirely to women in that musical field; in his general history of country music Malone (1031) mentions many female performers. Oerman and Bufwack (1165) concentrate on the women who performed in the rockabilly substyle, notably Brenda Lee, Jackie DeShannon, Wanda Jackson, and Jo-Ann Campbell.

See also nos. 368, 575, 660, 811, 889, 890, 1449, 1584, 1620.

Although deriving out of anthropology, the **life history** is a research technique which has particularly appealed to folklorists for various reasons (see nos. 786, 1504). Fewer life histories for women than for men have been published, but a number of women's life histories do exist, allowing us to view the female experience as lived and narrated by selected individuals in a few cultures at least. Some are of more direct interest to folklore studies than others. For example, Jordan (829) in her study of the folklore of a Mexican-American female informant and that of her family provides a life history and an analysis of that informant's life, and also relates the folklore to biography. Nos. 1369 and 1370 are of great interest because they present the life of "the Queen of the Gaelic storytellers," Peig Sayers, in addition to providing in themselves much folklore and folklife information. Jahner (786) is also of particular significance as this analyzes a woman's life history in folkloristic perspective and deals with the narrative that is that life history in terms of its providing "exemplary pattern."

Riddle, Abrahams, and Foss (1296) analyzes folklore repertoire partially in terms of life history. Pitseolak and Eber (1236) presents the life of a well-known Eskimo artist. The "Chinese working woman" whose life from 1867 to 1938 Pruit (1254) set down was also an informant for many oral narratives and accounts of folk customs; the life history, in fact, grew out of the collecting of information on customs. Ets (489) is unique in being a lengthy life history dealing with the American immigrant experience and with life in ethnic communities, though much of it deals with her informant's earlier life in Italy as a silkmaker; there is data on beliefs and oral folklore forms.

Smith (1421) includes a number of song texts, information on ritual, drumming, praise-singing, beliefs, foodways, marriage customs, etc.; it is interesting to note that this life history grew out of an attempt on the part of Smith to gather data from women in purdah to supplement her husband's Hausa research. Andreski (34) is a collection of over twenty-five short life stories of Ibibio women who grew up in a society in which there was "segregation of the sexes almost into two nations" and in which women were often rigidly repressed; there is information on magic, curing, customs, and traditional narrative.

Binford (156) briefly treats the life and divination rituals of an East African shaman and Sims (1411) the life of a black American healer. The Mexican Indian shaman Maria Sabina is the subject of a book-length study cum collection of the chants from the sacred ceremonies she conducts (Estrada, 488). Underhill (1537) is full of song texts and data on singing and dreams. Babb and Taylor (79) puts the subject into the larger context of folk healers and healing.

Other pioneering studies in women's life history include Parsons (1206) and Reichard (1279). Parsons' article is intended as a brief description of the life of Zuñi girls and women in terms of a fictional, composite individual, with emphasis placed on societal sex differences as expressed in speech, dress, ceremonials, work patterns, etc.; Parsons' initial personal comments on feminism and scholarship are of interest also. Reichard's work is a partially fictionalized, third-person account meant to illustrate aspects of Navajo life in general, including "marriage practices, house types, dress..., religious beliefs, recreation..., arts and crafts..., basic attitudes..., characteristic gestures..., the daily round of activities...." (Frisbie, 565: n.p.). See also nos. 57, 259, 332, 431, 512, 703, 729, 815, 839, 859, 869, 994, 1010, 1055, 1082, 1177, 1350, 1389, 1399, 1503, 1538, 1563, 1614.

Several women have written autobiographies of their lives within traditional societies and folk groups; Sugimoto (1491) in rural Japan, Chao (301) in urban China, East (464) in the Texas oil fields, Romero (1326) in the rural border country along the Rio Grande. Kingston's account (885) of her girlhood in the California Chinese community is especially rich in folklore; in relation to Kingston see Beh (127). See also Ritchie (1302), and Whyte (1622), the partial autobiography of a Scottish tale teller.

Several folklore journals have published short life histories or brief sketches of women; Brooks (231) consists of written memoirs of life in a Mormon village in Nevada; Franz (543) contains the recollections of a woman who cooked in Adirondack lumber camps, Del Bourgo and Botkin (402) recollections of New York City folklife; Nagorka (1134) deals with the life of a Polish immigrant and includes data on Easter eggs and whiskey making.

The Foxfire books contain a number of brief portraits of women in traditional society: Wigginton (1624: pp 17-30; 1625: pp. 18-27; 1626: pp. 221-244, 398-415, 465-481; 1627: pp. 15-50, 202-214, 319-333; 1628: pp. 17-76, 495-511).

For basic introductions to the life history method and related materials, see Gottschalk, Kluckhohn, and Angell (627) and Langness (946). Hammond and Jablow (676: pp. 147-149) provide a selected bibliography of women's life histories.

Female Folk Figures and Heroes: There are no women in Raglan's famous list of heroes (1257), nor in Rank's

(1265), and the question of female folk heroes and other
female figures in folklore is one which has not received
much attention from folklorists. Campbell (266) speaks of
the monomyth of the hero and may seem to be speaking of a
male figure, but he does in fact refer to the androgynous
nature of the hero. Leeming (966) is a collection of myths
organized according to various protagonists and centered
around "a simplifed form of [Campbell's] monomyth" and
includes narratives about such female figures as Cybele,
Penelope, and St. Agnes.

The most significant analysis undertaken to date is
that of Stone (1474), which is concerned with fairy tale
protagonists and compares the female figures in little-known
Anglo-American oral collections with those in popular
printed collections in terms of how passive or active the
female characters are. The heroines of the popular printed
collections were found to be passive, whereas the women in
the Anglo-American oral tales were much more active. Stone
concludes that most people in modern American society have
not been exposed to the type of female hero in the oral
tales, only to the more passive female who fits in with an
ideal of the passive woman; see also Stone (1471).

Coffin (318) deals with the female hero also, although
the focus of this book remains a bit unclear, as does the
author's conception of folklore and legend. He deals mostly
with historical figures who have become "legendary," such as
Cleopatra, Belle Starr, and Mae West, though comic strip
characters, ballad women, and such mythic figures as Helen
of Troy are also included, with material being drawn from a
wide variety of literary, historical, and folkloric sources.
An attempt is made to categorize female heroes through
catchy chapter titles like Black Magic, Grotesque Roses, and
Golden Girl. Abernethy (2) is in a similar vein for a more
limited geographical area, Texas, and includes such
non-folkloric people as Babe Didrikson Zaharias, sculptor
Elizabeth Ney, and the Dallas Cowboy cheerleaders; unlike
Coffin, the book contains articles by individual writers;
those most relevant to folklore are listed separately.

Green (640: pp. 194-201, 374-376, and passim) in her
major survey of the Indian as an image in American folk and
popular culture considers the dual image of the Indian
woman, as "princess" and as "squaw," a subject treated in
more concentrated form in a later article (641); see also
no. 516. Garbaty (577) links Chaucer's wife of Bath to a
figure in folk tradition, and Schlauch (1377) studies the
figure of the innocent, persecuted queen as found in Chaucer
but also in other medieval literature including folk
material; Fowler (536: pp. 218-234) discusses the same
figure in connection with a ballad. Lady Godiva is discussed
by Davidson (385); see also Lancaster (937). Joan of Arc is
an historical figure whose "legendary" status makes her of
interest to folklorists; see Warner (1571) for a sound study
of her "image" both during and after her life.

Historical women who have become folklore figures,
usually locally, have been treated by Pike (1234; a female
hermit), Adlard (10; the actress Nell Gwyn), Peterson (1225;

the author's great-great-grandmother, a hoodoo woman),
Bolton (181; Christina of Sweden), and De Nio (405; a female
recluse). Legendary women with supernatural powers include
Aunt Caroline Dye, the fortune teller mentioned in "St.
Louis Blues" (Wolf, 1642; Dorson, 427: p. 208; de Caro, 393;
see also no. 899), and Biddy Early, a "woman of knowledge"
who has become a fixture in Irish oral tradition (Schmitz,
1380). Wiseby (1640) and Collins (327) also deal with
figures of local legend. Langlois has discussed Belle
Gunness, a "lady Bluebeard" in several works (942, 943,
945). Clark discusses a Nez Perce tradition of an Indian
woman who aided Lewis and Clark; and Ives (775) considers
the Sonoran legend which says that a white woman was
kidnapped by the Seri Indians and eventually became their
"queen"; he suggests that the motif of a White Queen of
non-white, "native" peoples is found in various parts of the
world, although he does not provide any references. Lunt
(1005) discusses a local legend of a wild woman said to live
in Indiana woods, Modi (1109) the legendary women of Eastern
tradition whose bodies were poisoned so that men having
sexual congress with them died.

See also nos. 105, 146, 221, 228, 320, 369, 481, 639:
pp. 241-278, 1120, 1197, 1301, 1351, 1501.

Female Supernatural Figures: Classical and other
goddesses have been discussed in many volumes by classical
scholars, mythologists, anthropologists, and others, and no
attempt has been made to survey that body of material
thoroughly for this bibliography. Dean (390) is a recent
bibliography of goddess-related materials, and Weigle (1607)
is a major trove of information on women· and mythology, a
sort of anthology of texts of various kinds skillfully woven
together by connecting commentary in seven chapters. Many
illustrations, in themselves illuminating, are included and
there is an extensive bibliography. The dictionary of
folklore by Leach (957) contains numerous entries for
particular goddesses; Graves (636) contains comprehensive
accounts of the exploits of various Greek goddesses as well
as gods and gives copious references to classical sources.
There are also a number of relevant entries in Cavendish
(294), an "encyclopedia of the supernatural." Monaghan
(1111) is a useful dictionary-format directory for goddesses
and related female heroic figures.

Basic works on goddesses and related mythology include
the folowing: Patai (1212) is a good, short,
folkloristically-oriented discussion of the Hebrew goddess
Lilith (see also Patai, 1213, Rivlin, 1303, and Weiner,
1609). The goddesses of classical antiquity are discussed in
the classic work of Harrison (690: pp. 59-127; 691: pp.
257-321) and by Zuntz (1664). Other works, all with a
folkloristic emphasis, which treat figures from classical
mythology and legend include Abercromby (1; Amazons), Berg
(134; the story of Pandora in the context of archaic Greek
culture "with special emphasis on attitudes toward women"),
Coote (339; the Fates), Crooke (360; Penelope), Suhr (1492;
Athena). Lefkowitz (967) considers the limited roles
classical myths offered women. Spretnak (1444) reconstructs

from fragmentary sources the myths of pre-Hellenic goddesses
and provides short introductions to each. Suhr (1493) covers
the art of spinning in ancient Greece in relation to its
symbolism and connection with the goddess Aphrodite. Hillman
(773) is a collection of psychological essays on mythology,
the majority of which deal with goddesses or other female
figures from classical myth: Downing (435; Ariadne), Hillman
(734; Athene), Kerényi (875; Artemis), Kirksey (888;
Hestia), Miller (1083; Rhea).

For a book length survey of Amazons (ancient sources,
Amazons in literature and art, consideration of the factual
basis of the Amazon legends) see Sobol (1429). Chesler (308)
and Malamud (1030) bring the perspectives of psychology to
considering Amazons.

Spretnak (1445) is a feminist-oriented collection of
essays, etc., on spirituality in the women's movement, which
contains several essays relevant to women and folklore noted
separately, includes a section (Appendix II) which is an
exchange of views on the Great Goddess, myth and matriarchy.
One of the participants in that exchange, Binford, has also
commented elsewhere (157) on the Goddess and matriarchy from
the perspective of modern anthropology. Stone (1484) is a
recent feminist account of the Great Goddess and how men
suppressed the women's rites conected with her worship; see
also Stone (1482).

The subject of ancient goddess worship has been a
controversial one since Bachofen (81) used ancient myth to
suggest ancient matriarchy as a dominant social institution.
Volume 2, number 1, issue 5 (revised edition 1982) of
Heresies is devoted to the Great Goddess; included are
poetry, art works, and other creative contributions as well
as short interpretive essays. Rose (1335) is an outdated discussion of the evidence for mother-right but includes interesting information on a number of supposedly related customs. For the cult of the Great or Mother Goddess see also
nos. 267, 279, 280, 363, 590, 705, 788, 842, 1139, 1157.

Harrison (689) is a structural-symbolic analysis of the
major female supernaturals of the Navajo and considers them
in the light of kinship relations and the position of women.
O'Flaherty (1168) deals with Hindu mythology, especially
myths about women, in an interesting consideration of sexual
metaphors and animal symbols as indicative of male-female
relationships. McKay (1061) presents the evidence for the
existence of an ancient deer-goddess cult in Scotland. Reik
(1284) deals with the "myth of Eve," and Lederer (962)
discusses such figures as Lilith and the Hindu goddess,
Kali. Voeglin (1556) is a short discussion/description of
the Shawnee female creator deity. Graves (637) is a somewhat
eccentric account of the "white goddess" whom he associates
with poetic creativity as well as various particular mythic
and legendary figures. Harding (683) considers moon
goddesses from a Jungian perspective, Thompson (1514)
details the Mayan and Mexican moon goddesses, and Downing
(436) provides a somewhat personal and imaginative treatment
of the meaning of goddesses to her own life. See also nos.
65, 145, 252, 270, 340, 355, 469, 480, 549, 563, 591, 605,

651, 769, 876, 1170, 1246, 1255, 1336, 1417, 1483, 1573, 1589, 1592, 1603. Benwell and Waugh (133) deal with mermaids.

Warner (1570) is an excellent study of the Christian figure of the Virgin Mary, and Ashe (72) is also a useful historical study of Mary and her cult; this work sees an early Christian cult of Mary (as a renascent form of the Goddess) served by priestesses and appealing mostly to women. Budge provides translations of Ethiopic and Syraic legends of the Virgin Mary (247, 248). See also nos. 204, 394, 712, 1338, 1575, 1594, 1641. Brewster (209) discusses the legend of St. Marcella, who died rather than submit to incestuous relations with her father, Gutch (661) St. Martha and other saints. Weigle (1587, 1591) discusses the "death angel" figure of the penitentes of New Mexico and Colorado, Doña Sebastiana.

Two ghostly females have received concerted attention from American folklorists: La Llorona, the Mexican figure who is alternately female victim searching for her lost children and dangerous spectre who lures and destroys men; and the Vanishing Hitchhiker, the ghost who is picked up by a driver at a certain spot. Barakat (96, 97) Leddy (960, 961), and Kirtley (894) discuss the general background of La Llorona, as do Agogino, Stevens, and Carlotta (12), Horcasitas and Butterworth (755), and West (1615). Hawes (701), Jordan (833), and Kearney (866, 867) are concerned with how La Llorona relates to particular cultural and symbolic contexts; see also Espinosa (487: p. 401). (Blaffer, 167, considers a Central American male supernatural figure who victimizes women.) For basic discussion of the Hitchhiker, see Beardsley and Hankey (116, 117) and Jones (817). More recently Brunvard (24) has made the Hitchhiker part of the title of a volume on urban legends which considers her in addition to much other material in the context of modern American culture. Luomala (1007) notes how in Hawaii the Hitchhiker has been conflated with the goddess Pele.

Of course there are innumerable female ghosts and revenants in world folk tradition (see for example, nos. 982, 1196, 1539).

Briggs' encyclopedia (217) of fairies and the like contains a number of relevant entries, such as Gooseberry Wife, Swan Maiden, Seal Maiden, Mab, Fairy Brides. See also nos. 214, 215, 216.

See also nos. 50, 122, 144, 282, 295, 479, 694,: pp. 37-92, 255-332, 987, 1017, 1283, 1604, 1605.

The Library of Congress Archive of Folk Song has published several short but very useful bibliographies relating to **folksong and music** relevant to women; Corimer (347) is the most recent of these and is a general bibliography of the area; Hefner (710) is a list of songs about women in prison; no. 47 deals with the songs of the women's suffrage movement; no. 35 lists works which contain the famous line "She is more to be pitied than censured."

Women in narrative song, either as individual characters or as types, have been discussed in various works. Cunningham (369) deals with the stereotype of the "murdered girl," who appears in a number of standard American ballads. One particular murdered girl, the historical Pearl Bryan, is treated in a book-length study by Cohen (319), who deals not only with ballads but with newspaper treatments and the inter-relationships of these two media. A model for certain kinds of folklore analysis, this work raises interesting questions about how women and their actions are stereotyped. Green (639: pp. 241-278) discusses the song "The Death of Mother Jones" in relation to the life of that legendary labor activist. Kealy (865) treats the ballad heroine in general terms, Poole (1241) women in the medieval Spanish ballad. The sentimental ballad of "The Blind Girl" is the subject of Ellis (481). Krauss (920) is a structural study of "ballads of family opposition to lovers" and is relevant to questions of sex roles and societal expectations of women. In considering clothing symbols in ballads, Rogers (1322) includes women's dress. Fife and Fife (517) consists mostly of texts of western songs in which women figure.

Traditional laments and mourning songs are exclusively or largely the domain of women in some societies. For women's laments as a song genre there are Alexiou (17) and Caraveli-Chaves (273) for Greece; Tiwary (1519) for India; Honko (751) and Leino (971) for Finland; and Croker (358) for Ireland. See also nos. 49, 200. Nenola-Kallio (1138) discusses wedding laments and the related Finnish custom of shoeing the bride, and Blake (168) considers the laments traditionally sung by Chinese brides, beginning several days before the wedding; these laments often express yearnings toward a mother left behind after marriage and Blake also notes how the songs reflect a patriarchal social system. Although not focusing upon laments, Upadhyaya (1540, 1542) shows the position of a young woman in her own home and in her husband's and also deals with mother-daughter relations, in both cases as these are depicted in folksongs; see also no. 1541.

The pioneering, controversial work done by Lomax in cantometrics, an attempt to link musical style to other aspects of culture, is of direct relevance to a consideration of women and folk music, as he argues that social sexual codes and the position of women are closely related to musical style (993, 996, 997).

The ideology and the stereotype of the self-sacrificing woman as found in American country music is treated in Sims (1410), and McGinty (1059) deals with another country-western stereotype, the honky-tonk angel. See also no. 1630. Jackson (779) discusses the contributions of Afro-American women to American traditional music in such genres as lullabies and worksongs, Alloy (25) the songs of women in the textile trades (in the notes in what is essentially a song book), Glavan (595) the singing traditions of American college sororities.

In discussing the motif of craving for a child in Indian folksong, Vatuk (1548) goes so far as to suggest that Indian folk tradition has mainly been preserved by women.

The distinction traditionally drawn between "heroic" and
"women's" songs in Serbo-Croatian culture is examined and
criticized by Coote (341); this distinction is found to
often not apply. An important analysis of women's songs and
female singing traditions is McLeod and Herndon (1063). In
the context of Maltese society, the inter-relationships
between sex roles, singing, singing bars, prostitution, and
a particular song genre are carefully worked out. The
ntsomi, a genre dominated by women in Xhosa society, is the
subject of Scheub (1373), and the song and dance performance
of a troop of women performers from Zaire is noted by
Robinson (1315). Women's role (a somewhat passive one) in
the huapango, a Mexican song contest, is treated by
Johnson (810), and Elder (477) considers male calypso
singing as a "projection of...conflict over desirable social
roles between the male and the female."

As a genre, the blues comment upon relations betwen the
sexes and sex roles; the form as developed by female
performers has been commented upon in various works. The
performances of several singers of the "classic blues," a
synthesis of folk and popular styles, is the focus of
Spitzer (1439); the classic blues singer is viewed here as
an icon representing "black women." Stewart-Baxter (1464) is
a well-illustrated history of the development of the classic
blues singer. In his study of recorded coal-mining songs,
Green (639: pp. 371-380) treats Trixie Smith's unique
"Mining Camp Blues." For autobiographies, biographies, and
studies of the individual major blues singers, see Albertson
(16), Moore (1117), and Oliver (1173) for Bessie Smith;
Chilton (310) and Holiday and Dufty (743) for Billie
Holiday; and Waters and Samuels (1574) for Ethel Waters.
Driggs (441) is a brief survey of the careers and influence
of women jazz musicians.

The lullaby (for general comments see Brakely, 199),
often thought of as a women's genre, has been insightfully
discussed by Hawes (702); she deals with the lexical content
and function of lullabies in classifying songs as such and
also discusses child-rearing patterns as related to content.
Folk lullabies express the great complexity of mother-child
relations according to McDowell (1056) and may express
"tension, anxiety and depression." Khayyat (882), a
collection with commentary of Iraqi Jewish lullabies, points
out that the songs reflect the hard lives of the women who
sing them. Lopez and Joly (1002) analyze a Kuna lullaby in
social context and use their material to point out how
previous analyses of Kuna art have given a biased picture.
Collections of lullabies include Cass-Beggs and Cass-Beggs
(290); Commins (353), which has texts with translations and
notes; and Daiken, Hillis, and Brown (375), which includes a
general and historical introduction. Tracey (1523) traces
the East African origins of a lullaby apparently originally
introduced into a Southern white family by a slave nanny.
Lemaire (972) notes her research into the tradition of
women's lyrical songs in agrarian communities. Epic has not
been thought of as a woman's genre but the nineteenth
century novelist Butler (260) did make a case for the author

of the Odyssey being a woman. There are many works on folk
dance (for example, nos. 19, 765, 860, 951, 1522: pp.
312-376), a genre which involves both men and women. The
attention paid to women's roles in the dance varies.

See also nos. 27, 73, 120, 162, 175, 184, 245, 271,
283, 331, 442, 519, 552, 579, 631, 632, 633, 634, 649, 680,
797, 799, 808, 838, 854, 935, 1031, 1116, 1127, 1163, 1189,
1243, 1291, 1302, 1342, 1400, 1409, 1494, 1536, 1572, 1597,
1618.

Prose Narrative: Kay F. Stone has considered some
of the controversy over fairy tale heroines (1481); and in
other works (1474, 1475), she herself has dealt with the
fairy tale heroine, noting that active female characters
often appear in oral tales but seldom in popular
collections. Oliver (1174) also analyzes fairy tales from a
feminist perspective and criticizes Bettelheim (152).

Other feminist commentators upon fairy tales include
Rowe (1345), who sees the tales as making "female
subordination seem...romantically desirable" and as
promoting the paradigm of the passive woman, and
Waelti-Walters (1562), who also views the fairy tales as
providing a negative model; see also nos. 338, 1092.
Robinson (1316) announces on-going research on Snow White,
Walt Disney, and female roles. Girardot (593) analyzes the
tale of Snow White in terms of its revealing initiatory
patterns and shows some awareness of specifically female
initiation. Lüthi (1012: pp. 21-34, 109-119, passim) also
deals with female initiation in fairy tales and with female
characters in tales.

For a Jungian analysis of "the feminine" in fairy
tales, see von Franz (1558). Cox (353) and Rooth (1327) are
major studies of Cinderella and are primarily comparative
and historic-geographic, but given the importance of
Cinderella as a symbolic female figure, both are valuable
sources for the study of women in fairy tales. A recent
casebook (Dundes, 452) contains a selection of important
writings on the Cinderella tale. Travers (1525) prints six
versions of Sleeping Beauty and provides an essay analyzing
the Sleeping Beauty figure and theme. Thompson (1515) is, of
course, useful in any consideration of female figures in
fairy tales. Phelps (1231) has attempted to assemble a
collection of tales which contain strong female
protagonists; these are drawn from a number of cultures.

In a series of studies Mitchell has discussed female
joke-telling patterns (1096, 1098, 1099, 1103). Green
discusses the bawdy lore of Southern women, including
humorous narratives. (For general comments on women's humor,
see nos. 238, 269, 371, 699, 1610, 1612, 1613; nos. 976 and
1467 consider female stand-up comedians.) Pentikäinen
(1220), in discussing the "rhythm" of storytelling, analyzes
two variants of a narrative told by a female narrator.
Cothran (350) considers women's tall tales. Jordan (828)
includes discussion of supernatural legends told by
Mexican-American women. Personal narratives revealing of
women's experiences and women's styles of narration are the
focus of Kalčik (849), who deals with them in the context of

a contemporary women's group, and Bromberg-Ross (224)
reports on the role of storytelling in the contemporary
women's consciousness-raising group.

Kirshenblatt-Gimblett (892) analyzes in great detail
part of one particular narrative session in which a woman is
the central figure; this person's larger tale repertoire is
also considered. The roles played in the narration process
by the female relations of a male narrator are noted by Beck
(121). Roemer (1320) calls attention to the stories mothers
tell about their children's faux pas. Monteiro's
discussion of "nursing lore" (1112) deals mainly with
narratives told by female nurses. Several motifs which
express the longings of pregnant women for certain things
have been studied by Gilbert (589), who suggests that
"cravings play an important part in the psychological
acceptance of pregnancy." Mills (1098) deals with narratives
(from a Muslim society) in which persons of one sex dress
like those of the other; considering tales told by both a
male and a female, she draws conclusions about male and
female attitudes.

The relation of women in tales to their place in
society has been considered by Fischer (524) in dealing with
male/female social status in Truk and Ponape, and by Davis
(384), who uses personal narratives in assessing traditional
female roles in a company town. Bannan (95) relates
Southwestern Indian tales to the female life cycle and Howe
and Hirshfeld (763) analyze a Kuna narrative in relation to
sex roles in that society. In a major study, Dwyer (462)
uses a corpus of Moroccan folktales to analyze male/female
relations, "sexual selfhood," and related ideologies.

Jordan (833) has discussed Mexican-American legends of
serpents who invade women's vaginas, connecting these to
cultural attitudes and women's views of themselves and to
another legend cycle, that of La Llorona; also relevant to
the vaginal serpent legends are nos. 101, 277, 836. Nagy
(1135) considers the large tale repertoire of a female
narrator to deal with the informant's personality and her
relationship to her community.

In dealing with the narratives of American policemen
Barnes (100) touches upon the narrators' attitudes toward
women, while for Nahuat oral tradition Taggart (1502)
details "how men change their image of women in folktales
when women improve their position in a male dominant family
system." The position of women in Indian society as seen in
tales has been the subject of work by Upadhyaya (1544,
1545). The figure of the slandered wife in tales is dealt
with by Bawden (113) and Wood (1647), that of the innocent,
persecuted heroine by Dan (377), and the submissive or
silent wife by Allen (22) and Dawkins (388).

So-called modern legends as they reveal female
attitudes and concerns have been accorded some attention. In
a recent book-length volume (244) Brunvand considers a
number of these legends and their meanings in American
society. Women play roles as actors in a number of these
legends and are narrators of such tales, and Carpenter (284)
specifically calls attention to how women are often victims

of one sort or another in modern legends. Dundes (449)
provides an analysis of a legend told primarily by
college-age women and interprets it in terms of teenage
sexuality, social pressures on women, and symbolic
castration, an interpretation which has been considered
"sexocentric" by Jordan de Caro (837). Crane (354) considers
the legend of The Room Mate's Death as communicating
conflicting messages regarding what American society expects
of young females.

In an attempt to examine and redefine the legend genre,
Greenberg (646) examines the legend of the female college
student who while on a blind date is drugged and raped or
almost raped. Edwards considers a particular modern legend
(told most often by women) to examine "sex- and
genre-specific devices." The vagina dentata motif as it
appears in modern legend contexts has been briefly noted by
Jordan (825, 827), and Steed (1452) (see also nos. 777,
1079). Roemer (1319) provides a general analysis of a form
of supernatural legend told by females from the ages of ten
to twenty at slumber parties and in dorms and camps. The
legend of the young woman who has difficulty in getting out
of her vagina a tampax which is stuck there is noted briefly
by Marlin (1038) and MacLaughlin (1018). MacLaughlin (1019)
notes legends about terrible things happening to babies as
functioning to warn and scare young mothers, and Jordan
(826) the appearance of a well-known legend as a short story
in a feminist magazine. Hand (678) deals with the legend of
women who lure to their train compartments railroad
travellers, who are then drugged and robbed and who wake up
at destinations not theirs; this seems, however, to be a
legend told primarily by males.

See also nos. 76, 96, 98, 105, 116, 117, 140, 228, 304,
385, 399, 403, 437, 440, 457, 652, 694, 701, 725: pp.
385-404, 817, 828, 829, 832, 866, 924, 942, 943, 945, 960,
961, 1007, 1095, 1101, 1120, 1121, 1258, 1349, 1383, 1459,
1479, 1480, 1501, 1529, 1530, 1531, 1539, 1560, 1587.

Closely allied to prose narrative is women's **oral
history** (though of course oral history as such is not
necessarily folklore and much oral history collecting has
not been very relevant to folklore studies). The topic of
women's oral history in a folklore context was raised
briefly by Yocum (1654) and Goldstein and Dwyer-Shick (612);
both provide bibliography. No. 53 lists resources for the
study of women's oral history: bibliography, existing
collections, sample questionnaires and forms. Gluck (600)
suggests that oral history is a necessary aspect of women's
history in general because other documentary sources often
do not exist for women; she also discusses the interview
process. Several articles which appear in the same issue
(devoted to women's oral history) of _Frontiers_ magazine
are of interest to folklorists: Armitage, Bonfield, and
Jacobs (66), Silverman (1406), and Yung (1659) are concerned
with the oral history of folk groups of the North American
West, respectively, black women in Colorado, women on the
Alberta frontier, and Chinese women immigrants. Elsasser,
MacKenzie, and Tixler y Vigil (483) detail the oral history

of the women of an Hispanic American community, focusing on the problems of preserving tradition in the move away from traditional society.

Of course general oral history projects may garner information on the lives of women in folk and other societies; for example, Shiloh (1398), compiled by a women's group aiming to record general immigrant/ethnic oral history, includes female informants who tell of their lives in that historical context. See also nos. 185, 256, 299, 895, 1487, 1550.

The issue of **women's speech**, how it differs from men's speech, and what the implications for culture are of speech differences according to sex is an important one for folklorists as so much folklore lies within the realm of verbal art. Kramer (917) briefly surveys some of the research on "sex-related differences in speech" and includes discussion of the "folk-view" of how men and women "should" speak. Key (879) provides a cogent and readable discussion and includes a bibliography. Henley and Thorne (720) is an extensive bibliography for this area. For general discussion of language difference and sex and sexism in language, see Henley and Thorne (719), Nilsen, Bosmajian, Gershuny, and Stanley (1156), and Orasanu, Slater, and Adler (1181). The question of language as a tool for sexual domination was raised over thirty-five years ago by Furfey (569), who stated in a study based mainly on data from pre-literate cultures that "it may be tentatively suggested that language sometimes serves as a tool of sex dominance." This question has been recently intensely discussed by feminists and others, such as Spender, most influentially by Lakoff (934).

In the area of folk speech, the proverb usage of individual women has been discussed in two works: Jordan (829: pp. 174-190) examines the proverb use of a Mexican-American informant and Brandes (202) examines the proverb repertoire of a Spanish woman, relating her choice of proverbs to social and individual values. Two proverbial expressions about women, "No house is big enough for two women," and "maids' leading apes in hell," are the subject of, respectively, Taylor (1505) and Needham (1137), but there have been few attempts to analyze the image of women in the proverb corpus of any particular culture; notable is Webster (1579), an analysis of Moroccan proverbs which reveal the culturally held views of women, sex, and marriage. Canziani (271) does provide a list of Italian proverbs "in dispraise of women," where, she notes, the negative view of women contrasts to that found in courtship songs. Another individual proverb about women ("We rule the world and we are ruled by women.") is noted by Kryzyzanowski (924), who discusses it in relation to narratives. Some of the Ponapean proverbs in Riesenberg and Fischer (1298) relate to sex role expectations.

A corpus of riddles collected from two Indian males serves Upadhyaya (1543) in a consideration of family structure, including the position of women. Jones (818: pp. 113-120) provides a sketchy account of women orators in Native American culture. The traditional street cry of

female fishmongers in Edinburgh is discussed from a
linguistic perspective by Speitel (1433). Vernacular
expressions for menstruation from several American groups
are noted by Joffe (804), by Ernhester (485), who drew
material from the University of California at Berkeley
Folklore Archive, and by Nichols (1152). Maurer (1050)
discusses why female prostitutes seem to have developed
little of the argot affected by "other criminal
professions." Mitchell-Kernan's analysis of the
Afro-American conversational strategy of signifying relies
on female informants (1106, 1107). Kalčik (851) notes
differences between the nicknames ("handles") men and women
use over citizen's band radio and discusses the significance
of this; Rossi (1344) also deals with naming, though not in
a folkloric context. Page-Hollander (1191) considers sex
role, speech, and status in the context of telephone
conversations. Women commonly have been unfairly stereotyped
as gossips; for perspectives on gossip see nos. 1341, 1653.
      See also nos. 87, 921, 1227, 1418, 1498, 1510, 1601.
      For sex-related factors in non-verbal communication,
see nos. 147, 158: pp. 39-46, 718, 879: pp. 147-156, 880,
1602.
      Female initiation **rituals** have been noted in many
ethnographies. Brown (234) has studied a number of these
cross-culturally in order to determine why only some
societies have such rites and why there is such variety in
the nature of the rites; she attempts to assess the
relationships between the rites and such factors as a girl's
continued residence in her mother's home after marriage and
sex identity conflict. Brown's findings have, however, been
criticized by Driver (445; see also nos. 235, 236, 446).
Kloos (901) demonstrates the applicability of Brown's ideas
by studying the relationship between female initiation rites
and matrilocality and the economic importance of women among
the Caribs.
      Richards (1295) is a classic study, "the most detailed
description ever made of a girls' initiation ceremony";
Richards analyzes the expressed and symbolic purposes of an
African ritual and relates it to other aspects of the
culture in question. Blacking also gives a very full
description (with many photographs) of African girls'
initiation "schools," although his series of articles (163,
164, 165, 166) is essentially ethnographic documentation
rather than analysis. He deals with a number of expressive
genres which are part of the initiation schools, at which
the girls learn esoteric female knowledge, etiquette, and
social and sexual behavior patterns.
      Driver (444) considers the female puberty rites of
Western American Indians, and Driver and Riesenberg (447)
consider the puberty rites of girls in North and South
America in relation to an item of material culture. Frisbie
(564) is a major study of the Navajo girls' puberty
ceremony, and Farrer (502, 505) and Basso (109) have treated
those of the Apache. Ancient Greek rituals of female
initiation into the Eleusinian mysteries are the subject of
Skov (1415). Rigby (1299) provides a study of the structure

of girls' puberty rites, making a distinction between these
and other kinds of initiation rites and relating them to
marriage and kin stucture.

The initiation rituals of an American high school
sorority are dealt with by Schwartz and Merton (1382). Also
in the context of the modern, urban world are discussions of
the creation or the reinterpretation of rituals by feminists
by Turner (1535) and Broner (225). Charles (302) touches on
the involvement of women in the "drama" related to primitive
warfare.

For short, very general articles on initiation and
related rituals (both male and female), see nos. 59, 926,
1078, 1557. Bettelheim's lengthy psychoanalytic study of
puberty rites gives some consideration to girls' ceremonies
(151: pp. 239-260). Recently Schlegel and Barry (1379) have
indicated that evidence suggests that initiation ceremonies
for boys are no more common than those for girls (as has
been thought by many). Carmody (280) in surveying "women's
roles in traditional religious societies," deals with
various rituals and ceremonies, though her emphasis is on
the major religions.

Gough (628) and Reminick (1287) consider the question
of ritual defloration in specific cultures and Yates (1652)
deals with this broadly in psychoanalytic perspective.
LaFontaine (933) studies the ritual associated with first
menstruation, marriage, and first childbirth among the
Bugisu, noting the relation between bodily changes and
social status; ritual defloration is a central event and
symbolically elaborate and signifies men's control of women.
The rituals surrounding pregnancy and childbirth in Central
Indian villages are seen by Jacobson (784) as stressing that
in a male dominated society women do have the powerful role
of producing children.

Zelman (1662) is a cross-cultural study of sixty
cultural groups which sees female pollution-avoidance
rituals and male rituals associated with female reproduction
in terms of the social need to maximize or minimize sex
differences. Henderson (716) notes that women have an
extensive range of ritual roles in Onitsha Igbo society but
concentrates on funerary rites; the role of women in the
death rituals of the Black Cribs is carefully described by
Kerns (877). Women's rituals among the Luvale of Zambia
symbolically dispell the loss of children and disorders of
the reproduction system; they create unity among the women
of the group and serve to teach female esoteric knowldege
(Spring, 1446).

Ardener (62) deals convincingly with the problem of
anthropology's failure to perceive the cultural roles of
women, the models having been derived from the male world,
while he discusses African women's rites and the relation of
these rites to social boundaries as drawn by each sex.

Kluckhohn (902), noting that students of culture have
generalized about participation in culture on the basis of
male informants, comments on the knowledge that Navajo women
have of ceremonials even when they do not participate in
them. Bastien (110) investigates a "sex-specific ritual and

the woman diviner who performed it" in an Andean society
where rituals are sex-specific. A striking aspect of the
rituals of the cult of Dionysus was the conspicuous role
played by women, though this aspect has been largely ignored
by the scholarship; Kraemer (916) explains in the context of
Greek society why women were attracted to these rites.

Various rituals of women in India are studied by Wadley
(1561), who deals with a calendrical cycle of family and
household rites (which are contrasted to more public male
rituals), and Freeman (551), who deals with the roles women
play in the rituals of the Jagannatha cult, roles which have
received little attention in the large body of literature on
that cult. Jaskoski (797) surveys women's relation to
ceremonial life in various Native American tribal groups,
concentrating on healing songs. The English milkmaids'
ceremony is traced to ancient practices by Phillips (1232),
the rites relating to St. Agatha in Sicily are traced to the
deity of an ancient women's cult by Alford (18). Betteridge
(153) considers an Islamic ritual of Iran which can be
partaken in by all-female groups. See also nos. 143, 156,
438, 478, 488, 713, 738, 1180, 1396, 1534.

For the roles women play in rituals which are not
women's rituals, see, for example, nos. 367, 533, 723, 1262,
1293, 1586: esp. pp. 145-146.

Marriage, of course, involves both sexes, but as the
roles of bride and wife have often been seen as primary ones
for women, **courtship and marriage customs** are important
in the context of women's folklore. Compiling compendia of
marriage customs seems to have been especially popular
during the last century and there are several
nineteenth-century surveys, beginning with Hamilton (674).
Wood (1646) is "a record of the marriage ceremonies,
customs, superstitions, and folk-lore of many countries" and
Hutchinson (773) is similar. More recent is Braddock (195),
a popular assemblage of information on various customs
surrounding marriage, drawn from ethnographic sources as
well as literary and historical works. All four works are
useful for source material, though the care with which
references to primary material are given varies.

Westermarck (1616) presents a very full description of
marriage ceremonies in Morocco, dealing carefully with both
male and female roles. Baker (86) is a readily available,
brief but helpful survey, though it is restricted mostly to
British materials. Scott (1386) provides a compendium of
customs largely out of context. Turner (1533) provides a
popular and whimsical history of courtship, drawn largely
from literary sources. Earle (463) and Cole (325) provide
brief discussions of New England wedding customs, Seckar
(1388) a description of a typical Slovak-American wedding
(with song texts included), and Davis (383) of a
Polish-American one.

For various other customs and beliefs surrounding
marriage see nos. 36 (France), 361 (the custom of lifting
the bride), 650 (Scotland), 932 (Osage Indians), 1559. Joffe
(805) provides a short, general survey of the folklore,
mostly customs, of brides, and Jameson, Voegelin, and Foster

(794) briefly survey the folklore of marriage. Nevadomsky (1140) studies changes in the wedding rituals of East Indians in Trinidad as a means of showing how the position of women has changed in that society. For the practice of bundling, see nos. 48, 1465. The use of traditional riddling conversation and other formulas by blacks courting on Southern plantations is described in nos. 41 and 92.

Love magic and beliefs and superstitions about courtship and marriage (such as methods of divining the identity of one's future mate) have been treated in a number of articles: nos. 21, 80, 125, 314, 500, 586, 999, 1145, 1242, 1354, 1408, 1509, 1638. Of course many other compendia of superstitions contain similar items.

See also nos. 414, 529, 659, 663, 873, 1146, 1159, 1333, 1334, 1348, 1443, 1522: pp. 122-145.

There is also a body of lore relating to women's **reproductive functions**, including **menstruation, birth practices, and child care**. Joffe, Voegelin, and Foster (806) is a very brief survey of folk beliefs, customs, and narratives associated with menstruation. Lupton, Toth, and Delaney (1008) is a book-length cultural history. Young and Bacdayan (1658) and Stephens (1456, 1457) treat menstrual taboos cross-culturally in terms, respectively, of the social need to restrict women and assert male dominance, and of the extent of castration anxiety in the cultures in question.

Based on research in Wales, Skultans (1416) comments on the symbolic significance of menstruation and menopause, while Gross (656) notes that menstruation and childbirth are both marked by important female rituals among Australian aborigines (even men mark these events by imitative rituals). Kamsler (853) examines various Jewish menstrual taboos, no. 37 Alaskan Eskimo taboos.

Weideger (1581) is a very full discussion of the physiology and psychology of menstruation which also touches on related social issues. Snow (1424) and Snow and Johnson (1425, 1426) deal with some of the implications of folk beliefs about menstruation to modern scientific medicine. Grinnell (655) briefly notes Cheyenne customs having to do with menstruation as well as marriage and childbirth.

Pregnancy beliefs and birth customs and practices are detailed in nos. 693, 731, 824, 1149, 1158, 1179. Ayres (75) deals with pregnancy taboos placed upon parents of both sexes. Chodorow (313) sees mothering as a culturally learned activity. Frankel (542) is a very full study of "the folklore of the procreative process and infancy" of black women in Philadelphia. Stekert (1455) points out the need to examine the traditional beliefs and practices of Southern mountain women in northern cities in order to provide proper health care for them. Snow, Johnson, and Mayhew (1427) consider the role of traditional beliefs and attitudes in understanding the knowledge women have about reproduction.

In dealing with the knowledge of birth control in pre-industrial England and France, Ranum and Ranum (1266) touch on traditional beliefs. Songs and chants form the basis for a discussion of attitudes toward childbirth in

Africa by Nwoga (1160). Potter and Foster (1247) provide a brief general survey of the folklore of childbirth and Smith (1419) details briefly purification ceremonies following childbirth. Patai (1210, 1211) deals with Jewish cures for barrenness. Parsons wrote two pioneering articles (1201, 1205) dealing with Zuni beliefs and practices relating to conception, pregnancy, and the care of young children.

Various superstitions related to conception, pregnancy, and childbirth are noted in nos. 535, 548, 560, 1102, 1190. Dawson (389) and Newman (1148) deal with couvade, the custom whereby males imitate childbirth; the first is a book-length survey, the second details literary sources. Hand (677) notes that the couvade as such is not found in non-aboriginal North America but discusses a number of customs and beliefs which seem symbolically related. See Litoff (989) for a history of American midwives.

See also nos. 188, 420, 433, 434, 525, 531, 550, 665, 737, 750, 823, 881, 891, 974, 977, 1060, 1198, 1311, 1329, 1337, 1476, 1590, 1625: pp.274-303, 1631, 1634.

In many cultures women have been regarded as healers and adept practitioners of folk medicine; it has been suggested that in the West there has been a struggle between the male "scientific" medical establishment and the female traditional healing sorority, with the males having won out in recent centuries (Ehrenreich and English, 475, 476), and with the male doctors sometimes using their position to subjugate women. Fox (539) in discussing women in Christian science also discusses women healers in traditional societies, and Hughes (766) deals with them in medieval European society. Snow (1423) is based on an in-depth interview with a female folk healer with a multi-ethnic clientele in a southwestern city, and LaBarbera (930) also discusses the folk medical practices of one woman (not a professional healer). Although not concerned with female healers, O'Nell and Selby (1178) note how a folk illness, susto, functions as an escape mechanism for people who suffer stress in regard to sex role performance and that women show a much greater incidence of this "disease." See also nos. 42, 56, 79, 189, 205, 620, 630, 864, 986, 992, 1100, 1147, 1225, 1352, 1624: pp. 349-355, 1645.

There is an enormous body of literature on witchcraft and no attempt has been made to survey it all for the present bibliography. This is certainly an area of relevance to women, folklore, and culture, however, for as Parrinder has pointed out:

Everywhere women are believed to be the majority in witchcraft. Complementary to this is the fact that witch-doctors are practically always men. (1200: p. 191)

However, Gray (638) points out that although in Europe witches are most commonly thought of as female, on a world-wide basis witches are more likely to be male. The persecution of women as witches during the great European witch hunts is dealt with by Monter (1114), who sees this along with the courtly love ethic as relating to a male view of women as passive; by Matalene (1046), who considers the

general question of why the accused witches were so often
women (as does VanVuren, 1547: pp. 77-116); and by Heinshahn
and Steiger (711), who argue that the persecution especially
involved midwives and was an attempt to suppress female
knowledge of birth control and female control over
reproduction. Parrinder (1200) and Mair (1026) are both
sensible and readable introductions to the subject by
British anthropologists and both contain short
bibliographies. Madsen and Madsen (1022) deal with
witchcraft as reflecting sexual anxieties. For a short,
cogent discussion of mostly recent literature in several
fields which attempts to focus on the problem of why witches
are predominantly women, see Garrett (581). Robbins (1308)
is a more extensive survey of the literature of witchcraft
in general. Bruford (240) is a type-index of Gaelic witch
stories.

See also nos. 40, 54, 55, 459, 514, 771, 772, 801, 884,
1020, 1141, 1142, 1248, 1343, 1390, 1657.

Girls' and women's **games and play activities** have
been recognized as significant factors in shaping sex role
behavior and female identity, although only a few of the
studies relevant to this area of folklore attempt to
document the correlation. The most forceful attempt to do so
is by Cardozo-Freeman (275) who deals with how the games
played by Mexican girls reflect a very negative view of
relations with the male sex. The symbolic structures of
these games suggest that Mexican women lead "a life of
invasion, betrayal, abandonment, and forced seclusion."

Prendergast (1252) is an excellent study of a game
played by adult women in rural England, stoolball, a sort of
female version of cricket said to have been invented by
milkmaids; the author deals with the role of the game in the
lives of village women and also with male attitudes. Roberts
and Sutton-Smith (1312) contains information on statistical
relationships between sex, game preference, and social
attitudes. Rosenberg and Sutton-Smith (1339) see game
preference as a way of examining what boys and girls see as
their appropriate sex role behavior; in looking at both folk
and non-folk games they find preference changing because sex
role expectations are in a fluid state. Brady (198) views
the play of black girls in order "to discover the
culture-specific patterns of socialization and enculturation
which reveal themselves through play"; for a related article
see no. 468.

Sutton-Smith's important collection of essays on games
also incudes data on sex differences in play and other
relevant material (1497: esp. pp. 262-281, 405-415,
465-490). Virtanen (1554) deals with gender and game choice,
and Lever (975) studied fifth graders to determine whether
there were sex differences in the organization and meaning
of their games and what impact any such differences might
have on adult performance roles. Conn (334) interviewed
children to determine the relationship between awareness of
sex differences and game preference; both traditional and
non-traditional games are mentioned. Only non-traditional
games were studied by Montemayor (113), who determines that

for both boys and girls game performance is best when the
game is thought to be "sex appropriate."

Kelsey (871) describes a particualr singing game,
suggesting that it mirrors the stages of female life. The
performance competence of black girls engaged in play
activities in relation to socialization and enculturation is
considered by Brady (197). Diamond (412) is not a study of
games as such, but investigates the sociology of gender
differences through the use of an adult parlor game,
charades. The play activity of Eskimo girls called
storyknifing, which involves the narrating of stories while
illustrating them in snow or mud with a pointed object, has
been examined by Ager (11) and Oswalt (1187). See also no.
1551.

Jump-rope rhymes are almost exclusively a girls' genre;
the most complete compilation is Abrahams (3), which also
contains bibliography ; see also Ainsworth (14) and Speroni
(1435). Howard (760) deals with hopscotch as played in
Australia; Howard (761) with jacks in Australia.

On the American play-party see nos. 27, 184, 579, 1189,
1572.

The relatively recent concept of **family folklore**
covers a wide range of genres and ideas. Because women are
members of families and, further, because female roles have
traditionally been conceived of as household- and
family-oriented, family folklore studies should be of direct
interest to anyone concerned with women's folklore.
Boatright (176) is a pioneering study in this area. The best
bibliography to date is that which appears in the model
outline for a family folklore course circulated by the
Maryland Arts Council (Kotkin and Cutting-Baker, 915). The
very interesting collection of family narratives assembled
by the Family Folklore Project of the Festival of American
Folklife (Cutting-Baker, Gross, Kotkin, and Zeitlin, 374)
also contains bibliographical notes. Zeitlin, Gross, and
Cutting-Baker (1661) is a smaller collection of family
narratives. Baldwin (88) is a major study of the lore of a
particular family. Baldwin has also considered women's role
in family storytelling (90), and family poets, including
women (89). Roberts (1313) is a pioneering work in this area
but the folklore included comes mainly from male members of
the family in question.

See also nos. 203, 573, 582, 919, 1120, 1121, 1218,
1302, 1563.

Works devoted to the consideration of **sexual
folklore** necessarily involve the consideration of women,
though such studies may view them from a biased, male point
of view. Legman has made monumental contributions in this
generally neglected area of study. No. 968 is his most
general contribution, a collection of essays on such topics
as bawdy songs, collections of erotica, and the limerick.
Nos. 969 and 970 are more narrowly focused on obscene jokes;
in each volumne the author discusses an astonishing number
of jokes, arranging them under such sections and subsections
as Homosexuality, Women, Prostitution, Vagina Dentata.

Zumwalt's study (1663) of jokes told by children about adult sexuality includes data from female informants. In dealing with the issue of what is considered obscene in Yoruba culture, Qlajubu (1171) considers aspects of female sexuality in folklore. For a general bibliography on sexual customs, see Goodland (617). Hoffman (740) has dealt with folklore-related elements in erotic film and his type and motif index of Anglo-American erotica (741) is a basic reference source. Evans-Pritchard (490) treats the use of obscene songs by women in ceremonial context. Green (642) provides amusing and perceptive insights into Southern women's sexual humor. McMurtie (1065) reprints several North American Indian narratives which recount Lesbian love. Gulzow and Mitchell (658) report on recent legends about the vagina dentata and a strain of incurable syphillis as heard by soldiers in Viet Nam; they include a number of texts. Leach (955, 956) briefly deals with the folkloric aspects of chastity and chastity tests and no. 793 does the same for kissing. See also Crooke (362), who deals with symbolic sex change, Osberg (561), who deals with aspects of traditional sexual symbolism, as does Gunda (659), and nos. 46, 142, 1097, 1264, 1583.

There is a fairly extensive body of writing on women's **material culture**, though only a small fraction of it written by folklorists (no doubt because Anglo-American folklorists have given little attention to folklife and material folklore until relatively recently). Many of the traditional art forms created by women stem from women's domestic activities (a factor which may account for the relative wealth of information on women's material culture; these arts and crafts in the eyes of commentators have seemed appropriate to women's roles and hence have received attention; of course, it may also be that such activities are more public than many other kinds of women's lore and are thus more easily observed by researchers, especially male researchers). Though in the minds of outsiders many of these traditional arts and crafts of the world have principally an ethnic identity and may not be thought of as "women's art" (indeed, even intensive studies of these arts may not give much attention to the identity of the artists), they are practiced exclusively or chiefly by women. For example, American Indian baskets are largely the product of women (Mason, 1045, is the basic work on Indian baskets, but see also nos. 103, 495; Allen, 20, includes the life history of the author, a Pomo basketmaker, and photos of craftswomen at work on baskets; Pomo baskets have been thought of generally as among the supreme examples of the art; non-Indian baskets in America are more likely to be made by men; see no. 1507).

The less well-known quill art, the decoration chiefly on skins with dyed and natural porcupine quills, an art replaced by beadwork, was exclusively done by women (see nos. 149, 1013, 1182). And of course women are the weavers of the famous and much sought after Navajo blankets (see nos. 28, 131, 141, 458, 791, 845, 1087: pp. 58-76, 1278;

Gladys Reichard actually learned how to weave a blanket from Navajo women and her account, 1282, is particularly good). Throughout the world women are often the weavers of textiles or other products, such as mats. Anderson (32), Bjerregaard (161), Cason and Cahlender (289), and Katzenberg (861) all deal with different areas of the Americas. Osborne (1186) is particularly comprehensive on Guatemala and El Salvador, though as with most of these studies the emphasis is upon product rather than producer. Ryesky (1355) deals with women weavers in socioeconomic perspective and Jopling (821) with the different norms followed by men and women artists. Adams (6, 7) and Strange (1485) deal with Asian weaving, and Larsen, Bühler, Solyom, and Solyom (947) with the arts of dyeing textiles in Indonesia and elsewhere. For Africa see Kent (874) and Sieber (1404) and for the New Zealand Maori Mead (1070). In Asia women are sometimes the weavers of rugs, including kinds well-known and highly prized in the West (Chattopadhyay, 306; Gans-Ruedin, 576; Martin, 1042; Attenborough, 74: pp. 89-103). A detailed study of an American weaver of rag rugs is provided by Johnson (809); this essay probes deeply into the weaver's life and aesthetic.

The molas, appliqued decorative panels for clothing produced by the Kuna Indians of Panama, have been extremely popular in the United States and Europe, and they are of course produced by women. Salvador (1361, 1362) and Parker and Aron (1195) are particularly extensive treatments of this art form; Parker and Aron include very full notes on particular designs. Hirschfield (736) is a Marxist-structuralist analysis of molas which attempts to relate artistic and political-economic structures. See also Hoover (753), and Salvador (1363, 1364); Swain (1499) discusses differing male and female conceptions of ethnicity among the Kuna.

Women have often been potters, for example, among the Pueblo Indians (Bunzel, 251, is a classic study of Pueblo pottery). Litto (991) is an extensive survey, country by country, town by town, of western South American pottery, some of which is made by women. Kruckman (922) considers the effects which the establishment of a pottery industry had upon economics and sex roles in a Latin American village. MacGaffey (1015) studies two Bakongo potters in a culture where all of the potters are female; see also 1016. See also nos. 285, 486, 855, 1153.

Various forms of needlework are kinds of traditional women's art which have been given little attention by folklorists (perhaps partly because of difficulties in distinguishing folk from popular in this realm, but no doubt also because of a general neglect of women's folk art and because some kinds of needlework perhaps seemed neither particularly dramatic nor colorful, nor have they seemed particularly exotic or rural). One folklorist has dealt at length with American samplers (Fratto, 544, 546) and with the verse displayed on samplers, which is seen as bearing a relationship to contemporary commonplace books (545). Bolton and Coe (180), Colby (321), Curry (370), Huish (768), and

Krueger (923) also deal with samplers. Kopp and Kopp (914) attempt to call attention to American hooked and sewn rugs as a significant genre of American folk art, and Pocius (1230), working with Canadian hooked rugs, notes how basic design types mirror elements of hierarchical and egalitarian social structure. Dewhurst, MacDowell, and MacDowell (410) and Little (990) deal with various kinds of American folk art by women, including needlework. Swan (1500) is a profusely illustrated social history of American women which ties in with a discussion of their needlework. Harbeson (682) is a history of American needlework from the sixteenth to the twentieth centuries.

The following works come at the subject of needlework from a variety of perspectives and are listed as examples of the sort of published material available in an area which should be of greater interest to folklorists: nos. 112, 293, 381, 585, 624, 625, 626, 819, 1123, 1154, 1451 (embroidery); 778, 1051, 1192, 1251, 1546 (lace making); 292, 679, 681, 767, 1035, 1375.

Folk costume is an area of direct relevance to women in traditional societies, not only in that women wear distinctive costumes but also in that they are customarily the makers of clothing not only for themselves but for the male members of the group as well. There are a great many works on folk costume, most of them purely descriptive, such as nos. 29, 345, 346, 538, 657, 669, 1428, 1454, 1524, 1629. Flugel (530: pp. 103-121, 198-215) considers the significance of clothing in designating sex differences and Roberts (1310) and Kunzle (925) debate the question of how dress in a particular historical period reflected and molded sex roles. Molloy (1110), though a how-to-dress book, is very perceptive on the social significance of certain kinds of women's dress in modern American society. See also nos. 281, 724.

There has been a certain amount of attention paid to such female "folk" artists as Grandma Moses (Kallir, 852) and Clementine Hunter (Bacot, 85), but folklorists would generally prefer to classify such artists as "naive" or "primitive" rather than folk. More in keeping with the folklorist's conception of a folk (that is, traditional) artist is Maria Montoye Martinez, the noted potter of San Ildefonso whose life and art have ben chronicled in various works, beginning with Marriott (1039); see also nos. 1224, 1441. See also Stone (1477) on a well-known Polish weaver.

The Foxfire books contain various articles on women's crafts and on craftswomen: cheesemaking (1627: pp. 385-393), soapmaking (1624: pp. 151-158), butter churning (1624: pp. 185-188), cornshuck working (1626: pp. 451-464), and the process of weaving (as well as sheep herding, shearing, etc.) (1625: pp. 172-255).

Women also engage in folklife activities which may not be commonly regarded as "art" or "craft" (and which by and large have not been accorded the attention they deserve), such activities as cooking, gardening, and interior decoration. Walker (1564) has suggested that gardening was the only realm for artistic expression open to many black women in slavery times and after, and Hess (727) has raised the question of interior decoration as an art form. Patterson (1216) has written on Aran Island interiors as showing a woman's aesthetic and has linked that aesthetic to similar expression in the famous sweaters knitted in the Arans. These are interesting areas for investigation. Gardening and/or cooking are also discussed in nos. 470, 609, 692, 1047, 1356, 1357, 1532, 1624: pp. 159-164, 1627: pp. 150-193. Friedlander (559) discusses cooking in a particular Mexican village in relation to political oppression.

Weigle (1606) suggests several references on women's tattooing, Fox (537) discusses tattooing in a women's prison, and Bernstein (148) provides a brief portrait of a New York City female tattooist. Layard (953) notes that in South India tattoo artists are exclusively women, tying this fact in with a discussion of labyrinths and threshold designs. In various cultures women create threshold designs; see, for example, nos. 93, 1259.

Though not concerned with traditional art as such, Bovenscen (190), Castanis (291), Lippard (985), and Meyer and Schapiro (1080) are important, relevant statements on women's aesthetics.

Ladden (931) suggests that the role of martyr which women have sometimes had to assume has had an impact on women's art. Teilhet (1506) discusses the restrictions which female traditional artists labor under (though these may allow women to be more innovative). Hollister and Weatherford (745) note the absence of information on women's ritual art and call for further information in this area. Feinberg, Goldberg, Gross, Lieberman, and Sacre (508) attempt to relate the social/political position of women to the status of their textile making in several societies. Maksymowicz (1029) tries to relate myth to the sexual division of labor, which often has women making pottery. Jopling (822) points out how in one Mexican instance the low status of craftswomen in a particular craft has enabled them to obtain an economic advantage. The history and symbolism of the apron is briefly sketched by Siskind (1412). The "major visual art" of Bali, colorful cotton mantles produced by women, is through an analysis of structural principles seen to relate to the forms "preferred ... by the local culture" in Adams (9).

Of course numerous general works on folk art and other forms of material culture contain information on the material folk creations of women, even if they are not necessarily labeled as such. For example, in dealing with New Mexican wood carvers Briggs (212) discusses both male and female craftspersons, and the photographs in Nabokov (1133) make it clear that both men and women have a role in the adobe-making process, though this booklet is devoted largely to an explanation of the techniques involved rather than to the persons who perform them. A recent exhibition catalogue of Vermont folk arts and crafts (Beck, 128) contains information on numerous items produced by women, including such female folk art as paper dolls and rugs.

Nylén (1161), a compendious and careful survey of Swedish handcrafts, includes much data on the work of women, and in dealing with Norwegian peasant art Arneberg actually published two separate volumes, one for women's handcrafts (68), one for men's. A recent study of Senufo art (sculpture, ornaments, masks) in relation to culture by Glaze (597) contains separate chapters on how the art fits, respectively, into the lives of women and men. Even a work such as Jenkins (800), devoted largely to the crafts of male workers, includes some information on craftswomen, noting, for example, women as straw plaiters (pp. 144-148) and having a role in domestic weaving (pp. 181-184). For an extensive bibliography on American material culture see Glassie (594). Weatherford (1578) is a short but useful bibliography of works relating to women's traditional arts.

For women as architects, see Cole (324) and Weatherford (1577). Andersen (31) details the depiction of erotic female figures in medieval vernacular sculpture.

See also nos. 8, 15, 51, 52, 78, 232, 257, 258, 305, 382, 397, 466, 548, 596, 635, 672, 708, 713, 1009, 1049, 1052, 1235, 1236, 1245: pp. 100-103, 1274: pp. 114-122, 1325, 1347, 1453, 1508: pp. 79-112, 1552, 1566, 1591, 1648.

The traditional art whiich has received the most attention at least in the United States is **quilt making**, an art which has particularly flourished in North America. Recent interest in quilting stems in part from a recognition of patchwork quilt makers as percursors of modern abstract painters and as "pioneers in abstract design" (Dewhurst, MacDowell, and MacDowell, 410: p. xvii; see also Holstein, 746, 747). Mainardi (1023, 1024) has criticized that view, however, insisting that to view quilt makers in that manner is to value their art and aesthetic largely in terms of the male aesthetic of modern painting; Mainardi's writings have influenced feminists to an appreciation of quilts, however, as they turn to a "formerly ignored artistic heritage" (Weidlich, 1582: p. 7).

Quilting is certainly a folk art, but it has been little written upon by folklorists (nos. 45, 207, 208, 317, 443, 498, 1090, 1305, 1306, 1462 do represent folkloristic approaches), and one must turn to non-folklorists for most of the basic sources, although the best bibliography on quilting was compiled by two folklorists (Roach and Weidlich, 1304); this contains hundreds of references, only a few of which appear also in the present bibliography. Finley (520) has been called "the definitive text on patchwork quilts" and provides much information on historical and social dimensions of quilt making, as well as a variety of other data (the development of designs and names, etc.).

Various other works include historical and general information, such as Robertson (1314), Ickis (774), and Bacon (84), which also provides information on collecting, caring for, and repairing quilts. Orlofsky and Orlofsky (1183) is very well illustrated and provides a history of quilting, a bibliography, a very full discussion of techniques, and a list of quilt collections. Their comments on the social context of quilting are also available in a separate article (1184). Colby (322) contains illustrations of a number of historic quilts with notes on each, as well as discussion of design, construction methods, and materials; Colby (323) is more of a how-to book but with some history of the English quilt. Safford and Bishop (1358) discuss coverlets as well as quilts. Dunton (456) is good on certain patterns. Hall and Kretsinger (670) contains a brief, romantic text and many illustrations.

Several works have dealt with the quilts of a region or group or with otherwise specialized quilts: Bishop and Safanda (160) and Haders (666) Amish quilts, Clarke (317) those of Kentucky, Roach-Lankford (1305) those of Louisiana, and Johnson, Conor, Rogers, and Sidford (807) baby and doll quilts (see also no. 264).

Though older works on quilting tended to concentrate on the product rather than the producers, a number of more recent works have focused upon the artists who make the quilts. Cooper and Buferd (337) is a particularly impressive portrait of quilting women. The authors interviewed and observed a number of quilters in west Texas and New Mexico and much of the book is made up of excerpts from the interviews themselves. Together with excellent photos, the text gives a fine picture of these women's lives (see also nos. 336, 1253). Kalčik (847), Mayotte (1053), and Stone (1472) are also interviews with quilters, and quilters are also quoted by Lewis (978) and by Travis (1526). Individual quilters are also discussed in nos. 443, 1085, 1462, 1656. The social dimension of quilting or quilts as a form of communication is considered by Kirkland (887), Milspaw (1091), and Maines (1025; see also Eff, 473). Roach-Lankford (1306) is a particularly insightful treatment of a quilting bee as a process and the meanings family members may ascribe to a quilt. Hedges (709) draws upon the diaries of nineteenth century women for information on their quilts and quilting. No. 58 considers the changes in social context that affect the quilting of three Applachian women migrant to urban Michigan.

See also nos. 44, 159, 233, 237, 278, 376, 401, 467, 471, 527, 547, 613, 662, 735, 748, 758, 907, 948, 988, 1040, 1057, 1058, 1062, 1219, 1226, 1229, 1307, 1321, 1381, 1463, 1478, 1521, 1555, 1585, 1619, 1649.

Bowden (192), Dégh (400), Howard (762), and Reich, Buss, Fein, and Kurtz (1277) all deal with various kinds of women's **written folklore**. Dundes and Pagter (453) is the basic collection with commentary of "Xerox" folklore, traditional photocopied materials which circulate mainly in offices; because of the large numbers of women office workers this material is certainly of potential relevance.

There is not a large body of literature on **women folklorists**, but for that matter there is not a great deal of writing from the biographical or intellectual historical perspective on male folklorists either. As with male folklorists, obituaries are often the principal source for biographical information, as with the following: Armstrong (67) for Violet Alford, Banks (94) for Edith Guest, Boggs

(177) for Virginia Rodriguez Rivera, Boyer (194) for A.H. Gayton, Bronson (230), Dean Smith (391), and Rhodes (1292) for Maud Karpeles, Brunvard (243) for Maria Leach, Burne (253) for Lucy Catherine Lloyd and (254) Marian Roalfe Cox, Coote Lake (342) for Mary Macleod Banks, (343) Estella Canziani, and (344) Barbara Freire Marreco, Crowley (366) for Suzanne Comhaire-Slyvain, Davidson (386) for Nora Chadwick and (387) Katharine Briggs, Goldfrank (607) for Gladys Reichard, Hartland (645) for Charlotte Burne, James (789) for Margaret Murray and (790) Sona Rose Burstein, James (792) for Eloise Ramsay, Karpeles (858) for Anne Geddes Gilchrist, Kekis (868) for Maria Cadilla de Marinez, Knight (904) for Marjorie Lansing Porter, Leach (954) for Grace Partridge Smith, Marett (1037) for Edith Carey and (1036) Eleanor Hull, Newall (1144) for Katharine Briggs, Percival (1222) for B.M. Blackwood, Sanderson (1368) for Mary Williams, Wright (1650) for Adela Spoer and (1651) Eliza Gutch.

However, several women in the field of folklore have received more attention, including full-length biographies. For example, Zora Neale Hurston is the subject of a recent extensive biographical study (Hemenway, 715) and she has also been considered in several articles, partly because of her eminence as a novelist and literary figure (nos. 169, 261, 599, 995). Martha Young is the subject of a book (Hoole, 752). Dorothy Scarborough is the subject of both a thesis (Muncy, 1126) and a dissertation (Neatherlin, 1136), though here too the emphasis is upon her novels and literary reputation rather than her work as a folklorist. Her novel, The Wind, was recently republished, however, with a biographical introduction by a folklorist (Grider, 653). Ruth Crawford Seeger's eminence as a composer seems to have been more responsible for recent writing about her than her work in ethnomusicology (Gaume, 584; Jepson, 802), though that aspect of her life and work is not neglected. Modéll (1108) is a biographical study of Ruth Benedict, who contributed much to the field of anthropology as well as to that of folklore, but Briscoe (222) focuses specifically upon Benedict as folklorist. There is also much biographicl information in an anthology of Benedict's work edited by Margaret Mead (129). For Benedict, see also nos. 704: pp. 358-365, 964. Elsie Clews Parsons, something of a legendary figure in folkloristics, is considered by Lurie (1011), Chambers (300), Dorson (429, 430), and Reichard (1280); Reuss (1289) in discussing the "folklore of folklorists" specifically deals with her as a figure of professional legend. For Constance Rourke, not really a folklorist but one whose important writings certainly touch on folklore materials, see Bluestein (170). Known primarily as a dancer and choreographer, Katherine Dunham did do fieldwork as a young woman under the direction of Melville Herskovits; she is the subject of a biography by Beckford (124); see also Aschenbrenner (71). As a woman traveller in Africa Mary Kingsley has received some attention, for example from Oliver (1172).

Helen Creighton has published her autobiography (356), as did Margaret Murray (1130), and twelve women are among the contributors to Reuss and Lund (1290), a collection of autobiographical essays in which folklorists explain how they became interested in the field. In discussing her fieldwork and data, Scarborough (1371, 1372) includes autobiographical information, as does Hurston (772). Margaret Mead has, of course, written a celebrated autobiography (1069), but Mead is rather peripheral to folklore as such.

Other women folklorists whose lives and work have been written upon include Frances Densmore (Lurie, 1011; Archabel, 61), Maude Minnish Sutton (Patterson, 1215), Lucy Broadwood (Bassin, 108), Mary Henderson Eastman (McNeil, 1066), Violeta Parra (Agosin and Payne, 13), Martha Warren Beckwith (Luomala, 1006), Fannie Hardy Eckstorm (Ring, 1300; Whitten, 1621), Charlotte Burne (Burne, 255; Bronner, 227), and Alice Marriott (Kobler, 905). In his history of British folkloristics Dorson (428: pp. 277-283, 318-331, 333-336, 360-366, 381-387) deals with various women in the field, such as Lady Alice Bertha Gomme, Charlotte Burne, and Mary Frere. For women folklorists who have been involved in the study of the folklore of Mexico and other Latin American countries, including a few North Americans, there is Rodríguez Rivera (1318), a collection of short biographical articles in Spanish.

Reuss (1288) deals with the role women have played in American folklore study and in the American Folklore Society and de Caro (395, 396) with the "women's movement" in the American Folklore Society in the early 1970's.

See also nos. 218, 239, 265, 507, 834, 872, 1104, 1128, 1353, 1470.

There is a small body of literature concerning **women as fieldworkers** and, more generally, **sex and gender in the fieldwork situation**, although the personal aspects of fieldwork are little discussed by folklorists per se. Among folkloristic discussions of fieldwork, Georges and Jones (587) argue that sex, age, and so on need not affect the collecting situation. Toelken (520) argues just the opposite, that the fieldworker must take into account the way factors, such as the sex of the collector, informant, and others present in the collecting situation, affect the data collected, and he offers some strategies for dealing with specific problems. Yocum (1655) sensitively discusses doing fieldwork with members of her own family; this article includes interesting photodocumentation. See Goldstein (610) for a discussion of the woman in the field as wife and female assistant. Lee (963) includes a description of the different responses male and female informants made to her collecting. Eastman (465) and McNeil (1066) include some fieldwork experiences of a pioneer folklore collector, Mary Henderson Eastman.

Among anthropological discussions of fieldwork Helm (714) concerns women in early anthropology. Powdermaker (1250) and especially Bovin (191) discuss sex and gender as they affect fieldwork. The latter lists the advantages and

disadvantages usually ascribed to male and female
fieldworkers and discusses as well the neutral role a
culture may assign a stranger who does not fit into its sex
role pattern. Both articles mention the need to use a team
approach in some societies. Frisbie in nos. 566, 567
examines a specific area of fieldwork, the effects and
problems of taking a child into the field. Pettigrew (1228)
recounts her experience doing fieldwork with Sikhs.

Recently anthropologists have argued that the personal
experiences of fieldwork are significant in the study of
anthropology and in understanding ethnographies and other
products of anthropological study. Many have begun to
publish such experiences in their ethnographies, in
discussions of fieldwork, and in collections of fieldwork
experiences. See nos. 213, 757, 939, 1249, 1576, and the
ground-breaking Bowen (193). Dancer and choreographer
Katherine Dunham also published an account of her Caribbean
fieldwork as a young woman (454). Golde's collection (604)
is specifically devoted to the experiences of women
anthropologists in the field. The essays included discuss a
wide variety of experiences, different cultural expectations
placed on women fieldworkers, advantages and disadvantages
of being female in the field, strategies for dealing with
various situations, and so on. It is the most comprehensive
and thoughtful study of sex and gender in fieldwork at the
present time. See especially no. 940. See Kalčik (848) for a
more detailed review.

Other collections of fieldwork experiences include nos.
150, 288, 534, 553, 820, 883, 1437. In these, see
especially: Dube (448), which includes a useful exploration
of the problems of an insider when studying her own culture;
Diamond (413) on working in a male-oriented society; Gallin
and Gallin (574) on the husband and wife team and taking
children into the field; Gonzalez (614), which mentions how
the relationship between men and women in the host society
affects fieldwork, and (615) on fieldwork with children; and
Spindler and Spindler (1438) for husband and wife team
fieldwork. See Kalčik (850) for a working bibliography on
sex roles and fieldwork.

Other resources: Useful journals and magazines (not
necessarily still being published at this time) include:
Folklore Women's Communication (formerly Folklore
Feminists Communication), Lady-Unique-Inclination-of-the-
Night (devoted to the subject of goddesses), Signs:
Journal of Women in Society and Culture, Women: A Journal
of Liberation, Paid My Dues: A Quarterly Journal of Women
and Music, Country Women, Abstracts of Women's Studies,
Concerns: Newsletter of the Women's Caucus for the Modern
Languages, Aphra: The Feminist Literary Magazine,
Frontiers: A Journal of Women Studies, Heresies: A
Feminist Publication in Art and Politics, Feminist Art
Journal, National Women's Anthropology Newsletter, Women
and Language News, and the International Journal of
Women's Studies.

For film, see reviews and comments by Susan Dwyer-Shick
and others in various issues of Folklore Feminists

Communication (no. 6: pp. 8, 24; no. 7: pp. 20-21; no. 8: pp. 13-14; no 9: pp 9-13) and Folklore Women's Communication (no. 15: p. 24; no. 16: p. 19; no. 21: p. 10; no. 22: pp. 21-23; no. 24: pp. 23-24; no. 26: pp. 8, 9-10; nos. 27-28: pp. 18, 19-20). See also National Women's Anthropology Newsletter, vol. 3, no. 3, and the collection of reviews in American Anthropologist vol. 79: pp. 192-212. Beh (126) discusses the Women's Film Archive.

Farrell (501) discusses one particular research center as a source for raw data in studying women in country music. The Women's History Research Center in Berkeley, California, maintains a library and archive.

In 1979 a Conference on Women and Folklore was held in Philadelphia; see Reimensnyder (1285) for details.

Several courses on women and folklore have been offered at various American universities. For detailed descriptions including syllabi, see nos. 276, 330, 352, 643, 893, 944.

Lange (941) discusses career opportunities outside teaching for women folklorists.

BIBLIOGRAPHY

CITATIONS

1.   Abercromby, John. "An Amazonian Custom in the Caucasus." Folk-Lore 2 (1891): 171-181.

2.   Abernethy, Francis Edward, ed. Legendary Ladies of Texas. Publications of the Texas Folklore Society, No. 43. Dallas: E-Heart, 1981.

3.   Abrahams, Roger D. Jump Rope Rhymes: A Dictionary. American Folklore Society Bibilographical and Special Series, No. 20. Austin: University of Texas Press, 1969.

4.   ----------. "Personal Power and Social Restraint in the Definition of Folklore." Journal of American Folklore 84 (1971): 16-30.

5.   Adamec, Cannie Stark, ed. In press. Sex Roles: Origins, Influences and Implications for Women. Proceedings of the Inaugural Institute on Women, Ottawa, Canada. St. Albans, Vt.: Eden Press.

6.   Adams, Marie Jean. System and Meaning in East Sumba Textile Design: A Study in Traditional Indonesian Art. Southeast Asia Studies, Cultural Reports, No. 16. New Haven: Yale University, 1969.

7.   ----------. "Designs in Sumba Textiles: Local Meanings and Foreign Influences." Textile Museum Journal 3, no 2. (1971): 28-37.

8.   ----------. "Work Patterns and Symbolic Structures in a Village Culture, East Sumba, Indonesia." Southeast Asia 1 (1971): 321-334.

9.   ----------. "Structural Aspects of Village Art." American Anthropologist 75 (1973): 265-279.

10.   Adlard, John. "A Note on Nell Gwyn." Folklore 83 (1972): 61-67.

11.   Ager, Lynn Price. "Storyknifing: An Alaskan Eskimo Girl's Game." Journal of the Folklore Institute 11 (1975): 187-198.

12.   Agogino, George A., Stevens, Dominique E., and Carlotta, Lynda. "Doña Marina and the Legend of La Llorona." Anthropological Journal of Canada 11 (1973): 27-29.

13.   Agosin, Marjorie, and Payne, Sylvia (trans.). "Violeta Parra: Her Life and Her song." Folklore Women's Communication 24 (1981): 12-14.

14.   Ainsworth, Catherine Harris. "Jump Rope Verses around the United States." Western Folklore 20 (1961): 179-199.

15.   Aitken, Robert. "Agricultural Implements Drawn by Women." Scottish Studies 3 (1959): 232-233.

16.   Albertson, Chris. Bessie. New York: Stein and Day, 1972.

17.   Alexiou, Margaret. The Ritual Lament in Greek Tradition. Cambridge: Cambridge University Press, 1974.

18.   Alford, Violet. "The Cat Saint." Folk-Lore 52 (1941): 161-183.

19.   Alford, Violet, and Gallop, Rodney. The Traditional Dance. London: Methuen, 1935.

20.   Allen, Elsie. Pomo Basketmaking: A Supreme Art for the Weaver. Heraldsburg, Cal.: Naturegraph, 1972.

21.   Allen, Prudence. "Love and Marriage in York State Lore." New York Folklore Quarterly 5 (1949): 257-267.

22.   Allen, Shirley S. "The Griselda Tale and the Portrayal of Women in the Decameron." Philological Quarterly 56 (1977): 1-13.

23.   Allison, Lelah. "Folk Beliefs Regarding Weather in Southeastern Illinois." Journal of American Folklore 61 (1948): 68-70.

24.   ----------. "Folk Beliefs Collected in Southeastern Illinois." Journal of American Folklore 63 (1950): 309-324.

25.   Alloy, Evelyn, ed. Working Women's Music: The Songs and Struggles of Women in the Cotton Mills, Textile Plants and Needle Trades. Hatboro, Pa.: Legacy Books, 1976.

26.   Al-Qazzaz, Ayad. Women in the Middle East and North Africa. Middle East Monographs, No. 2. Austin: Center for Middle Eastern Studies, University of Texas, 1977.

27.   Ames, Mrs. L.D. "The Missouri Play-Party." Journal of American Folklore 24 (1911): 295-318.

28.   Amsden, Charles A. Navaho Weaving, Its Technique and History. Santa Ana, Cal.: Fine Arts Press, 1934.

29.   Andersen, Ellen. Folk Costumes in Denmark. Copenhagen: Hassing, 1952.

30.   Andersen, Flemming G., and Pettitt, Thomas. "Mrs.

Brown of Falkland: A Singer of Tales?" _Journal of American Folklore_ 92 (1979): 1-24.

31.   Andersen, Jorgen. _The Witch on the Wall: Medieval Erotic Sculpture in the British Isles_. Copenhagen and London: Rosenkilde and Bagger and George Allen and Unwin, 1977.

32.   Anderson, Marilyn. _Guatemalan Textiles Today_. New York: Watson-Guptill, 1978.

33.   Andors, Ellen B. "The Rodi: Female Associations among the Gurung of Nepal." Ph.D. dissertaion, Columbia University, 1976.

34.   Andreski, Iris. _Old Wives Tales_. New York: Schocken, 1970.

35.   Anonymous. "A Brief List of Works Containing 'She is more to be pitied than censured' (by William B. Gray, 1898)." Washington: Library of Congress Archive of Folk Song (pamphlet), n.d.

36.   ----------. "A Rural Wedding in Lorraine." _Folk-Lore Record_ 3, no. 2 (1880): 258-274.

37.   ----------. "Confining Maidens in Alaska." _Journal of American Folklore_ 1 (1888): 168-169.

38.   ----------. "English Folk-Tales in America." _Journal of American Folklore_ 2 (1889): 213-218.

39.   ----------. "Gypsy Queen in America." _Journal of American Folklore_ 2 (1889): 156.

40.   ----------. "Beliefs of Southern Negroes Concerning Hags." _Journal of American Folklore_ 7 (1894): 66-67.

41.   ----------. "Courtship Formulas of Southern Negroes." _Journal of American Folklore_ 8 (1895): 155-156.

42.   ----------. "Negro Superstitions in South Carolina." _Journal of American Folklore_ 8 (1895): 251-252.

43.   ----------. "Abenaki Witchcraft Story." _Journal of American Folklore_ 15 (1902): 62-63.

44.   ----------. "American Patchwork Quilts." _Newark Museum_ January, 1930: 89-92.

45.   ----------. "The Art of Patchwork." _Tennessee Folklore Society Bulletin_ 16 (1950): 54-61.

46.   ----------. "Scatological Lore on Campus." _Journal of American Folklore_ 75 (1962): 260-262.

47.   ----------. "Sources for Songs of the Woman's Suffrage Movement: With Library of Congress Call Numbers."
Washington: Library of Congress Archive of Folk Song
(pamphlet), 1969.

48.   ----------. "Bundling." In no. 957, pp. 639-640.

49.   ----------. "Keen." In no. 957, p. 573.

50.   ----------. "Loathly Lady." In no. 957, pp. 639-640.

51.   ----------. "Traditional Women's Art Forms at the
Metropolitan." Folklore Feminists Communication 4 (1974):
13.

52.   ----------. "Doll Making." Folklore Feminists
Communication 9 (1976): 5.

53.   ----------. "Women's Oral History Resource Section."
Frontiers 2, no. 2 (1977): 110-128.

54.   ----------. "'A Feast of Witches.'" Folklore Women's Communication 14 (1978): 21.

55.   ----------. "'Witches Bringing a Shower of Rain.'"
Folklore Women's Communication 14 (1978): inside cover.

56.   ----------. "More on Mitchell's Note." Folklore
Women's Communication 17 (1979): 23-24.

57.   ----------. "A Woman's Ways: An Interview with Judy
Swamp." Parabola 5, no. 4 (1980): 52-61.

58.   ----------. "From Bed to Wall: The Quilt Making of
Three Appalachian Women in Michigan." Folklore Women's
Communication 26 (1982): 5-7.

59.   Anonymous and Foster, George M. "Adolescence Ceremonies." In no. 957, pp. 11-12.

60.   Anton, Ferdinand. Women in Pre-Columbian America.
New York: Abner Schram, 1973.

61.   Archabel, Nina Marchetti. "Frances Densmore: Pioneer
in the Study of American Indian Music." In Women of
Minnesota: Selected Biographical Essays, ed. Barbara
Stuhler and Gretchen Greuter, pp. 94-115. St. Paul:
Minnesota Historical Society Press, 1977.

62.   Ardener, Edwin. "Belief and the Problem of Women."
In The Interpretation of Ritual: Essays in Honour of A. I.
Richards. ed. J.S. LaFontaine, pp. 135-158. London:
Tavistock, 1972.

63.   Ardener, Shirley G. "Sexual Insult and Female

Militancy." Man: Journal of the Royal Anthropological Institute 8 (1973): 422-440.

64.   ----------, ed. Perceiving Women. New York: John Wiley and Sons, 1975.

65.   Arguelles, Miriam, and Arguelles, Jose. The Feminine: Spacious as the Sky. Boulder, Colo., and London: Shambhala, 1977.

66.   Armitage, Sue, Banfield, Theresa, and Jacobus, Sarah. "Black Women and Their Communities in Colorado." Frontiers 2, no. 2 (1977): 45-51.

67.   Armstrong, Lucille. "Violet Alford, Her Life and Work, A Tribute." Folklore 84 (1973): 104-110.

68.   Arneberg, Halfdan. Norwegian Peasant Art: Women's Handicrafts. Oslo: Fabritus and Sonner, 1949.

69.   Arnold, Marigene. "Mexican Women: The Anatomy of a Stereotype in a Mestizo Village." Ph.D. dissertation, University of Florida, 1973.

70.   Arthur, Marilyn B. "Review Essay: Classics." Signs: Journal of Women in Culture and Society 2 (1976): 382-403.

71.   Aschenbrenner, Joyce. "Katherine Dunham: A Biographical Note." Dance Research Annual 12 (1981): 11-13.

72.   Ashe, Geoffrey. The Virgin. London and Henley: Routledge and Kegan Paul, 1976.

73.   Atkinson, Robert M. "Songs Little Girls Sing: An Invitation to Violence." Northwest Folklore 2 (1967): 2-8.

74.   Attenborough, David. The Tribal Eye. New York: W.W. Norton, 1976.

75.   Ayres, Barbara. "Pregnancy Magic: A Study of Food Taboos and Sex Avoidances." In Cross-Cultural Approaches: Readings in Comparative Research, ed. Clellan S. Ford, pp. 111-125. New Haven: HRAF Press, 1967.

76.   Axler, David. Untitled note on jokes about feminists. Folklore Women's Communication 23 (1980): 37-38.

77.   Azadovskii, Mark. A Siberian Tale Teller, trans. James R. Dow. Center for Intercultural Studies in Folklore and Ethnomusicology Monographs, No. 2. Austin: University of Texas, 1974.

78.   Aziz, Barbara Nimri. "Nepal Hill Art and Women's Traditions." Heresies 4 (1978): 93-95.

79.   Babb, Jewel, and Taylor, Pat Ellis. Border Healing Woman: The Story of Jewel Babb. Austin: University of Texas Press, 1981.

80.   Babcock, W.H. "Charms for Young Women." Journal of American Folklore 1 (1888): 164-165.

81.   Bachofen, Jacob. J. Myth, Religion and Mother Right. Trans. Ralph Manheim. Princeton: Princeton University Press, 1967.

82.   Backus, E.M. "Negro Ghost Stories." Journal of American Folklore 9 (1896): 228-230.

83.   Bacon, Alice. Japanese Girls and Women. Boston and New York: Houghton Mifflin, 1891.

84.   Bacon, Lenice Ingram. American Patchwork Quilts. New York: William Morrow, 1973.

85.   Bacot, H. Parrott. Louisiana Folk Art. Baton Rouge: Anglo-American Art Museum, Louisiana State University, 1972.

86.   Baker, Margaret. Discovering the Folklore and Customs of Love and Marriage. Aylesbury, England: Shire Publications, 1974.

87.   Baldwin, L. Karen. "A Sampling of Housewives' Proverbial Phrases from Levittown, Pennsylvania." Keystone Folklore Quarterly 10 (1965): 127-148.

88.   ----------. "Down on Bugger Run: Family Groups and the Social Base of Folklore." Ph.D. dissertation, University of Pennsylvania, 1975.

89.   ----------. "Rhyming Pieces and Piecin' Rhymes: Recitation Verse and Family Poem-Making." Southern Folklore Quarterly 40 (1976): 209-238.

90.   ----------. "'Woof!': A Word on Women's Roles in Family Storytelling." In no. 835.

91.   Ballou, Patricia K. "Review Essay: Bibliographies for Research on Women." Signs: Journal of Women in Culture and Society 3 (1977): 436-450.

92.   Banks, Frank D. "Plantation Courtship." Journal of American Folklore 7 (1894): 147-149.

93.   Banks, M.M. "Threshold Designs." Folk-Lore 48 (1937): 268-269.

94.   ----------. Obituary for Edith Guest. Folk-Lore 53 (1942): 80.

95.   Bannan, Helen M. "Spider Woman's Web: Mothers and Daughters in Southwestern Native American Literature." In no. 226, pp. 268-279.

96.   Barakat, Robert A. "Aztec Motifs in 'La Llorona.'" Southern Folklore Quarterly 29 (1965): 288-296.

97.   ----------. "Wailing Women of Folklore." Journal of American Folklore 82 (1969): 270-272.

98.   Barbeau, Marius. "Bear Mother." Journal of American Folklore 59 (1945): 1-12.

99.   Barker, Diane Leonard, and Allen, Sheila, eds. Sexual Divisions and Society: Process and Change. London: Tavistock, 1976.

100.   Barnes, B.S. "Policelore." Louisiana Folklore Miscellany 5, no. 2 (1982): 34-47.

101.   Barnes, Daniel R. "The Bosom Serpent." Journal of American Folklore 85 (1972): 111-122.

102.   Barnes, Gertrude. "Superstitions and Maxims from Dutchess County, New York." Journal of American Folklore 36 (1923): 16-22.

103.   Barrett, S.A. "Pomo Indian Basketry." University of California Publications in American Archaeology and Ethnology 7 (1908): 133-308.

104.   Barrick, Mac E. "The Verse Competition Jest in Central Pennsylvania." Journal of American Folklore 85 (1972): 73.

105.   ----------. "The Helen Keller Joke Cycle." Journal of American Folklore 93 (1980): 441-449.

106.   Barry, H.H., Bacon, M.K., and Child, I.L. "A Cross-Cultural Survey of Some Sex Differences in Socialization." Journal of Abnormal and Social Psychology 63 (1957): 327-332.

107.   Baruch, Grace K. "The Traditional Feminine Role: Some Negative Effects." The School Counselor March, 1974: 285-289.

108.   Bassin, Ethel. "Lucy Broadwood, 1858-1929: Her Contribution to the Collection and Study of Gaelic Traditional Song." Scottish Studies 9 (1965): 145-152.

109.   Basso, Keith H. The Gift of Changing Woman. Bureau of American Ethnology, Anthropological Papers, No. 76. Washington: Bureau of American Ethnology, 1966.

110.   Bastien, Joseph W. "Rosinta, Rats, and The River:

Bad Luck is Banished in Andean Bolivia." In no. 494, pp.
260-274.

111.   Bataille, Gretchen. "Bibliography on Native American
Women." Concerns 10, no. 2 (1980): 16-28.

112.   Bath, Virginia Churchill. Embroidery Masterworks.
Chicago: Regenry, 1972.

113.   Bawden, C.R. "The Theme of the Calumniated Wife in
Mongolian Popular Literature." Folklore 74 (1963):
488-497.

114.   Baxandall, Rosalyn, Gordon, Linda, and Reverby
Susan. America's Working Women. New York: Random House,
1976.

115.   Bayliss, Clara Kern. "Witchcraft." Journal of
American Folklore 21 (1908): 263.

116.   Beardsley, Richard K., and Hankey, Rosalie. "The
Vanishing Hitchhiker." California Folklore Quarterly 1
(1942): 303-335.

117.   ----------. "A History of the Vanishing Hitchhiker."
California Folklore Quarterly 2 (1943): 13-25.

118.   Beauchamp, W.M. "Onondaga Tales." Journal of American Folklore 1 (1888): 44-48.

119.   ----------. "Iroquois Women." Journal of American
Folklore 13 (1900): 81-91.

120.   Bebey, Francis. African Music. London: Harrap,
1975.

121.   Beck, Ervin. "Telling the Tale in Belize." Journal
of American Folklore 93 (1980): 417-434.

122.   Beck, Jane C. "The White Lady of Great Britain and
Ireland." Folklore 81 (1970): 292-306.

123.   ----------. Always in Season: Folk Art and Traditional Culture in Vermont. Montpelier: Vermont Council on
the Arts, 1982.

124.   Beckford, Ruth. Katherine Dunham: A Biography.
Foreword Arthur Mitchell. New York and Basel: Marcel Dekker,
1979.

125.   Beckwith, Martha Warren. "Signs and Superstitions
Collected from American College Girls." Journal of American
Folklore 36 (1923): 1-15.

126.   Beh, Siew Hua. "The Women's Film Archive." Folklore
Feminists Communication 8 (1976): 12.

127.   ----------. "Growing Up with Legends of the Chinese Swordswomen." In no. 1445, pp. 121-126.

128.   Bell, Michael J. "Tending Bar at Brown's: Occupational Role as Artistic Performance." Western Folklore 35 (1976): 93-107.

129.   Benedict, Ruth Fulton. An Anthropologist at Work: Writings of Ruth Benedict, ed. Margaret Mead. New York: Greenwood Press, 1966.

130.   Bennett, Lynn. "Mother's Milk and Mother's Blood: The Social and Symbolic Roles of Women among the Brahmans and Chetris of Nepal." Ph.D. dissertaion, Columbia University, 1977.

131.   Bennett, Noel. The Weaver's Pathway: A Clarification of the "Spirit Trail" in Navajo Weaving. Flagstaff: Northland Press, 1935.

132.   Benson, Mary Sumner. Women in Eighteenth-Century America: A Study of Opinion and Social Usage. New York: Columbia University Press, 1935.

133.   Benwell, Gwen, and Waugh, Arthur. Sea Enchantress: The Tale of the Mermaid and Her Kin. London: Hutchinson, 1961.

134.   Berg, William. "Pandora: Pathology of a Creation Myth." Fabula 17 (1976): 1-25.

135.   Bergen, Fanny D. "English Folk-Tales in America II: Johnny-Cake." Journal of American Folklore 2 (1889): 60-62.

136.   ----------. "Some Customs and Beliefs of the Winnebago Indians." Journal of American Folklore 9 (1896): 51-54.

137.   ----------. "Two Negro Witch Stories." Journal of American Folklore 12 (1890): 145-147.

138.   ----------. "Two Witch Stories." Journal of American Folklore 12 (1899): 68-69.

139.   Bergen, Fanny D., and Newell, W.W. "Weather Lore." Journal of American Folklore 2 (1889): 203-208.

140.   Berkman, Susan C.J. "'She's Writing Antidotes': An Examination of Hospital Employees' Uses of Stories about Personal Experiences." In Occupational Folklore and the Folklore of Working, ed. Catherine Swanson and Philip Nusbaum, pp. 48-54. Folklore Forum 11, no. 1. Bloomington: Folklore Forum, 1978.

141.   Berlant, Anthony, and Kahlenberg, Mary Hunt. Walk in Beauty. New York: Graphic Society, 1977.

142.   Bernard, H. Russell. "Otomi Obscene Humor: Preliminary Observations." Journal of American Folklore 88 (1975): 383-392.

143.   Berndt, Catherine H. Women's Changing Ceremonies in Northern Australia L'Homme: Cahiers d'Ethnologie, de Geographie et de Linguistique, No. 1. Paris: Marmann et Cie, 1950.

144.   ----------. "The Ghost Husband: Society and the Individual in New Guinea Myth." Journal of American Folklore 79 (1966): 244-277.

145.   Berndt, Ronald M. "The Wuradilagu Song Cycle of North-Eastern Arnhem Land." Journal of American Folklore 79 (1966): 195-243.

146.   Berne, Eric. "The Mythology of Dark and Fair: Psychiatric Use of Folklore." Journal of American Folklore 72 (1959): 1-13.

147.   ----------. What do You Say after You Say Hello? The Psychology of Human Destiny. New York: Bantam, 1973.

148.   Bernstein, A.A. "Queen of the Bowery." New York Folklore Quarterly 23 (1967): 196-201.

149.   Berry, Carolyn. "Quill Art." Heresies 4 (1978): 112-113.

150.   Beteille, Andre, and Madan, T.N., eds. Encounter and Experience: Personal Accounts of Fieldwork. Honolulu: University of Hawaii Press, 1975.

151.   Bettelheim, Bruno. Symbolic Wounds: Puberty Rites and the Envious Male. Glencoe, Ill.: Free Press, 1954.

152.   ----------. The Uses of Enchantment: The Meaning and Importance of Fairy Tales. New York, Knopf, 1976.

153.   Betteridge, Anne H. "The Controversial Vows of Urban Muslim Women in Iran." In no. 494, pp. 141-155.

154.   Bick, M.J.A. "Power and the Allocation of Rights of Women in African Societies." Ph.D. dissertation, Columbia University, 1974.

155.   Biggar, Jeanne C. Bibliography on the Sociology of Sex Roles. Charlottesville: Department of Sociology, University of Virginia, 1970.

156.   Binford, Martha B. "Julia: An East African Diviner." In no. 494, pp. 3-21.

157.   Binford, Sally R. "Myths and Matriarchies." Human Behavior 8, no. 5 (1979): 62-66.

158.   Birdwhistell, Ray. Kinesics and Context. Philadelphia: University of Pennsylvania Press, 1970.

159.   Bishop, Robert. New Discoveries in American Quilts. New York: E.P. Dutton, 1975.

160.   Bishop, Robert, and Safanda, Elizabeth. A Gallery of Amish Quilts: Design Diversity from a Plain People. New York: E.P. Dutton, 1976.

161.   Bjerregaard, Lena. Techniques of Guatemalan Weaving. New York: Van Nostrand Reinhold, 1977.

162.   Blackburn, Stuart H. "Oral Performance: Narrative and Ritual in a Tamil Tradition." Journal of American Folklore 94 (1981): 207-227.

163.   Blacking, John. "Songs, Dances, Mimes and Symbolism of Venda Girls' Initiation Schools, Part 1: Vhusha." African Studies 28 (1969): 3-35.

164.   ----------. "Songs, Dances, Mimes and Symbolism of Venda Girls' Initiation Schools, Part 2: Milayo." African Studies 28 (1969): 69-118.

165.   ----------. "Songs, Dances, Mimes and Symbolism of Venda Girls' Initiation Schools, Part 3: Domba." African Studies 28 (1969): 149-199.

166.   ----------. "Songs, Dances, Mimes and Symbolism of Venda Girls' Initiation Schools, Part 4: The Great Domba Song." African Studies 28 (1969): 215-266.

167.   Blaffer, Sarah C. The Black-man of Zinacantan: A Central American Legend. Austin: University of Texas Press, 1972.

168.   Blake, C. Fred. "The Feelings of Chinese Daughters towards the Mothers as Revealed in Marriage Laments." Folklore 90 (1979): 91-97.

169.   Blake, Emma L. "Zora Neale Hurston: Author and Folklorist." Negro History Bulletin 29 (1966): 149-150.

170.   Bluestein, Gene. "Constance Rourke and the Folk Sources of American Humor." Western Folklore 26 (1967): 77-87.

171.   Blum, Harold P., ed. Female Psychology: Contemporary Psycholanalytic Views. New York: International Universities Press, 1977.

172.   Blumenthal, Walter Hart. Women Camp Followers of the American Revolution. Philadelphia: G.S. MacManus, 1952.

173.   Blumhagen, Grace Kathleen O'Connor. "The Relationship Between Female Identity and Feminism." Ph.D. dissertation, Washington University, 1975.

174.   Boag, Mrs. E.T. "De Secon' Flood." Journal of American Folklore 11 (1898): 237-238.

175.   Boas, Franz. "On Certain Songs and Dances of British Columbia." Journal of American Folklore 1 (1888): 49-64.

176.   Boatright, Mody C. "The Family Saga as a Form of Folklore." In The Family Saga and Other Phases of American Folklore, pp. 1-19. Urbana: University of Illinois Press, 1958.

177.   Boggs, Edna. Obituary for Virginia Rodriguez Rivera. Journal of American Folklore 82 (1969): 70.

178.   Bogin, Meg. The Women Troubadours. New York: Paddington Press, 1976.

179.   Boles, Jacqueline Miles. "The Nightclub Stripper: A Sociological Study of a Deviant Occupation." Ph.D. dissertation, University of Georgia, 1973.

180.   Bolton, Ethel Stanwood, and Coe, Eva Johnston. American Samplers. Boston: Massachusetts Society of the Colonial Dames of America, 1921.

181.   Bolton, Henry Carrington. "The Porta Magica, Rome." Journal of American Folklore 8 (1895): 73-78.

182.   Borun, Minda, McLaughlin, Molly, Oboler, Gina, Perchonock, Norma, and Sexton, Lorraine. Women's Liberation: An Anthropological View. Pittsburgh: Know, Inc., 1971.

183.   Boserup, Ester. Women's Role in Economic Development. New York: St. Martin's Press, 1970.

184.   Botkin, B.A. The American Play-Party Song. University Studies, No. 37. Lincoln: University of Nebraska, 1937.

185.   ----------, ed. Lay My Burden Down: A Folk History of Slavery. Chicago and London: University of Chicago Press, 1945.

186.   Boulding, Elise. The Underside of History: A View of Women through Time. Boulder, Colo.: Westview Press, 1976.

187.   Bourguignon, Erika, and Greenbaum, Lenora S.

Diversity and Homogeneity in World Societies. N.p.: HRAF
Press, 1973.

188.   Bourke, J.G. "Custom of 'Measuring' Sick Children."
Journal of American Folklore 5 (1892): 241-242.

189.   ----------. "Popular Medicine, Customs, and Supersti-
tions· of the Rio Grande." Journal of American Folklore 7
(1894): 119-146.

190.   Bovenscen, Silvia. "Is There a Feminine Aesthetic?"
Heresies 4 (1978): 10-12.

191.   Bovin, Mette. "The Significance of the Sex of the
Field Worker for Insights into the Male and Female Worlds."
Ethnos 31, supplement (1966): 24-27.

192.   Bowden, Betsy. "A Query about Slam Books." Folklore
Women's Communication 18 (1979): 15-17.

193.   Bowen, Elenore Smith [Laura Bohannan]. Return to
Laughter. Garden City: Doubleday and American Museum of
Natural History, 1964.

194.   Boyer, Ruth M. Obituary for Anna Hadwick Gayton.
Journal of American Folklore 91 (1978): 834-841.

195.   Braddock, Joseph. The Bridal Bed. London: Joseph
Hale, 1960.

196.   Braddy, Haldeen. "Queens of the Bullring." Southern
Folklore Quarterly 26 (1962): 107-112.

197.   Brady, Margaret, K. "'Gonna Shimmy Shimmy 'til the
Sun Goes Down': Aspects of Verbal and Non-Verbal
Socialization in the Play of Black Girls." Folklore Annual
6 (1974): 1-16.

198.   ----------. "This Little Lady's Gonna Boogaloo:
Elements of Socialization in the Play of Black Girls." In
Black Girls at Play: Folklore Perspectives on Child
Development, pp. 1-56. Austin: Southwest Educational
Development Laboratory, 1975.

199.   Brakeley, Theresa C. "Lullaby." In no. 957, pp.
653-654.

200.   ----------. "Mourning Songs." In no. 957, pp. 755-
757.

201.   Brand, John, and Ellis, Henry. Observations on
Popular Antiquities. 2 vols. London: F.C. and J. Rivington,
1813.

202.   Brandes, Stanley. "The Selection Process in Proverb
Use: A Spanish Example." Southern Folklore Quarterly 38

(1974): 167-186.

203.   ----------. "Family Misfortune Stories in American
Folklore." Journal of the Folklore Institute 12 (1975):
5-17.

204.   Brandon, S.G.F. "Mary." In no. 294, 13: 1747-1752.

205.   Brester, Paul G. "Folk Cures and Preventitives from
Southern Indiana." Southern Folklore Quarterly 4 (1940):
33-43.

206.   ----------. "More Songs from Indiana." Southern
Folklore Quarterly 4 (1940): 175-203.

207.   ----------. "Quilt Patterns." California Folklore
Quarterly 3 (1944): 61.

208.   ----------. "The Romance of Quilt Names." Hoosier
Folklore 9 (1950): 59-62.

209.   ----------. "The Legend of St. Marcella, Virgin
Martyr." Western Folklore 16 (1957): 179-183.

210.   Bridentahl, Renate and Konz, Claudia, eds. Becoming
Visible: Women in European History. Boston: Houghton
Mifflin, 1977.

211.   Briffault, Robert. The Mothers: The Matriarchal
Theory of Social Origins. New York: Mcamillan, 1927.

212.   Briggs, Charles L. The Wood Carvers of Códorva, New
Mexico: Social Dimensions of an Artistic "Revival".
Knoxville: University of Tennessee Press, 1980.

213.   Briggs, Jean L. Never in Anger: Portrait of an
Eskimo Family. Cambridge: Harvard University Press, 1970.

214.   Briggs, Katharine. The Anatomy of Puck: An Examination of Fairy Beliefs among Shakespeare's Contemporaries and
Successors. London: Routledge and Kegan Paul, 1959.

215.   ----------. Pale Hecate's Team: An Examination of
the Beliefs on Witchcraft and Magic among Shakespeare's
Contemporaries and His Immediate Successors. New York:
Humanities Press, 1962.

216.   ----------. The Fairies in English Tradition and
Literature. Chicago: University of Chicago Press, 1967.

217.   ----------. An Encyclopedia of Fairies: Hobgoblins,
Brownies, Bogies, and Other Supernatural Creatures. New
York: Pantheon, 1976.

218.   Briggs, Katharine M. "Christina Hole: An Appreciation." Folklore 90 (1979): 4-8.

219.   Brill, Tony. "A Storyteller from Hatzeg: Imagination and Reality in the Life and Magic Tales of Sînziana Ilona." In Studies in East European Folk Narrative, ed. Linda Degh, pp. 619-678. Publications of the American Folklore Society Bibliographical and Special Series, No. 30: Indiana University Folklore Monograph Series, No. 25. Bloomington: American Folklore Society and Indiana University, 1978.

220.   Brinton, D.G. Nagualism: A Study in Native American Folk-Lore and History. Philadelphia: MacCalla and Co., 1894.

221.   ----------. Maria Candelaria: An Historical Drama from American Aboriginal Life. Philadelphia: D. McKay, 1897.

222.   Briscoe, Virginia Wolf. "Ruth Benedict: Anthropological Folklorist." Journal of American Folklore 92 (1979): 445-476.

223.   Brittain, Alfred. Roman Women. Philadelphia: Rittenhouse, 1908.

224.   Bromberg-Ross, JoAnn. "Storying and Changing: An Examination of the Consciousness-Raising Process." Folklore Feminists Communication 6 (1975): 9-11.

225.   Broner, E.M. "Honor and Ceremony in Women's Rituals." In no. 1445, pp. 234-244.

226.   Broner E.M., and Davidson, Cathy N. The Lost Tradition: Mothers and Daughters in Literature. New York: Ungar, 1980.

227.   Bronner, Simon J. "Charlotte Sophia Burne, British Folklorist: A Reexamination." Folklore Women's Cummunication 24 (1981): 14-19.

228.   ----------. "Folklore and the News: A Volley of Billie Jean King Jokes." Folklore Women's Communication 25 (1981): 13-14.

229.   Bronson, Bertrand. "Mrs. Brown and the Ballad." California Folklore Quarterly 4 (1975): 129-140.

230.   ----------. Obituary for Maud Karpeles. Journal of American Folklore 90 (1977): 455-464.

231.   Brooks, Juanita. "Memories of a Mormon Girlhood." Journal of American Folklore 77 (1964): 195-219.

232.   Brotten, Bronwyn, and Lang, Ann. "Zulu Beadwork." African Arts Spring 1973: 8-13.

233.   Brown, Elsa. Creative Quilting. New York: Watson-Guptill, 1975.

234.   Brown, Judith K. "A Cross-cultural Study of Female Initiation Rites." American Anthropologist 65 (1963): 837-853.

235.   ----------. "'Girls' Puberty Rites': A Reply to Driver." American Anthropologist 72 (1970): 1450-1451.

236.   ----------. "Initiation Rites for Girls: A Further Reply." American Anthropologist 73 (1971): 1262-1263.

237.   Brown, Judy. "Crafts: And You Thought Quilting Was Dead." Foxfire 2 (1969): 22-24.

238.   Bruere, Martha Bensley, and Beard, Mary Ritter. Laughing Their Way: Women's Humor in America. New York: Macmillan, 1934.

239.   Bruford, Alan. "A Scottish Gaelic Version of 'Snow-White.'" Scottish Studies 9 (1965): 153-174.

240.   ----------. "Scottish Gaelic Witch Stories: A Provisional Type-List." Scottish Studies 11 (1967): 13-47.

241.   Brun-Gulbrandsen, Sverre. "Sex Roles and the Socialization Process." In The Changing Roles of Men and Woman, ed. Edmund Dahlstrom. Trans. Gunilla and Steven Anderman, pp. 59-78. Boston: Beacon Press, 1971.

242.   Brunvard, Jan H. The Study of American Folklore. New York: W.W. Norton, 1978.

243.   ----------. Obituary for Maria Leach. Journal of American Folklore 91 (1978): 703.

244.   ----------. The Vanishing Hitchhiker: American Urban Legends and Their Meanings. New York and London: W.W. Norton, 1981.

245.   Bryce, L.W. Women's Folk Songs of Rajputana. Delhi: Publications Division, 1964.

246.   Buchan, David D. The Ballad and the Folk. London: Routledge and Kegan Paul, 1972.

247.   Budge, E.A. Wallis. Legends of Our Lady Mary the Perpetual Virgin and Her Mother Hanna. Oxford: Oxford University Press, 1933.

248.   ----------. One Hundred and Ten Miracles of Our Lady Mary. Oxford: Oxford University Press, 1933.

249.   Bullough, Vern L., and Bullough, Bonnie. The Subordinate Sex: A History of Attitudes toward Women. Urbana:

University of Illinois Press, 1973.

250.   Bullough, Vern L., and Elcano, Barret Wayne. A
Bibliography of Prostitution. New York: Garland, 1977.

251.   Bunzel, Ruth. The Pueblo Potter: A Study of Creative Imagination in Primitive Art. New York: Columbia
University Press, 1929.

252.   Burland, Cottie A. "The Goddess Chalchihuitlicue as
an Expression of an Archetype in Ancient Mexican Religion."
In Sixth International Congress of Anthropological and
Ethnological Sciences, vol. 2, pp. 373-376. Paris: Musée de
l'Homme, 1964.

253.   Burne, C.S. Obituary for Lucy Catherine Lloyd.
Folk-Lore 26 (1915): 99-100.

254.   ----------. Obituary for Marian Emily Roalfe Cox.
Folk-Lore 27 (1916): 434-435.

255.   Burne, John C. "The Young Charlotte Burne: Author of
'Shropshire Folklore.'" Folklore 86 (1975): 167-174.

256.   Burnham, Dorothy. "The Life of the Afro-American
Woman in Slavery." International Journal of Women's
Studies 1 (1978): 363-377.

257.   Burnham, Harold B., and Burnham, Dorothy K. "Keep
Me Warm One Night": Early Handweaving in Eastern Canada.
Toronto: University of Toronto Press and Royal Ontario
Museum, 1972.

258.   Burnside, Madeline. "Weaving." Heresies 4 (1978):
27.

259.   Buss, Fran Leeper. La Partera: Story of a Midwife.
Ann Arbor: University of Michigan Press, 1980.

260.   Butler, Samuel. The Authoress of the Odyssey, intro. David Grene. Chicago: University of Chicago Press,
1967.

261.   Byrd, James W. "Zora Neale Hurston: A Novel Folklorist." Tennessee Folklore Society Bulletin 21 (1955):
37-41.

262.   Cabello-Argandoña, Roberto, Gómez-Quiñones, Juan,
and Durán, Patricia Herrera. The Chicana: A Comprehensive
Bibliographic Study. Los Angeles: University of California
Chicano Studies Center, 1975.

263.   Callan, Hilary. 1975. "The Premiss of Dedication:
Notes toward an Ethnography of Diplomats' Wives." In no. 64,
pp. 87-104.

264.   Camp, Charles. Review of A Child's Comfort: Baby and Doll Quilts in American Folk Art, by Bruce Johnson et al. Journal of American Folklore 91 (1978): 876.

265.   Campbell, J.L. "The Late Fr. Allan McDonald, Miss Goodrich Freer and Hebridean Folklore." Scottish Studies 2 (1958): 175-188.

266.   Campbell, Joseph. The Hero with a Thousand Faces. Bollingen Series, No. 17. Princeton: Princeton University Press, 1949.

267.   ----------. "Joseph Campbell on the Great Goddess." Parabola 5, no. 4 (1980): 74-85.

268.   Cantor, Aviva. A Bibliography on the Jewish Woman: A Comprehensive and Annotated Listing of Works Published, 1900-1978. Fresh Meadows, N.Y.: Biblio Press, 1982.

269.   Cantor, Joanne. "What is Funny to Whom? The Role of Gender." Journal of Communication 26, no. 3 (1976): 164-172.

270.   Cantrell, Carol. "Kuan-Yin, the Goddess of Mercy." Folklore Women's Communication 24 (1981): 4-8.

271.   Canziani, Estella. "Piedmontese Proverbs in Dispraise of Women." Folk-Lore 24 (1913): 91-96.

272.   Caplan, Patricia, and Bujra, Janet M., eds. Women United, Women Divided: Comparative Studies of Ten Contemporary Cultures. Bloomington: Indiana University Press, 1979.

273.   Caraveli-Chaves, Anna. "Bridge between Worlds: The Greek Women's Lament as Communicative Event." Journal of American Folklore 93 (1980): 129-157.

274.   Cardinale, Susan. Anthologies by and about Women. Westport, Ct.: Greenwood Press, 1982.

275.   Cardozo-Freeman, Inez. "Games Mexican Girls Play." Journal of American Folklore 88 (1975): 12-24.

276.   ----------. "Folklore Courses: The Folklore of Women." Folklore Feminists Communication 10 (1976): 14-19.

277.   ----------. "Serpent Fears and Religious Motifs among Mexican Women." Frontiers 3, no. 3 (1978): 10-13.

278.   Carlisle, Lillian. Pieced Work and Applique Quilts at the Shelburne Museum. Museum Pamphlet Series, no. 2. Shelburne, Vt.: Shelburne Museum, 1957.

279.   Carmody, Denise Lardner. The Oldest God: Archaic Religion Yesterday and Today. Nashville: Abingdon, 1981.

280.   ----------. Women and World Religions. Nashville: Abingdon, 1979.

281.   Carnes, Valerie. "Icons of Popular Fashion." In Icons of America, ed. Ray B. Browne and Marshall Fishwick, pp. 228-240. Bowling Green: Popular Press, 1978.

282.   Carpenter, Ann. "The Loathly Lady in Texas Lore." Journal of the American Studies Association of Texas 5 (1974): 48-53.

283.   ----------. "'The Burglar and the Old Maid': A Note on an Anti-Female Ballad." Folklore Feminists Communication 6 (1975): 6-7.

284.   ----------. "Woman as Victim in Modern Folklore." In no. 2, pp. 211-216.

285.   Carrilo, Rafael, and Pomar, Teresa. Artesanos y Artesanias del Esatado de Mexico. Toluca: Dirección de Promoción, Comercial y Artesenal del Gobierno del Estado de Mexico, 1972.

286.   Carroll, Berenice A., ed. Liberating Women's History: Theoretical and Critical Essays. Urbana: University of Illinois Press, 1976.

287.   Carter, Barbara Lillian. "On the Grounds: Informal Culture in a Girls Reform School." Ph.D. dissertation, Brandeis University, 1972.

288.   Casangre, Joseph B., ed. In the Company of Man: Twenty Portraits of Anthropologists. New York: Harper, 1960.

289.   Cason, Marjorie, and Cahlender, Adele. The Art of Bolivian Highland Weaving. New York: Watson-Guptill, 1976.

290.   Cass-Beggs, Barbara, and Cass-Beggs, Michael. Folk Lullabies. New York: Oak, 1969.

291.   Castanis, Muriel. "Are You a Closet Collector?" Heresies 4 (1978): 61.

292.   Caulfeild, S.F.A., and Saward, Blanche C. The Dictionary of Needlework. London: L. Upcott Gill, 1882.

293.   Cave, Oenone. English Folk Embroidery. New York: Taplinger, 1965.

294.   Cavendish, Richard, ed. Man, Myth and Magic: An Illustrated Encyclopedia of the Supernatural. 24 vols. New York: Marshall Cavendish, 1970.

295.   ----------. "Woman." In no. 294, 22: 3050-3059.

296.   Chafe, William Henry. The American Woman: Her
Changing Social, Economic, and Political Roles, 1920-1970.
London: Oxford University Press, 1972.

297.   Chamberlain, Alexander F. "Primitive Woman as Poet."
Journal of American Folklore 16 (1903): 205-221.

298.   Chamberlain, Isabel Cushman. "Contributions toward a
Bibliography of Folk-Lore Relating to Women." Journal of
American Folklore 12 (1899): 32-37.

299.   Chamberlain, Mary. Fenwomen: A Portrait of Women in
an English Village. London: Virago, 1975.

300.   Chambers, Keith S. "The Indefagitable Elsie Clews
Parsons--Folklorist." Western Folklore 32 (1973): 180-198.

301.   Chao, Buwei Yang. Autobiography of a Chinese
Woman. New York: John Day Publishing Company, 1947.

302.   Charles, Lucile Hoerr. "Drama in War." Journal of
American Folklore 68 (1955): 253-281.

303.   Charpenel, Mauricio. "Calling Cards for an Old
Profession." Folklore Annual 1 (1969): 16-19.

304.   Chase, Ellen. "Story of Betts Haddington." Journal
of American Folklore 11 (1898): 162-164.

305.   Chase, Judith Wragg. Afro-American Art and Craft.
New York: Van Nostrand Reinhold, 1971.

306.   Chattopadhyay, K. Carpets of India and Floor Cover-
ings. Bombay, Tapaporevala, 1969.

307.   Chesler, Phyllis. Women and Madness. New York:
Avon, 1972.

308.   ----------. "The Amazon Legacy." In no. 1445, pp.
97-113.

309.   Child, Francis J. The English and Scottish Popular
Ballads. Boston: Little Brown, 1882-1898.

310.   Chilton, John. Billie's Blues: A Survey of Billie
Holiday's Career, 1933-1959. London: Quartet Books, 1975.

311.   Chiñas, Beverly. The Isthmus Zapotecs: Women's
Roles in Cultural Context. New York: Holt, Rinehart and
Winston, 1973.

312.   ----------. "Teaching about Women Cross-Culturally:
A Critical Appraisal of the Anthropological Data." Feminist
Studies 3 (1975): 75-82.

313.   Chodorow, Nancy, The Reproduction of Mothering: Psychoanalysis and the Sociology of Gender. Berkeley: University of California Press, 1978.

314.   Christensen, Abigail M. Holmes. "Folk-Belief in the Virginia Lowlands." Journal of American Folklore 7 (1894): 153-154.

315.   Clark, Alice. Working Life of Women in the Seventeenth Century. London: Frank Cass, 1968.

316.   Clark, Ella E. "Watkuese and Lewis and Clark." Western Folklore 12 (1953): 175-178.

317.   Clarke, Mary Washington. Kentucky Quilts and Their Makers. Lexington: University Press of Kentucky, 1976.

318.   Coffin, Tristram Potter. The Female Hero in Folklore and Legend. New York: Seabury Press, 1975.

319.   Cohen, Anne. Poor Pearl, Poor Girl: The Murdered-Girl Stereotype in Ballad and Newspaper. American Folklore Society Memoirs, No. 58. Austin: University of Texas Press, 1973.

320.   Cohen, David Stern. "The Origin of the 'Jackson Whites.'" Journal of American Folklore 85 (1972): 260-266.

321.   Colby, Averil. Samplers. Newton Center, Mass.: C.T. Branford Co., 1964.

322.   ----------. Patchwork Quilts. New York: Scribner, 1965.

323.   ----------. Quilting. New York: Scribner, 1971.

324.   Cole, Doris. From Tipi to Skyscraper: A History of Women in Architecture. Boston: i press, 1973.

325.   Cole, Pamela McArthur. "New England Weddings." Journal of American Folklore 6 (1893): 103-107.

326.   Cole, William, and Robinson, Florett, eds. Women Are Wonderful: A History of Cartoons of a Hundred Years with America's Most Controversial Figure. Boston: Houghton Mifflin, 1956.

327.   Collins, Betty. "The Legend of Aunt Jane." Western Folklore 26 (1967): 55-56.

328.   Collins, Camilla A. "Research in Progress [on female hosiery mill workers]." Folklore Feminists Communication 1 (1973): 3.

329.   ----------. "Twenty-four to a Dozen: Occupational

Folklore in a Hosiery Mill." Ph.D. dissertation, Indiana
University, 1978.

330.   ----------. "Folklore and Women Syllabus." Folklore
Women's Communication 21 (1980): 13-17.

331.   Collinson, Francis. "The Musical Aspect of the Songs
of Nan MacKinnon of Vatersay." Scottish Studies 5 (1961):
40-42.

332.   Colson, E. Autobiographies of Three Pomo Women.
Berkeley: Archaeological Research Facility, Department of
Anthropology, University of California, 1974.

333.   Commins, Dorothy Berliner. Lullabies of the World.
New York: Random House, 1967.

334.   Conn, Jacob H. "Children's Awareness of Sex Differences: Play Attitudes and Game Preferences." Journal of
Child Psychiatry 2 (1951): 82-99.

335.   Cooper, Elizabeth. The Harim and Purdah: Studies of
Oriental Women. New York: Century, 1915.

336.   Cooper, Patricia. "Patchwork of the Pioneer West."
Historic Preservation 31, no. 1 (1979): 12-17.

337.   Cooper, Patricia, and Buferd, Norma Bradley. The
Quilters: Women and Domestic Art, An Oral History. Garden
City: Doubleday, 1977.

338.   Cooper, Susan. Review of Womenfolk and Fairytales,
by Rosemary Minard. New York Times Book Review April 13,
1975: 8.

339.   Coote, Henry Charles. "The Neo-Latin Fay." Folk-
Lore Record 2 (1879): 1-18.

340.   ----------. "Indian Mother-Worship." Folk-Lore
Record 3, no. 2 (1880): 117-123.

341.   Coote, Mary P. "Women's Songs in Serbo-Croatian."
Journal of American Folklore 90 (1977): 331-338.

342.   Coote Lake, E.F. Obituary for Mary McLeod Banks.
Folk-Lore 63 (1952): 42-43.

343.   ----------. Obituary for Estella Canziani. Folklore
75 (1964): 206-208.

344.   ----------. Obituary for Barbara Freire Marreco
(Mrs. Robert Aitken). Folklore 77 (1967): 305-306.

345.   Cordry, Donald Bush, and Cordry, Dorothy M. Costumes and Weaving of the Zoque Indians of Chiapas, Mexico.
Southwest Museum Papers, No. 15. Los Angeles:

Southwest Museum, 1941.

346.   ----------. Mexican Indian Costumes. Austin: University of Texas Press, 1969.

347.   Corimer, Holly, comp. "Women and Folk Music: A
Select Bibliography." Washington: Library of Congress
Archive of Folk Song (pamphlet), 1978.

348.   Cornelisen, Ann. Women of the Shadows. New York:
Vintage, 1976.

349.   Cornillon, Susan Koppelman, ed. Images of Women in
Fiction: Feminist Perspectives. Bowling Green: Popular
Press, 1972.

350.   Cothran, Kay L. "Women's Tall Tales: A Problem in
the Social Structure of Fantasy." St. Andrew's Review 2,
no. 1 (1972): 21-27.

351.   ----------. Review of The First Sex, by Elizabeth
Gould Davis. Journal of American Folklore 87 (1974):
89-93.

352.   Cothran, Kay L., Green, Rayna, and Baldwin, Karen.
"Women and Folklore Courses." Folklore Feminists
Communication 1 (1973): 6-8.

353.   Cox, Marian Roalfe. Cinderella. Publications of
the Folk-lore Society, No. 31. London: David Nutt, 1893.

354.   Crane, Beverly. "The Structure of Value in 'The
Roommate's Death': A Methodology for Interpretive Analysis
of Folk Legends." Journal of the Folklore Institute 14
(1977): 133-149.

355.   Crawford, O.G.S. The Eye Goddess. London: Phoenix
House, 1957.

356.   Creighton, Helen. A Life in Folklore. Toronto:
McGraw-Hill Ryerson, 1975.

357.   Crihfield, Liza. "The Institution of the Geisha in
Modern Japanese Society." Ph.D. dissertation, Stanford
University, 1978.

358.   Croker, T. Crofton, ed. and trans. The Keen of the
South of Ireland as Illustrative of Irish Political and
Domestic History, Manners, Music and Superstitions. Percy
Society Early English Poetry, Ballads and Popular Literature
of the Middle Ages, No. 13, part 1. London: Percy Society,
1844.

359.   Cromwell, Ida M., Rogers, Eleanor T., Coffin, Tristram P., and Bayard, Samuel P. "Songs I Sang on an Iowa
Farm." Western Folklore 17 (1958): 229-247.

360.   Crooke, W. "The Wooing of Penelope." Folk-Lore 9 (1898): 97-133.

361.   ----------. "The Lifting of the Bride." Folk-Lore 13 (1902): 226-251.

362.   ----------. "Simulated Change of Sex to Baffle the Evil Eye." Folk-Lore 24 (1913): 385.

363.   ----------. "The Cults of the Mother Goddess in India." Folk-Lore 30 (1919): 282-308.

364.   Cross, Tom Peete. "Folk-Lore from the Southern States." Journal of American Folklore 22 (1909): 251-255.

365.   Crow, Martha Foote. The American Country Girl. New York: Frederick A. Stokes, 1915.

366.   Crowley, Daniel J. Obituary for Suzanne Comhaire-Sylvain. Journal of American Folklore 91 (1978): 700-701.

367.   Crumrine, N. Ross, and Crumrine, M. Louise. "Ritual Symbolism in Folk and Ritual Drama: The Mayo Indian San Cayetano Velación, Sonora, Mexico." Journal of American Folklore 90 (1977): 8-28.

368.   Cunningham, Agnes "Sis," and Rose, Madeline B. "Sis Cunningham: Songs of Hard Times." Ms. March, 1974: 29-32.

369.   Cunningham, Keith Kermit, Jr. "A Study of the Southern Folk Song Style Area Sweetheart Murder Ballad: The Search for an Oicoclass." Ph.D. dissertation, Indiana University, 1976.

370.   Curry, David Park. Stitches in Time: Samplers in the Museum's Collection. Miscellaneous Publications of the Museum of Art, No. 98. Lawrence: University of Kansas Museum of Art, 1975.

371.   Curry, Jane. "The Ring-Tailed Roarers Rarely Sang Soprano." Frontiers 2, no. 3 (1977): 129-140.

372.   Curtin, Jeremiah. "European Folk-Lore in the United States." Journal of American Folklore 2 (1889): 56-59.

373.   Cutting, Edith E. "York State Farm Lore." New York Folklore Quarterly 7 (1951): 4-77.

374.   Cutting-Baker, Holly, Gross, Sandra, Kotkin, Amy, and Zeitlin, Steven. Family Folklore. Washington: Smithsonian Institution and National Park Service, 1976.

375.   Daiken, Leslie, Hillis, Mary, and Brown, Sebastian. The Lullaby Book. London: Edmund Ward, 1959.

376.   Daingerfield, Elizabeth. "Patch Quilts and Philosophy." The Craftsman 14 (1908): 523-527.

377.   Dan, Ilana. "The Innocent Persecuted Heroine: An Attempt at a Model for the Surface Level of the Narrative Structure of the Female Fairy Tale." In Patterns in Oral Literature, ed. Heda Jason and Dimitri Segal, pp. 13-30. The Hague: Mouton, 1977.

378.   D'Andrade, Roy G. "Sex Differences and Cultural Institutions." In The Development of Sex Differences, ed. Eleanor E. Maccoby, pp. 174-204. Stanford: Stanford University Press, 1966.

379.   Dasgupta, Kalpana, Usha. M.C., Saxena, Rajni, and Mathur, Neera. Women on the Indian Scene: An Annotated Bibliography. New Delhi: Abhinav Publications, 1976.

380.   Davis, Elizabeth Gould. The First Sex. New York: G.P. Putnam, 1971.

381.   Davis, Mildred J. Early American Embroidery Designs. New York: Crown, 1969.

382.   Davis, Natalie Zemon, "Women in the Crafts in Sixteenth-Century Lyon." Feminist Studies 8 (1982): 46-80.

383.   Davis, Susan G. "Old-Fashioned Polish Weddings in Utica, New York." New York Folklore 4 (1978): 89-102.

384.   ----------. "Women's Roles in a Company Town: New York Mills, 1900-1951." New York Folklore 4 (1978): 35-47.

385.   Davidson, H.R. Ellis. "The Legend of Lady Godiva." Folklore 80 (1969): 107-121.

386.   ----------. Obituary for Nora Kershaw Chadwick. Folklore 83 (1972): 254-255.

387.   ----------. Obituary for Katharine M. Briggs. Folklore 92 (1981): 110-112.

388.   Dawkins, R.M. "The Silent Princess." Folk-Lore 63 (1952): 129-142.

389.   Dawson, Warren R. The Custom of Couvade. Manchester: Manchester University Press, 1929.

390.   Dean, Nancy. "A Bibliography and Selected Review of Goddess-Related Materials." Lady-Unique-Inclination-of-the-Night 3 (1978): 73-80.

391.   Dean-Smith, Margaret. Obituary for Maude Karpeles. Folklore 88 (1977): 110-111.

392.   de Beauvoir, Simone. The Second Sex, trans. H.M. Parshley. New York: Knopf, 1953.

393.   de Caro, F.A. "Finding a Lost Watch." Indiana Folklore 1 (1968): 25-27.

394.   ----------. "Indiana Miracle Legends: A Survey." Indiana Folklore 2 (1969): 36-53.

395.   ----------. "The Women's Movement in A.F.S.: A Brief Chronology (1971-1973)." Folklore Historian 1 (1974): 1-4; reprinted Folklore Feminists Communication 5 (1975): 4, 20-23.

396.   ----------. "The Women's Movement in A.F.S.: A Correction." Folklore Feminists Communication 9 (1976): 6.

397.   de Caro, F.A., and Jordan, R.A. Louisiana Traditional Crafts. Baton Rouge: Louisiana State University Union Gallery, 1980.

398.   Deegan, Dorothy. Stereotype of the Single Woman in American Novels. New York: Octagon, 1968.

399.   Dégh, Linda. Folktales and Society: Story-Telling in a Hungarian Peasant Community. Trans. Emily M. Schossberger. Bloomington: Indiana University Press, 1969.

400.   ----------. "Two Letters from Home." Journal of American Folklore 91 (1978): 808-822.

401.   DeGraw, Imelda G. Quilts and Coverlets. Denver: Denver Art Museum, 1974.

402.   Del Bourgo, Fanya, and Botkin, B.A. "Love in the City." New York Folklore Quarterly 21 (1965): 165-178.

403.   Demetracopoulou, D. "The Loon Woman Myth: A Study in Synthesis." Journal of American Folklore 46 (1933): 101-128.

404.   Demetracopoulou, D. and du Bois, Cora. "A Study of Wintu Mythology." Journal of American Folklore 45 (1932): 373-500.

405.   De Nio, Pierre. "The Strange Life of Fannie Read." New York Folklore Quarterly 17 (1961): 287-292.

406.   De Pauw, Linda Grant, Hunt, Conover, and Schneir, Miriam. Remember the Ladies: Women in America, 1750-1815. New York: Viking Press and the Pilgrim Society, 1976.

407.   Derrickson, Mrs. S.D. "Various Superstitions." Journal of American Folklore 5 (1892): 243-244.

408.   Deutsch, Helene. Psychology of Women. New York:

Grune & Stratton, 1944.

409.   Dew, Joan. Singers and Sweethearts: The Women of Country Music. New York: Dolphin, 1977.

410.   Dewhurst, C. Kurt, MacDowell, Betty, and MacDowell, Marsha. Artists in Aprons: Folk Art by American Women. New York: Dutton and Museum of American Folk Art, 1979.

411.   Dexter, Elisabeth Anthony. Colonial Women of Affairs: A Study of Women in Business and the Professions before 1776. Boston: Houghton Mifflin, 1924.

412.   Diamond, John Timothy. "On the Social Structure of Imagery: The Case of Gender." Ph.D. dissertation, Ohio State University, 1977.

413.   Diamond, Norma. "Fieldwork in a Complex Society: Taiwan." In no. 1437, pp. 113-141.

414.   Dick, Ernst S. "The Bridesman in the Indo-European Tradition: Ritual and Myth in Marriage Ceremonies." Journal of American Folklore 79 (1966): 338-347.

415.   Dickinson, Joan Younger. "The Role of Immigrant Women in the U.S. Labor Force 1890-1910." Ph.D. dissertation, University of Pennsylvania, 1975.

416.   Diner, Helen. Mothers and Amazons: the First Feminine History of Culture. New York: Julian Press, 1965.

417.   Dingwall, Eric John. The American Woman: An Historical Study. New York, Rinehart, 1957.

418.   Dixson, Miriam. The Real Matilda: Woman and Identity in Australia, 1788 to 1975. Harmondsworth: Penguin, 1976.

419.   Doering, Susan Graves. "Femininity Scales and First Pregnancy." Ph.D. dissertation, Johns Hopkins University, 1975.

420.   Donegan, Jane B. Women and Men Midwives: Medicine, Morality and Misogyny in Early America. Westport, Ct.: Greenwood Press, 1978.

421.   Donovan, Frances R. The Woman Who Waits. Boston: R.G. Badger, 1920.

422.   ----------. The Saleslady. Chicago: University of Chicago Press, 1929.

423.   ----------. The Schoolma'am. New York: Frederick A. Stokes, 1938.

424.   Dorson, Richard M. "Aunt Jane Goudreau, Roup-Garou

Storyteller." Western Folklore 6 (1947): 13-27.

425.   ----------. "Negro Tales of Mary Richardson." Mid-
west Folklore 6 (1956): 1-28.

426.   ----------. Buying the Wind: Regional Folklore in
the United States. Chicago: University of Chicago Press,
1964.

427.   ----------. American Negro Folktales. Greenwich,
Ct.: Fawcett, 1967.

428.   ----------. The British Folklorists: A History.
London: Routledge and Kegan Paul, 1968.

429.   ----------. "Elsie Clews Parsons: Feminist and
Folklorist." AFFword 1 (1971): 1-4.

430.   ----------. "Elsie Clews Parsons: Feminist and
Folklorist." Folklore Feminists Communication 2 (1974): 4,
22-25.

431.   Dougherty, Molly C. Becoming a Woman in Rural Black
Culture. New York: Holt, Rinehart and Winston, 1978.

432.   Douglas, Ann.   The Feminization of American Culture. New York: Knopf, 1977.

433.   Douglas, Mary. Purity and Danger: An Analysis of
Concepts of Pollution and Taboo. London: Routledge and
Kegan Paul, 1966.

434.   ----------. "Couvade and Menstruation: The Relevance
of Tribal Studies." In Implicit Meanings: Essays in
Anthropology, pp. 60-72. London: Routledge and Kegan Paul,
1975.

435.   Downing, Chris. "Ariadne, Mistress of the Labyrinth." In no. 733, pp. 135-149.

436.   Downing, Christine. The Goddess: Mythological Images of the Feminine. New York: Crossroad, 1981.

437.   Doyle, Charles Clay. "Where I Have No Nose." Folklore Women's Communication 15 (1978): 21-23.

438.   Drake, Ann Minick. "Illness, Ritual, and Social
Relations among the Chewa of Central Africa." Ph.D.
dissertation, Duke University, 1976.

439.   Dresser, Norine. "'Is it Fresh?': An Examination of
Jewish-American Shopping Habits." New York Folklore
Quarterly 27 (1971): 153-160.

440.   Dressler, Janet N. "Exempla Usage in Catholic
Parochial Schools." Folklore Forum 8 (1975): 130-141.

441.   Driggs, Frank. Women in Jazz: A Survey. Brooklyn: Stash Records, 1977.

442.   Drinker, Sophie. Women and Music. New York: Coward-McCann, 1948.

443.   Driscoll, Eleanor. "Quilts in Moore County." North Caroline Folklore 4 (1956): 11-15.

444.   Driver, Harold E. "Girls' Puberty Rites in Western North America." University of California Anthropological Records 6 (1941): 21-90.

445.   ----------. "Girls' Puberty Rites and Matrilocal Residence." American Anthropologist 71 (1969): 905-908.

446.   ----------. "Brown and Driver on Girls' Puberty Rites Again." American Anthropologist 73 (1971): 1261-1262.

447.   Driver, Harold E., and Riesenberg, Saul. Hoof Rattles and Girls' Puberty Rites in North and South America. Indiana University Publications in Anthropology and Linguistics, No. 4. Bloomington: Indiana University Press, 1950.

448.   Dube, Leela. "Woman's Worlds--Three Encounters." In no. 150, pp. 157-177.

449.   Dundes, Alan. "On the Psychology of Legend." In American Folk Legend: A Symposium, ed. Wayland D. Hand, pp. 21-36. Berkeley and Los Angeles: University of California Press, 1971.

450.   ----------. "The Crowing Hen and the Easter Bunny: Male Chauvinism in American Folklore." In Folklore Today: A Festchrift for Richard M. Dorson, ed. Linda Dégh, Henry Glassie, and Felix J. Oinas, pp. 123-138. Bloomington: Indiana University Research Center for Languange and Semiotic Studies, 1976.

451.   ----------. Folklore Theses and Dissertations in the United States. American Folklore Society Bibliographical And Special Services, No. 27. Austin: University of Texas Press, 1976.

452.   ----------, ed. Cinderella: A Casebook. New York: Garland, 1982.

453.   Dundes, Alan, and Pagter, Carl R. Work Hard and You Shall Be Rewarded: Urban Folklore from the Paperwork Empire. Bloomington: Indiana University Press, 1978.

454.   Dunham, Katherine. Journey to Accompong. New York: Holt, 1946.

455.   Dunn, John J. "Jean Ritchie: A Clear Voice." Country Dance and Song 3 (1970): 23-28.

456.   Dunton, William Rush, Jr. Old Quilts. Catonville,
Md.: The Author, 1946.

457.   DuToit, Brian M. "Gadsup Culture Hero Tales." Journal of American Folklore 77 (1964): 315-330.

458.   Dutton, Bertha P. Navajo Weaving Today. Santa Fe:
Museum of New Mexico Press, 1961.

459.   Dworkin, Andrea. "What Were Those Witches Really
Brewing?" Ms. April, 1974: 52-55, 89-90.

460.   ----------. Woman Hating. New York: Dutton, 1974.

461.   Dwyer, Daisy Hilse. "Women's Conflict Behavior in a
Traditional Moroccan Setting: An Interactional Analysis."
Ph.D. dissertation, Yale University, 1973.

462.   ----------. Images and Self-Images: Male and Female
in Morocco. New York: Columbia University Press, 1978.

463.   Earle, Alice Morse. "Old Time Marriage Customs in
New England." Journal of American Folklore 6 (1893):
97-102.

464.   East, Lorecia. The Boomers: The Autobiography of a
Roughneck's Wife. Baton Rouge: Legacy, 1976.

465.   Eastman, Mary Henderson. Dahcotah: or, Life and
Legends of the Sioux around Fort Snelling. New York: John
Wiley, 1849.

466.   Eaton, Allen H. Handicrafts of the Southern Highlands, ed. Rayna D. Green. New York: Dover Publications,
1973.

467.   Echols, Margit. The New American Quilt: An Innova-
tion in Contemporary Quilt Design. Garden City: Doubleday,
1976.

468.   Eckhardt, Rosalind. "From Handclap to Line Play." In
Black Girls at Play: Folkloric Perspectives on Child
Development, pp. 57-101. Austin: Southwest Educational
Development Laboratory, 1975.

469.   Economou, George D. The Goddess Natura in Medieval
Literature. Cambridge: Harvard University Press, 1972.

470.   Edelheit, Martha, comp. "Conversations and Reminiscences." Heresies 4 (1978): 72-88.

471.   Edelson, Carol "Quilting: A History." Off Our Backs

May, 1973: 13-14.

472.   Edwards, Carol L. "Metanarration and Women's Narratives." Folklore Women's Communication 24 (1981): 6-11.

473.   Eff, Elaine. "Response to Quilting Article." Folklore Feminists communication 8 (1976): 8.

474.   Eggan, Fred. "Ritual Myths Among the Tinguian." Journal of American Folklore 69 (1956): 331-339.

475.   Ehrenreich, Barbara, and English, Deirdre. Complaints and Disorders: The Sexual Politics of Sickness. Glass Mountain Pamphlets, No. 2. Old Westbury, N.Y.: Feminist Press, 1973.

476.   ----------. Witches, Midwives, and Nurses: A History of Women Healers. Oyster Bay, N.Y.: Glass Mountain Pamphlets, 1973.

477.   Elder, Jacob D. "The Male/Female Conflict in Calypso." Caribbean Quarterly 14, no. 3 (1968): 23-41.

478.   Eliade, Mircea. Birth and Rebirth: The Religious Meaning of Initiation in Human Culture. Trans. W.R. Trask. New York: Harper, 1958.

479.   ----------. Images and Symbols: Studies in Religious Symbolism. New York: Sheed and Ward, 1969.

480.   ----------. Gods, Goddesses, and Myths of Creation. New York: Harper and Row, 1974.

481.   Ellis, Bill. "The 'Blind Girl' and the Rhetoric of Sentimental Heroism." Journal of American Folklore 91 (1978): 657-674.

482.   Ellis, Havelock. Man and Woman. 8th ed. London: William Heinemann, 1934.

483.   Elsasser, Nan, MacKenzie, Kyle, and Tixler y Vigil, Yvonne. Las Mujeres: Conversations from a Hispanic Community. Old Westbury, N.Y.: Feminist Press, 1981.

484.   Epstein, Cynthia Fuchs. Woman's Place: Options and Limits in Professional Careers. Berkeley: University of California Press, 1971.

485.   Ernster, Virginia L. "American Menstrual Expressions." Sex Roles: A Journal of Research 1 (1975): 3-13.

486.   Espejel, Carlos. Cerámica Popular Mexicana. Mexico City: Editorial Blume and Museo Nacional de Artes e Industrias Populares, 1975.

487.   Espinosa, Aurelio M. "New Mexican Spanish Folk-Lore." Journal of American Folklore 23 (1910): 395-418.

488.   Estrada, Alvaro. Maria Sabina: Her Life and Chants. Trans. Henry Munn, essay by R. Gordon Wasson, preface Jerome Rothenberg. Santa Barbara: Ross-Erikson, 1981.

489.   Ets, Marie Hall. Rosa: The Life of an Italian Immigrant. Minneapolis: University of Minnesota Press, 1970.

490.   Evans-Pritchard, E.E. "Some Collective Expressions of Obscenity in Africa." Journal of the Royal Anthropological Institute 59 (1929): 311-331.

491.   ----------. The Position of Women in Primitive Societies. New York: Free Press, 1965.

492.   Ewing, Curtis Kinney. "Freud and Engels: A Comparison of Sex Roles." Ph.D. dissertation, University of New Mexico, 1975.

493.   Fairchild, Johnson E., ed. Women, Society and Sex. Greenwich, Ct.: Fawcett, 1962.

494.   Falk, Nancy Auer, and Gross, Rita M., eds. Unspoken Worlds: Women's Religious Lives in Non-Western Cultures. San Francisco: Harper and Row, 1980.

495.   Fallon, Carol. The Art of the Indian Basket in North America. Lawrence: University of Kansas Museum of Art, 1975.

496.   Faragher, Johnny, and Stansell, Christine. "Women and Their Families on the Overland Trail to California and Oregon, 1842-1847." Feminist Studies 2, no. 2/3 (1975): 150-166.

497.   Faragher, John Mack. Women and Men on the Overland Trail. New Haven: Yale University Press, 1979.

498.   Farb, Joanne. "Piecin' and Quiltin': Two Quilters in Southwest Arkansas." Southern Folklore Quarterly 39 (1975): 363-375.

499.   Farr, Sidney Saylor. Appalachian Women: An Annotated Bibliography. Lexington: University Press of Kentucky, 1981.

500.   Farr, T.J. "Middle Tennessee Folk Beliefs Concerning Love and Marriage." Southern Folklore Quarterly 2 (1938): 165-174.

501.   Farrell, Frances M. "The John Edwards Memorial Foundation as a Raw Data Source for the Study of Women in Country Music." JEMF Quarterly 13 (1977): 161-167.

502.   Farrer, Claire R. "Performances of the Mescalero Apache 'Clowns.'" Folklore Annual 4 and 5 (1972-1973): 135-151.

503.   ----------. "Introduction: Women and Folklore: Images and Genres." Journal of American Folklore 88 (1975): v-xv.

504.   ----------, ed. Women and Folklore. Austin: University of Texas Press, 1975.

505.   ----------. "Singing for Life: The Mescalero Apache Girls' Puberty Ceremony." In Southwestern Indian Ritual Drama, ed. Charlotte Frisbie, pp. 125-157. Albuquerque: University of New Mexico Press, 1980.

506.   Farrer, Claire R., and Kalčik, Susan J. "Women: A Selected Bibliography from the Journal of American Folklore, 1888-1973." Folklore Feminsts Communication 1 (1973): 12-28.

507.   Fee, Elizabeth. "The Sexual Politics of Victorian Social Anthropology." Feminist Studies Winter/Spring, 1973: 23-29.

508.   Feinberg, Jean, Goldberg, Lenore, Gross, Julie, Lieberman, Bella, and Sacre, Elizabeth. "Political Fabrications: Women's Textiles in 5 Cultures." Heresies 4 (1978): 28-37.

509.   Ferguson, Mary Anne, ed. Images of Women in Literature. Boston: Houghton Mifflin, 1973.

510.   Fernea, Elizabeth Warnock. Guests of the Sheik. Garden City: Doubleday, 1969.

511.   ----------. A Street in Marrakech. Garden City: Doubleday, 1975.

512.   Fernea, Elizabeth Warnock, and Bezirgan, Basima Qattan, eds. Middle Eastern Muslim Women Speak. Austin: University of Texas Press, 1977.

513.   Ferrante, Joan M. Woman as Image in Medieval Literature. New York and London: Columbia University Press, 1975.

514.   Ffennell, Margaret C. "The Shrew Ash in Richmond Park." Folk-Lore 9 (1898): 330-336.

515.   Fife, Austin E. "Pioneer Mormon Remedies." Western Folklore 16 (1957): 153-162.

516.   Fife Austin E., and Redden, Francesca. "The Pseudo-Indian Folksongs of the Anglo-American and French-Canadian." Journal of American Folklore 67 (1954): 239-251, 379-394.

517.   Fife, Austin, and Fife, Alta. "Pug-Nosed Lil and the Girl with the Blue Velvet Band: A Brief Medley of Women in Western Songs." American West 7, no. 2 (1970): 32-37.

518.   Filene, Peter Gabriel. Him, Her, Self: Sex Roles in Modern America. New York: Harcourt Brace Jovanovich, 1974.

519.   Fillmore, John Comfort. "A Woman's Song of the Kwakiutl Indians." Journal of American Folklore 6 (1893): 285-290.

520.   Finley, Ruth. Old Patchwork Quilts and the Women Who Made Them. Philadephia and London: J.B. Lippincott, 1929.

521.   Finnegan, Ruth. Oral Poetry: Its Nature, Significance and Social Context. Cambridge: Cambridge University Press, 1977.

522.   Firestone, Shulamith. The Dialectic of Sex: The Case for Feminist Revolution. New York: Bantam, 1970.

523.   Fischer, Christiane, ed. Let Them Speak for Themselves: Women in the American West, 1849-1900. Hamden, Ct.: Archon Books, 1977.

524.   Fischer, J.L. "The Position of Men and Women in Truk and Ponape: A Comparative Analysis of Kinship Terminology and Folktales." Journal of American Folklore 69 (1956): 55-62.

525.   Fish, Lydia. "The Old Wife in the Dormitory--Sexual Folklore and Magical Practices from State University College." New York Folklore Quarterly 28 (1972): 30-36.

526.   Fishburn, Katherine. Women in Popular Culture: A Reference Guide. Westport, Ct.: Greenwood Press, 1982.

527.   Fitz-Randolph, Mavis. Tradtitional Quilting: Its Story and Practice. London: B.T. Batsford, 1954.

528.   Flanagan, Cathleen C., and Flanagan, John T. American Folklore: A Bibliography, 1950-1974. Metuchen, N.J., and London: Scarecrow Press, 1977.

529.   Fletcher, Alice C. "Leaves from my Omaha Note-Book." Journal of American Folklore 2 (1889): 219-226.

530.   Flugel, J.C. The Psychology of Clothes. New York: International Universities Press, 1969.

531.   Fock, Niels. "South American Birth Customs in Theory and Practice." In Cross-Cultural Approaches: Readings in Comparative Research, ed. Clellan S. Ford, pp. 126-144. New Haven: HRAF Press, 1967.

532.   Ford, Clellan, and Beach, Frank. Patterns of Sexual Behavior. New York: Harper, 1972.

533.   Foster, George M. "The Fire Walkers of San Pedro Manrique, Soria, Spain." Journal of American Folklore 68 (1955): 325-332.

534.   Foster, George, and Kemper, Robert, eds. Anthropologists in Cities. Boston: Little Brown, 1974.

535.   Fowler, Alice. "Influence of an Expectant Mother." Folklore 28 (1917): 322-323.

536.   Fowler, David C. A Literary History of the Popular Ballad. Durham, N.C.: Duke University Press, 1968.

537.   Fox, James Gordon. "Self-Imposed Stigmata: A Study of Tattooing among Female Inmates." Ph.D. dissertation, State University of New York at Albany, 1976.

538.   Fox, Lilla M. Folk Costumes of Southern Europe. London: Chatto, Boyd and Oliver, 1972.

539.   Fox, Margery Q. "Power and Piety: Women in Christian Science." Ph.D. dissertation, New York University, 1973.

540.   Fox, Robin. Kinship and Marriage: An Anthropological Perspective. Harmondsworth: Penguin, 1967.

541.   Frank, Blanche Beverly. "The American Orthodox Jewish Housewife: A Generational Study in Ethnic Survival." Ph.D. dissertation, City University of New York, 1975.

542.   Frankel, Barbara. Childbirth in the Ghetto: Folk Beliefs of Negro Women in a North Philadelphia Hospital Ward. San Francisco: R & E Research Associates, 1977.

543.   Franz, Eleanor. "Adirondack Lady." New York Folklore Quarterly 24 (1968): 194-202.

544.   Fratto, Toni Flores. "Samplers: The Historical Ethnography of an American Popular Art." Ph.D. dissertation, University of Pennsylvania, 1971.

545.   ----------. "'Remember Me': The Sources of American Sampler Verses." New York Folklore 2 (1976): 205-222.

546.   ----------. "Samplers: One of the Lesser American Arts." Feminist Art Journal 5, no. 4 (1976-1977): 11-15.

547.   Frazer, Dorothy. The Quilting Primer. Radnor, Pa.: Chilton Book Co., 1974.

548.   Frazer, James G. "Notes on Harvest Customs." Folk-Lore Journal 7 (1889): 47-53.

549.   ----------. The Golden Bough: A Study in Comparative Religion. 12 vols. London: Macmillan, 1907-1915.

550.   ----------. "Women Fertilized by Stone." Folklore 29 (1918): 254.

551.   Freeman, James M. "The Ladies of Lord Krishna: Rituals of Middle-Aged Women in Eastern India." In no. 494, pp. 110-126.

552.   Freiert, William Kendall. "The Motifs of Confrontation with Women in Homer's 'Odyssey.'" Ph.D. dissertation, University of Minnesota, 1972.

553.   Freilich, Morris, ed. Marginal Natives: Anthropologists at Work. New York: Harper and Row, 1970.

554.   Frey, Linda, Frey, Marsha, and Schneider, Joanne, comps. Women in Western European History: A Select Chronological, Geographical, and Topical Bibliography from Antiquity to the French Revolution. Westport, Ct.: Greenwood Press, 1982.

555.   Fried, Morton H. "Mankind Excluding Woman." Science 165 (1969): 883-884.

556.   Friedan, Betty. The Feminine Mystique. New York: Dell, 1963.

557.   Friedl, Ernestine. "The Position of Women: Appearance and Reality." Anthropological Quarterly 40, no. 3 (1967): 97-108.

558.   ----------. Women and Men: An Anthropologist's View. New York: Holt, Rinehart and Winston, 1975.

559.   Friedlander, Judith. "The Aesthetics of Oppression: Traditional Arts of Women in Mexico." Heresies 4 (1978): 3-9.

560.   Friedman, Albert B. "Grounding a Superstition: Lactation as Contraceptive." Journal of American Folklore 95 (1982): 200-208.

561.   Friedman, Albert B., and Osberg, Richard H. "Gawain's Girdle as Traditional Symbol." Journal of American Folklore 90 (1977): 301-315.

562.   Friedman, Leslie. Sex Role Stereotyping in the Mass

Media: An Annotated Bibliography. New York: Garland, 1977.

563.   Friedrich, Paul. The Meaning of Aphrodite. Chicago: University of Chicago Press, 1978.

564.   Frisbie, Charlotte Johnson. Kinaalda: A Study of the Navaho Girls' Puberty Ceremony. Middleton, Ct.: Wesleyan University Press, 1967.

565.   ----------. "Introduction." Dezba: Woman of the Desert, by Gladys A. Reichard, n.p. Glorieta, N.M.: Rio Grande Press, 1971.

566.   ----------. "Fieldwork as a 'Single Parent': To Be or Not to Be Accompanied by a Child." In Collected Papers in Honor of Florence Hawley Ellis, ed. Theodore R. Frisbie, pp. 98-119. Papers of the Archaeological Society of New Mexico, No. 2. Norman, Okla.: University of Oklahoma Press, 1975.

567.   ----------. "Observations on a Preschooler's First Experience with Cross Cultural Living." Journal of Man 7 (1975): 91-112.

568.   Frost, John. Pioneer Mothers of the West: or, Daring and Heroic Deeds of American Women. Boston: Lee and Shepard, 1859.

569.   Furfey, Paul. "Men's and Women's Language." American Catholic Sociological Review 5 (1944): 218-223.

570.   Furness, Clifton. The Genteel Female: An Anthology. New York: Alfred A. Knopf, 1931.

571.   Fussell, G.E., and Fussell, K.R. The English Country-woman: A Farmhouse Social History, A.D. 1500-1900. New York: Benjamin Blom, 1971.

572.   Gale, Fay, ed. Woman's Role in Aboriginal Society. Australian Aboriginal Studies, No. 36. Canberra: Australian National Institute of Aboriginal Studies, 1970.

573.   Gallagher, Dorothy. Hannah's Daughters: Six Generations of an American Family. New York: Crowell, 1976.

574.   Gallin, Bernard, and Gallin, Rita Schlesinger. "The Rural-to-Urban Migration of an Anthropologist in Taiwan." In no. 534, pp. 223-248.

575.   Galvin, Corinne Brown. "Sojourner Truth, the Libyan Sibyl." New York Folklore Quarterly 6 (1950): 5-21.

576.   Gans-Ruedin, E. The Connoisseur's Guide to Oriental Rugs. Rutland, Vt.: Charles Tuttle, 1971.

577.   Garbaty, Thomas Jay. "Chaucer's Weaving Wife."

Journal of American Folklore 81 (1968): 342-346.

578.   Gardner, Emelyn E. "Folk-Lore from Schoharie County, New York." Journal of American Folklore 27 (1914): 304-325.

579.   ----------. "Some Play-Party Games in Michigan." Journal of American Folklore 33 (1920): 91-133.

580.   Garnett, Lucy M.J. The Women of Turkey and Their Folk-Lore. London: David Nutt, 1890.

581.   Garrett, Clarke. "Women and Witches: Patterns of Analysis." Signs: Journal of Women in Culture and Society 3 (1977): 461-470.

582.   Garrett, Kim. "Family Stories and Sayings." Publications of the Texas Folklore Society 30 (1961): 273-281.

583.   Gathorne-Hardy, Jonathan. The Unnatural History of the Nanny. New York: Dial, 1972.

584.   Gaume, Mary Matilda. "Ruth Crawford Seeger: Her Life and Works." Ph.D. dissertation, Indiana University, 1973.

585.   Geddes, Elisabeth. Blackwork Embroidery. Boston: Charles T. Branford, 1966.

586.   Gelber, Mark I. "Wishful Defloration at a Girls' School." Journal of American Folklore 84 (1971): 244.

587.   Georges, Robert A., and Jones, Michael O. People Studying People: The Human Element in Fieldwork. Berkeley: University of California Press, 1980.

588.   Giffen, Naomi M. The Roles of Men and Women in Eskimo Culture. Chicago: University of Chicago Press, 1930.

589.   Gilbert, Helen. "Pregnancy Cravings as a Motif in Folktales." Folklore Forum 5 (1972): 129-142.

590.   Gimbutas, Marija. The Goddesses and Gods of Old Europe, 7000 to 3500 B.C.; Myths, Legends and Cult Images. Berkeley: University of California Press, 1974.

591.   ----------. "Women and Culture in Goddess-Oriented Old Europe." In no. 1445, pp. 22-31.

592.   Ginat, Joseph. "A Rural Arab Community in Israel: Marriage Patterns and Woman's Status." Ph.D. dissertation, University of Utah, 1975.

593.   Girardot, N.J. "Initiation and Meaning in the Tale of Snow White and the Seven Dwarfs." Journal of American Folklore 90 (1977): 274-300.

594.   Glassie, Henry. Pattern in the Material Folk Culture of the Eastern United States. Philadelphia: University
of Pennsylvania Press, 1968.

595.   Glavan, Joyce. "Sorority Tradition and Song." Journal of the Ohio Folklore Society 3 (1968): 192-198.

596.   Glaze, Anita. "Power and Art in a Senufo Village."
African Arts Spring, 1975: 25-29, 64-67.

597.   ----------. Art and Death in a Senufo Village.
Bloomington: Indiana University Press, 1981.

598.   Glazer, Nona, and Waeher, Helen Youngelson, eds.
Woman in a Man Made World: A Socioeconmic Handbook.
Chicago: Rand McNally, 1972.

599.   Gloster, Hugh M. "Zora Neale Hurston, Novelist and
Folklorist." Phylon 4 (1943): 153-159.

600.   Gluck, Sherna. "What's So Special about Women?
Women's Oral History." Frontiers 2, no. 2 (1977): 3-17.

601.   Godden, G.M. "Mortuary Customs and Beliefs of South
Carolina Negroes." Journal of American Folklore 7 (1894):
318-320.

602.   Goffman, Erving. The Presentation of Self in Everyday Life. Garden City: Doubleday, 1959.

603.   ----------. Interaction Ritual. New York: Doubleday, 1967.

604.   Golde, Peggy, ed. Women in the Field: Anthropological Experiences. Chicago: Aldine, 1970.

605.   Goldenberry, Naomi R. Changing of the Gods: Feminism and the End of Traditional Religions. Boston: Beacon
Press, 1979.

606.   Golder, F.A. "Aleutian Stories." Journal of American Folklore 18 (1905): 215-222.

607.   Goldfrank, Esther S. Obituary for Gladys Amanda
Reichard. Journal of American Folklore 69 (1956): 53-54.

608.   Goldman, Marion Sherman. Gold Diggers and Silver
Miners: Prostitution and Social Life on the Comstock Lode.
Ann Arbor: University of Michigan Press, 1981.

609.   Goldstein, Elizabeth, and Green, Gail. "Pierogi- and
Babka-Making at St. Mary's." New York Folklore 4 (1978):
71-79.

610.   Goldstein, Kenneth. A Guide for Field Workers in

Folklore. Hatboro, Pa.: Folklore Associates, 1964.

611.   ----------. "The Verse Competition Jest in North-eastern Scotland." Journal of American Folklore 83 (1970): 351-353.

612.   Goldstein, Kenneth S., and Dwyer-Shick, Susan. "Women's Oral History: Some Bibliography Additions." Folklore Feminists Communication 8 (1976): 11.

613.   Gonin, Eileen, and Newton, Jill. Quiltmaking for Your Home. London: Octopus Books, 1974.

614.   Gonzales, Nancie L. Solien. "Cakchiqueles and Caribs: The Social Context of Fieldwork." In no. 553, pp. 153-184.

615.   ----------. "The City of Gentlemen." In no. 534, pp. 19-40.

616.   Goodale, Jane C. Tiwi Wives: A Study of the Women of Melville Island. American Ethnological Society Monographs, No. 51. Seattle and London: University of Washington Press, 1971.

617.   Goodland, Roger. A Bibliography of Sex Rites and Customs. London: G. Routledge and Sons, 1931.

618.   Goodwater, Leanna. Women in Antiquity: An Annotated Bibliography. Metuchen, N.J.: Scarecrow Press, 1975.

619.   Goody, Jack and Tambiah, S. J. Bridewealth and Dowry. Cambridge: Cambridge University Press, 1973.

620.   Gore, J. Howard. "The Go-Backs." Journal of American Folklore 5 (1892): 107-109.

621.   Gorfain, Phyllis, and Glazier, Jack. "Sexual Symbolism, Origins, and the Ogre in Mbeere, Kenya." Journal of American Folklore 91 (1978): 925-946.

622.   Gornick, Vivian. "Woman as Outsider." In no. 623, pp. 126-144.

623.   Gornick, Vivian, and Moran, Barbara K., eds. Woman in Sexist Society: Studies in Power and Powerlessness. New York: New American Library, 1971.

624.   Gostelow, Mary. Embroidery South Africa London: Mills and Boon, 1976.

625.   ----------. The Complete International Book of Embroidery. New York: Simon and Schuster, 1977.

626.   ----------. Embroidery of All Russia. New York: Scribner, 1977.

627.   Gottschalk, Louis, Kluckhohn, Clyde, and Angell, Robert. The Use of Personal Documents in History, Anthropology and Sociology. New York: Social Science Research Council, 1965.

628.   Gough, E. Kathleen. "Female Initiation Rites on the Malabar Coast." Journal of the Royal Anthropological Institute 85 (1955): 45-80.

629.   Gould, Jan. Women of British Columbia. Saanichton, B.C.: Hancock House, 1975.

630.   Gould-Martin, Katherine. "Women Asking Women: The Ethnography of Health Care in Rural Taiwan." Ph.D. dissertation, Rutgers University, 1976.

631.   Gower, Hershcel. "Jeannie Robertson: Portrait of a Traditional Singer." Scottish Studies 12 (1968): 113-126.

632. Gower, Herschel, and Porter, James. "Jeannie Robertson: The Child Ballads." Scottish Studies 14 (1970): 35-58.

633.   ----------. "Jeannie Robertson: The 'Other' Ballads." Scottish Studies 16 (1972): 139-159.

634.   ----------. "Jeannie Robertson: The Lyric Songs." Scottish Studies 21 (1977): 55-103.

635.   Grabenhorst-Randall, Terree. "The Woman's Building." Heresies 4 (1978): 44-46.

636.   Graves, Robert. The Greek Myths. 2 vols. Baltimore: Penguin, 1955.

637.   ----------. The White Goddess: A Historical Grammar of Poetic Myth. New York: Octagon, 1972.

638.   Gray, Patrick. "The Universality of the Female Witch." International Journal of Women's Studies 2 (1980): 541-550.

639.   Green, Archie. Only a Miner: Studies in Recorded Coal-Mining Songs. Urbana: University of Illinois Press, 1972.

640.   Green, Rayna. "The Only Good Indian: The Image of the Indian in American Vernacular Culture." Ph.D. dissertation, Indiana University, 1973.

641.   ----------. "The Pocahontas Perplex: The Image of Indian Women in American Culture." Massachusetts Review 16 (1975): 698-714.

642.   ----------. "Magnolias Grow in Dirt: The Bawdy Lore of Southern Women." Southern Exposure 4 (1977): 29-33.

643.   ----------. "Native American Studies 80: Native American Women Syllabus." Folklore Women's Communication 20 (1980): 22-25.

644.   ----------. "Review Essay: Native American Women." Signs: Journal of Women in Culture and Society 6 (1980): 248-268.

645.   ----------. Native American Women: A Bibliography. Wichita Falls, Tx.: Ohoyo Resource Center, 1981.

646.   Greenberg, Andrea. "Drugged and Seduced: A Contemporary Legend." New York Folklore Quarterly 29 (1973): 131-158.

647.   Greenwald, Harold. The Call Girl: A Social and Psychoanalytic Study. New York: Ballantine, 1958.

648.   Greenway, John. "Aunt Molly Jackson and Robin Hood: A Study in Folk Re-Creation." Journal of American Folklore 69 (1956): 23-38.

649.   ----------. American Folksongs of Protest. New York: A.S. Barnes, 1960.

650.   Gregor, Walter. "Some Marriage Customs in Cairnbulg and Inverallochy." Folk-Lore Journal 1 (1883): 119-121.

651.   Grether, Gertrude E. "The Divinity of Women in the Roman Imperial Families, 27 B.C.-235 A.D." Ph.D. dissertation, Cornell University, 1976.

652.   Grider, Sylvia Ann. "The Supernatural Naratives of Children." Ph.D. dissertation, Indiana University, 1976.

653.   ----------. "Foreword." To The Wind, by Dorothy Scarborough. Barker Texas History Center Series, No. 4. Austin and London: University of Texas Press, 1979.

654.   ----------. "A Select Bibliography of Childlore." Western Folklore 39 (1980): 248-265.

655.   Grinnell, George Bird. "Cheyenne Woman Customs." American Anthropologist 4 (1902): 13-16.

656.   Gross, Rita M. "Menstruation and Childbirth as Ritual and Religious Experience among Native Australians." In no. 494, pp. 277-292.

657.   Guðjónsson, Elsa E. "The National Costume of Women in Iceland." American-Scandinavian Review Winter, 1969-1970: 361-369.

658.   Gulzow, Monte, and Mitchell, Carol. "'Vagina Dentata' and 'Incurable Venereal Disease': Legends from the Viet

Nam War." Western Folklore 39 (1980): 306-316.

659.   Gunda, Bela. "Sex and Semiotics." Journal of American Folklore 86 (1973): 143-151.

660.   Gunning, Sarah Ogan. "My Name is Sarah Ogan Gunning...." Sing Out! 25, no. 2 (1976): 15-16.

661.   Gutch, Mrs. "Saint Martha and the Dragon." Folk-Lore 63 (1952): 193-203.

662.   Gutcheon, Beth, and Gutcheon, Jeffrey. The Quilt Design Workbook. New York: Rawson Associates, 1976.

663.   H., T.W. "Brides Dancing Barefoot." Journal of American Folklore 2 (1889): 66-67.

664.   Haber, Barbara. Women in America: A Guide to Books. Boston: G.K. Hall, 1978.

665.   Hackett, Marie L. "A Collection of Menstrual Lore." Folklore Women's Communication 15 (1978): 19-20.

666.   Haders, Phyllis. Sunshine and Shadow: The Amish and Their Quilts. New York: Universe, 1976.

667.   Hafkin, Nancy J., and Bay, Edna G., eds. Women in Africa: Studies in Social and Economic Change. Stanford: Stanford University Press, 1976.

668.   Hagood, Margaret Jarman. Mothers of the South: Portraiture of the White Tenant Farm Woman. Chapel Hill: University of North Carolina Press, 1939.

669.   Haire, Frances H. The Folk Costume Book. New York: A.S. Barnes, 1937.

670.   Hall, Carrie A., and Kretsinger, Rose G. The Romance of the Patchwork Quilt in America. Caldwell, Idaho: Caxton Printers, 1936.

671.   Hall, Edwin S. The Eskimo Storyteller: Folktales from Noatak, Alaska. Knoxville: University of Tennessee Press, 1975.

672.   Hall, Eliza Calvert. A Book of Hand-Woven Coverlets. Rutland, Vt., and Tokyo: Tuttle, 1966.

673.   Hamamsy, Laila S. "The Role of Women in a Changing Navajo Society." American Anthropologist 59 (1957): 101-111.

674.   Hamilton, Lady Augusta. Marriage Rites, Customs, and Ceremonies of All Nations of the Universe. London: Chapple and Son, Andrews, J. Bumpas and E. Barrett, 1822.

675.   Hammersmith, Sue Kiefer. "Being a Nun: Social Order and Change in a Radical Community." Ph.D. dissertation, Indiana University, 1976.

676.   Hammond, Dorothy, and Jablow, Alta. Women in the Cultures of the World. Menlo Park, Ca.: Cummings, 1976.

677.   Hand, Wayland D. "American Analogues of the Couvade." In Studies in Folklore, ed. W. Edson Richmond, pp. 213-229. Indiana University Publications, Folklore Series, No. 9. Bloomington: Indiana University Press, 1957.

678.   ----------. "Migratory Legend of 'The Cut-Out Pullman': Saga of American Railroading." New York Folklore Quarterly 27 (1971): 231-235.

679.   Hanley, Hope. Needlepoint in America. New York: Scribner, 1969.

680.   Hanna, Sami A. "Al-Jawārī Al-Mug-hanniyāt: The Singing Arab Maids." Southern Folklore Quarterly 34 (1970): 325-330.

681.   Harbeson, Georgiana Brown. "Shadow in the Thread: Embroidered Tapestries." House Beautiful 67 (1930): 731-735.

682.   ----------. American Needlework: The History of Decorative Stitching and Embroidery from the Late 16th to the 20th Century. New York: Coward-McCann, 1938.

683.   Harding, Esther. Woman's Mysteries, Ancient and Modern. London: Longmans, 1935.

684.   Harding, Susan. "Women and Words in a Spanish Village." In no. 1286, pp. 283-308.

685.   ----------. "Street Shouting and Shunning: Conflict between Women in a Spanish Village." Frontiers 3, no. 3 (1978): 14-18.

686.   Haring, Lee. "Performing for the Interviewer: A Study of the Structure of Context." Southern Folklore Quarterly 36 (1972): 383-398.

687.   Harper, Dee W., and Meeks, Catherine L. Bibliography for the Sociology of Sex Roles. State College, Miss.: Mississippi State University Department of Sociology and Anthropology, 1972.

688.   Harrington, M. Raymond. "An Abenaki 'Witch-Story.'" Journal of American Folklore 14 (1901): 160.

689.   Harrison, Edith Swan. "Women in Navajo Myth: A Study in the Symbolism of Matriliny." Ph.D. dissertation, University of Massachusetts, 1973.

690.   Harrison, Jane Ellen. Mythology. Boston: Marshall Jones, 1924.

691.   ----------. Prologomena to the Study of Greek Religion. New York: Meridian, 1959.

692.   Harrison, Phyllis. "Food and Auctions: We Are How We Eat." Folklore Women's Communication 23 (1980): 3-5.

693.   Hart, Donn V., Rajadhon, Phya Anuman, and Coughlin, Richard J. Southeast Asian Birth Customs: Three Studies in Human Reproduction. New Haven: HRAF Press, 1965.

694.   Hartland, Edwin S. The Science of Fairy Tales: An Inquiry into Fairy Mythology. London: W. Scott, 1891.

695.   ----------. Obituary for Charlotte S. Burne. Folklore 34 (1923): 99a ff.

696.   Hartley, Ruth. "Children's Concept of Male and Female Roles." Merrill-Palmer Quarterly 6 (1960): 83-91.

697.   Hartman, Mary S., and Banner, Lois W. Clio's Consciousness Raised: New Perspectives on the History of Women. New York: Harper and Row, 1974.

698.   Hartman, William S., Fithian, Marilyn, and Johnson, Donald. Nudist Society: An Authoritative, Complete Study of Nudism in America. New York: Crown, 1970.

699.   Hassett, James, and Houlihan, John. "Different Jokes for Different Folks: A Report on PT's Humor Survey." Psychology Today January, 1979: 64-71.

700.   Havlick, Margaret Jean. "Life Styles of Single Women." Ph.D. dissertation, Temple University, 1975.

701.   Hawes, Bess Lomax. "La Llorona in Juvenile Hall." Western Folklore 27 (1968): 153-170.

702.   ----------. "Folksongs and Function: Some Thoughts on the American Lullaby." Journal of American Folklore 86 (1974): 140-148.

703.   Hawkins, John. "An Old Mauma's Folk-Lore." Journal of American Folklore 9 (1896): 129-131.

704.   Hays, H.R. From Ape to Angel: An Informal History of Social Anthropology. New York: Knopf, 1958.

705.   ----------. In the Beginning: Early Man and His Gods. New York: Putnam, 1963.

706.   ----------. The Dangerous Sex: The Myth of Feminine Evil. New York: Putnam, 1964.

707.   Haywood, Charles. A Bibliography of North American Folklore and Folksong. New York: Greenberg, 1951.

708.   Heath, Deborah A. "Art, Objectivity, and the Problem of Depicting the Prosaic." Folklore Women's Communication 19 (1979): 14-17.

709.   Hedges, Elaine. "The Nineteenth-Century Diarist and Her Quilts." Feminist Studies 8 (1982): 293-299.

710.   Heffner, Susan R., comp. "A Selected List of Songs Dealing with Women in Prison." Washington: Library of Congress Archive of Folk Song (pamphlet), 1977.

711.   Heinsohn, Gunnar, and Steiger, Otto. "The Elimination of Medieval Birth Control and the Witch Trials of Modern Times." International Journal of Women's Studies 5 (1982): 193-214.

712.   Hellbom, Anna-Britta. "Las apariciones de la Virgen de Guadalupe en Mexico y en Espana: Un estudio comparativo." Ethnos 29 (1964): 58-72.

713.   ----------. "The Life and Role of Women in the Aztec Culture." Cultures 8, no. 3 (1982): 55-65.

714.   Helm, June, ed. Pioneers of American Anthropology: The Uses of Biography. Seattle: University of Washington Press, 1966.

715.   Hemenway, Robert E. Zora Neale Hurston: A Literary Biography. Urbana: University of Illinois Press, 1977.

716.   Henderson, Helen Kreider. "Ritual Roles of Women in Onitsha Igbo Society." Ph.D. dissertation, University of California, Berkeley, 1969.

717.   Henderson, Margaret Waller. "Woman in the Medieval French Epic." Ph.D. dissertation, New York University, 1965.

718.   Henley, Nancy M. "Power, Sex and Nonverbal Communication." Berkeley Journal of Sociology 18 (1973-1974): 1-23.

719.   Henley, Nancy M., and Thorne, Barrie, eds. Language and Sex: Difference and Dominance. Rowley, Mass.: Newbury House, 1975.

720.   ----------, comps. She Said / He Said: An Annotated Bibliography of Sex Difference in Language, Speech, and Non-Verbal Communication. Pittsburgh: Know, Inc., 1975.

721.   Henriques, Fernando. Prostitution and Society: A Survey. New York: Citadel, 1962.

722.   Henry, Mellinger Edward, and Matteson, Maurice. "Songs from North Carolina," _Southern Folklore Quarterly_ 5 (1941): 137-149.

723.   Hernandez, Juan. "Cactus Whips and Wooden Crosses." _Journal of American Folklore_ 76 (1963): 216-224.

724.   Herrera, Hayden. "Portrait of Frida Kahlo as a Tehuana." _Heresies_ 4 (1978): 57-58.

725.   Herskovits, Melville J., and Herskovits, Frances S. _Dahomean Narrative_. Evanston, Ill.: Northwestern University Press, 1958.

726.   Herskovits, Melville J., and Rogers, Morris J., Jr. "A Note on Present Day Myth." _Journal of American Folklore_ 42 (1929): 73-75.

727.   Hess, Jean. "A Query about Domestic Art." _Folklore Women's Communication_ 18 (1979): 17.

728.   Heyl, Barbara Sherman. "The House Prostitute: A Case Study." Ph.D. dissertation, University of Illinois, 1975.

729.   Heyman, Abigail. _Growing up Female: A Personal Photojournal_. New York: Holt, Rinehart and Winston, 1974.

730.   Higashi, Sumiko. _Virgins, Vamps, and Flappers: The Silent Movie Heroine_. St. Albans, Vt.: Eden Press, 1979.

731.   Hilger, M. Inez. "Chippewa Pre-natal Food and Conduct Taboos." _Primitive Man_ 9 (1936): 46-48.

732.   Hill, Blake. "Women and Religion: A Study of the Socialization in a Community of Catholic Sisters." Ph.D. dissertation, University of Kentucky, 1967.

733.   Hillman, James, ed. _Facing the Gods_. Irving, Tx.: Spring, 1980.

734.   ----------. "On the Necessity of Abnormal Psychology: Ananke and Athene." In no. 733, pp. 1-38.

735.   Hinson, Dolores A. _Quilting Manual: New Designer's Boutique_. New York: Hearthside Press, 1966.

736.   Hirschfield, L.A. "Art in Cunaland: Ideology and Cultural Adaptation." _Man_ n.s. 12 (1977): 104-123.

737.   Hobbie, Margaret. "Query [on putting babies outside to sleep]." _Folklore Feminists Communication_ 7 (1975): 4.

738.   Hoch-Smith, Judith, and Spring, Anita, eds. _Women in Ritual and Symbolic Roles_. New York: Plenum Press, 1978.

739.   Hoffer, Carol Pulley. "Acquisition and Exercise of Political Power by a Woman Paramount Chief of the Sherbro People." Ph.D. dissertation, Bryn Mawr College, 1971.

740.   Hoffmann, Frank A. "Prolegomena to a Study of Traditional Elements in Erotic Film." Journal of American Folklore 78 (1965): 143-148.

741.   ----------. "An Analytical Survey of Anglo-American Erotica." Ph.D. dissertation, Indiana University, 1968.

742.   Hoffs, Tamor. The Liberated Mother Goose. Millbrae, Cal.: Celestial Arts, 1974.

743.   Holiday, Billie, and Dufty, W.   Lady Sings the Blues. London: Barrie and Jenkins, 1973.

744.   Holliday, Carl. "Women's Life in Colonial Days." Ph.D. dissertation, American University, 1922.

745.   Hollister, Valerie, and Weatherford, Elizabeth. "'By the Lakeside There Is an Echo': Towards a History of Women's Traditional Arts." Heresies 4 (1978): 119-123.

746.   Holstein, Jonathan. Abstract Design in American Quilts. New York: Whitney Museum of American Art, 1971.

747.   ----------. American Pieced Quilts. Boston: New York Graphic Society, 1973.

748.   ----------. The Pieced Quilt: An American Design Tradition. Boston: New York Graphic Society, 1975.

749.   Holzberg, Carol S. "Anthropology: The Science of Man?" International Journal of Women's Studies 1 (1978): 438-444.

750.   Honeyman, A.M. "Midwifery in Dundee." Folklore 77 (1966): 132.

751.   Honko, Lauri. "Balto-Finnic Lament Poetry." Studia Fennica 17 (1974): 9-61.

752.   Hoole, William Stanley. Martha Young: Alabama's Foremost Folklorist. University, Ala.: Confederate, n.d.

753.   Hoover, F. Louis. Molas from the San Blas Islands. New York: Center for Inter-American Relations, 1969.

754.   Hopkins, Pandora. "Individual Choice and the Control of Musical Change." Journal of American Folklore 89 (1976): 449-462.

755.   Horcasitas, Fernando, and Butterworth, Douglas. "La Llorona." Tlalocan 4 (1963): 204-224.

756.   Horney, Karen. Feminine Psychology. New York: W.W. Norton, 1967.

757.   Hostetler, John A., and Huntington, Gertrude Enders. "The Hutterites: Fieldwork in a North American Communal Society." In no. 1437, pp. 194-219.

758.   Houck, Carter, and Miller, Myron. American Quilts and How to Make Them. New York: Scribner, 1975.

759.   Houghton, Ross C. Women of the Orient. Cincinnati: Cranston and Stowe, 1877.

760.   Howard, Dorothy. "Australian 'Hoppy' (Hopscotch)." Western Folklore 17 (1958): 163-175.

761.   ----------. "The Game of 'Knucklebones' in Australia." Western Folklore 17 (1958): 34-44.

762.   ----------. "Autograph Album Customs in Australia." Southern Folklore Quarterly 23 (1959): 95-107.

763.   Howe, James, and Hirschfeld, Lawrence A. "The Star Girls' Descent: A Myth about Men, Women, Matrilocality and Singing." Journal of American Folklore 94 (1981): 292-322.

764.   Huber, Joan. "Review Essay: Sociology." Signs: Journal of Women in Culture and Society 1 (1976): 685-697.

765.   Huet, Michel, and Paudrat, Jean-Louis. The Dance, Art and Ritual in Africa. New York: Pantheon, 1978.

766.   Hughes, Muriel J. "Women Healers in Medieval Life and Literature." Ph.D. dissertation, Columbia University, 1944.

767.   Hughes, Therle. English Domestic Needlework: 1660-1860. London: Abbey Fine Arts, n.d.

768.   Huish, Marcus B. Samplers and Tapestry Embroideries. New York and London: Longmans, Green and Co., 1913.

769.   Hull, Eleanor. "Legends and Traditions of the Cailleach Bheara or Old Woman (Hag) of Beare." Folklore 38 (1927): 225-254.

770.   Hultkrantz, Ake. "Bachofen and the Mother Goddess: An Appraisal after One Hundred Years." Ethnos 26 (1961): 75-85.

771.   Hurston, Zora Neale. "Hoodoo in America." Journal of American Folklore 44 (1931): 317-417.

772.   ----------. Mules and Men. Philadelphia: Lippincott, 1935.

773.   Hutchinson, H.N. Marriage Customs in Many Lands.
London: Seeley and Co., 1897.

774.   Ickis, Marguerite. The Standard Book of Quilt Making and Collecting. New York: Dover, 1949.

775.   Ives, Ronald L. "The Legend of the 'White Queen' of
the Seri." Western Folklore 21 (1962): 161-164.

776.   Jabbra, Nancy Walstrom. "The Role of Women in a
Lebanese Community." Ph.D. dissertation, Catholic
University, 1975.

777.   Jackson, Bruce. "Vagina Dentata and Cystic Terato-
ma." Journal of American Folklore 84 (1971): 341-342.

778.   Jackson, Mrs. F. Nevill. A History of Hand-Made
Lace. London: L. Upcott Gill, 1900.

779.   Jackson, Irene V. "Black Women and Afro-American
Tradition." Sing Out! 25, no. 2 (1976): 10-13.

780.   Jacobs, Melville. "A Few Observations on the World
View of the Clackamas Chinook Indians." Journal of American
Folklore 68 (1955): 283-289.

781.   ----------. "Titles in an Oral Literature." Journal
of American Folklore 70 (1957): 157-172.

782.   ----------. "The Romantic Role of Older Women in a
Culture of the Pacific Northwest Coast." Kroeber
Anthropological Society Papers 18 (1958): 79-85.

783.   Jacobs, Sue-Ellen. Women in Perspective: A Guide
for Cross-Cultural Studies. Urbana: University of Illinois
Press, 1974.

784.   Jacobson, Doranne. "Golden Handprints and Red-
Painted Feet: Hindu Childbirth Rituals in Central India." In
no. 494, pp. 73-93.

785.   Jacobson, Dorothy Ann. "Hidden Faces: Hindu and
Muslim Purdah in a Central Indian Village." Ph.D.
dissertation, Columbia University, 1970.

786.   Jahner, Elaine. "Woman Remembering: Life History as
Exemplary Pattern." In no. 835.

787.   Jain, Devaki, ed. Indian Women. New Delhi: Minis-
try of Information, Government of India, 1975.

788.   James, E.O. The Cult of the Mother Goddess. New
York: Praeger, 1959.

789.   ----------. Obituary for Margaret Murray. Folklore
74 (1963): 568-569.

790.   ----------. Obituary for Sona Rose Burstein. <u>Folk-lore</u> 82 (1971): 320-321.

791.   James, George W. <u>Indian Blankets and Their Makers</u>. Chicago: A.C. McClurg, 1914.

792.   James, Thelma G. Obituary for Eloise Ramsay. <u>Journal of American Folklore</u> 78 (1965): 155.

793.   Jameson, R.D., and Anonymous. "Kiss." In no. 957, pp. 582-583.

794.   Jameson, R.D., Voeglin, Erminie Wheeler, and Foster, George M. "Marriage." In no. 957, pp. 679-681.

795.   Jamison, Mrs. C.V. "A Louisiana Legend Concerning Will o' the Wisp." <u>Journal of American Folklore</u> 18 (1905): 250-252.

796.   Janeway, Elizabeth. <u>Man's World, Woman's Place: A Study in Social Mythology</u>. New York: Morrow, 1971.

797.   Jaskoski, Helen. "'My Heart Will Go Out': Healing Songs of Native American Women." <u>International Journal of Women's Studies</u> 4 (1981): 118-134.

798.   Javonovich, Joann, Littenberg, Ronnie, Maxfield, Alice, Muller, Gretchen, Resnick, Marlene, Rosenthal, Kris, Scharf, Karen, and Wortis, Sheli. <u>Women and Psychology</u>. Cambridge: Cambridge-Goddard Graduate School for Social Changes, 1972.

799.   Jayal, S. <u>Status of Women in Epics</u>. Mystic, Ct.: Lawrence Verry, 1966.

800.   Jenkins, J. Geraint. <u>Traditional Country Craftsmen</u>, illus. Winifred Mumford. New York and Washington: Praeger, 1966.

801.   Jennings, Hermione L.F. "A Cambridgeshire Witch." <u>Folk-Lore</u> 16 (1905): 187-190.

802.   Jepson, Barbara. "Ruth Crawford Seeger: A Study in Mixed Accents." <u>Feminist Art Journal</u> 6, no. 1 (1977): 13-16, 50-51.

803.   Jewell, Karen Sue Warren. "An Analysis of the Visual Development of a Stereotype: The Media's Portrayal of Mammy and Aunt Jemima as Symbols of Black Womanhood." Ph.D. dissertation, Ohio State University, 1976.

804.   Joffe, Natalie. "The Vernacular of Menstruation." <u>Word</u> 4 (1948): 181-186.

805.   ----------. "Bride." In no. 957, pp. 164-165.

806.   Joffe, Natalie F., Voegelin, Erminie W., and Foster, George F. "Menstruation." In no. 957, pp. 706-707.

807.   Johnson, Bruce, Conor, Susan S., Rogers, Josephine, and Sidford, Holly. A Child's Comfort: Baby and Doll Quilts in American Folk Art. New York and London: Harcourt Brace and Javanovich and the Museum of American Folk Art, 1977.

808.   Johnson, David. "Musical Traditions in the Forbes Family of Disblair, Aberdeenshire." Scottish Studies 22 (1978): 91-93.

809.   Johnson, Geraldine Niva. "It's a Sin to Waste a Rag: Rug Weaving in Western Maryland." In no. 835.

810.   Johnson, Jean B. "The Huapango: A Mexican Song Contest." California Folklore Quarterly 1 (1942): 233-244.

811.   Johnson, Robbie Davis. "Folklore and Women: A Social Interactional Analysis of the Folklore of a Texas Madam." Journal of American Folklore 86 (1973): 211-224.

812.   Johnson, Mrs. William Preston. "Two Negro Tales." Journal of American Folklore 9 (1896): 194-198.

813.   Jones, Bessie, and Hawes, Bess Lomax. Step It Down: Games, Songs and Stories from the Afro-American Heritage. New York: Harper and Row, 1972.

814.   Jones, Betty H., and Arthurs, Alberta. "The American Heroines and their Critics." International Journal of Women's Studies 1 (1978): 1-12.

815.   Jones, David E. Sanapia: Comanche Medicine Woman. New York: Holt, Rinehart and Winston, 1972.

816.   Jones, Hettie. Big Star Fallin' Mama: Five Women in Black Music. New York: Viking, 1974.

817.   Jones, Louis C. "Hitchhinking Ghosts in New York." California Folklore Quarterly 3 (1944): 284-292.

818.   Jones, Louis Thomas. Aboriginal American Oratory: The Tradition of Eloquence among the Indians of the United States. Los Angeles: Southwest Museum, 1965.

819.   Jones, Mary Eirwen. A History of Western Embroidery. London: Studio Vista, 1969.

820.   Jongmans, D.G., and Gutkind, P.C.W., eds. Anthropologists in the Field. Assen: Van Gorcum,. 1967.

821.   Jopling, Carol F. "Women Weavers of Yalalag: Their Art and Its Process." Ph.D. dissertation, University of Massachusetts, 1973.

822.   ----------. "Women's Work: A Mexican Case Study of Low Status as a Tactical Advantage." Ethnology 13 (1974): 187-195.

823.   Jordan, Brigitte. "Two Studies in Medical Anthropology. I. The Self-Diagnosis of Early Pregnancy: A Study of Lay Competence. II. A Crosscultural Investigation of Four Birthing Systems in Sociobiological Perspective." Ph.D. dissertation, University of California, Irvine, 1975.

824.   ----------. Birth in Four Cultures: A Crosscultural Investigation of Childbirth in Yucatan, Holland, Sweden and the United States. St. Albans, Vt.: Eden Press, 1978.

825.   Jordan, Rosan A. "More on the Dentata." Folklore Feminists Communication 3 (1974): 11.

826.   ----------. "Note about 'The Cat in the Bag.'" Folklore Feminists Communication 4 (1974): 13.

827.   ----------. "Query [on vagina dentata anti-rape device]." Folklore Feminists Communication 2 (1974): 10.

828.   ----------. "Ethnic Identity and the Lore of the Supernatural." Journal of American Folklore 88 (1975): 370-382.

829.   ----------. "The Folklore and Ethnic Identity of a Mexican-American Woman." Ph.D. dissertation, Indiana University, 1975.

830.   ----------. "Folklore Rewritten." Folklore Feminists Communication 5 (1975): 8.

831.   ----------. "Editorial Response to Women and Folklore." Folklore Feminists Communication 8 (1976): 4-5.

832.   ----------. "A Note on Stress and Success." Folklore Women's Communication 19 (1979): 9.

833.   ----------. "The Vaginal Serpent and Other Themes from Mexican-American Women's Lore." In no. 835.

834.   Jordan, Rosan, Farrer, Claire R., Weigle, Marta, Kodish, Deborah, LaRouge, Philip, and Westcott, Denise. "FWC Name Change." Folklore Women's Communication 24 (1981): 1-3.

835.   Jordan, Rosan A., and Kalčik, Susan J., eds. Women's Folklore, Women's Culture. Publications of the American Folklore Society. Philadelphia: University of Pennsylvania Press, forthcoming.

836.   Jordan de Caro, Rosan. "A Note about Folklore and Literature (The Bosom Serpent Revisited)." Journal of American Folklore 86 (1973): 62-65.

837.   ----------. "A Note on Sexocentrism in Folklore Studies." Folklore Feminists Communication 1 (1973): 5-6.

838.   Joseph, Terri B., trans. "Poetry as Sexual Strategy: Songs of the Moroccan Rif." Alcheringa n.s. 2, no. 1 (1976): 72-75.

839.   Joyce, Rosemary. "Query [on women's life histories]." Folklore Women's Communication 17 (1979): 15.

840.   Joyce, T. Athol, and Thomas, N.W. Women of All Nations: A Record of Their Characteristics, Habits, Manners, Customs and Influence. London: Cassell and Co., 1908.

841.   Juhasz, Suzanne. "The Feminine Mode in Literature and Criticism." Frontiers 2, no. 3 (1977): 96-103.

842.   Justin, Dena. "From Mother Goddess to Dishwasher." Natural History 82, no. 2 (1973): 40-45.

843.   Kaberry, Phyllis M. Aboriginal Women: Sacred and Profane. London: Routledge and Kegan Paul, 1939.

844.   ----------. Women of the Grassfields: A Study of the Economic Position of Women in Bamenda, British Cameroons. Colonial Research Publications, No. 14. London: Her Majesty's Stationery Office for the Colonial Office, 1952.

845.   Kahlenberg, Mary Hunt, and Berlant, Anthony. The Navajo Blanket. Los Angeles: Los Angeles County Museum and Praeger, 1972.

846.   Kahn, Kathy. Hillbilly Women. Garden City: Doubleday, 1973.

847.   Kalčik, Susan. "Interview: To Wash a Quilt." Folklore Feminists Communication 3 (1974): 8.

848.   ----------. "Women in the Field (Review Article)." Folklore Feminists Communication 4 (1974): 2, 14.

849.   ----------. "'...like Ann's gynecologist or the time I was almost raped': Personal Narratives in Women's Rap Groups." Journal of American Folklore 88 (1975): 3-11.

850.   ----------. "Sex Roles and Field Work: A Working Bibliography." Folklore Feminists Communication 7 (1975): 13-17, 23.

851.   ----------. "Women's Handles and the Performance of Identity in the CB Community." In no. 835.

852.   Kallir, Otto. Grandma Moses. New York: Abrams, 1973.

853.   Kamsler, Harold M. "Hebrew Menstrual Taboos." Journal of American Folklore 51 (1938): 76-82.

854.   Kaplan, Bernice A. "Changing Functions of the Huanacha Dance at the Corpus Christi Festival in Paracho, Michoacan, Mexico." Journal of American Folklore 64 (1951): 383-392.

855.   Kaplan, Flora. "Mexican Folk Pottery." Heresies 4 (1978): 1.

856.   Kaplan, Sydney Janet. Feminine Consciousness in the Modern British Novel. Urbana: University of Illinois Press, 1975.

857.   ----------. "Review Essay: Literary Criticism." Signs: Journal of Women in Culture and Society 4 (1979): 514-527.

858.   Karpeles, Maud. Obituary for Anne Geddes Gilchrist. Journal of American Folklore 68 (1955): 87-88.

859.   Katz, Jane B., ed. I Am the Fire of Time: The Voices of Native American Women. New York: Dutton, 1977.

860.   Katzarova-Kukudova, Raina, and Djenev, Kiril. Bulgarian Folk Dances. Cambridge: Slavica and Duquesne University Tamburitzans Instutute of Folk Arts, 1976.

861.   Katzenberg, Dena S. "And Eagles Sweep across the Sky": Indian Textiles of the North American West. Baltimore: Baltimore Musuem of Art, 1977.

862.   Katzman, David M. Seven Days a Week: Women and Domestic Service in Industrializing America. New York: Oxford University Press, 1978.

863.   Kavablum, Lea. Cinderella: Radical Feminist, Alchemist. Guttenberg, N.J.: The Auther, 1973.

864.   Kay, Margarita Artschwager. "Health and Illness in the Barrio: Women's Point of View." Ph.D. dissertation, University of Arizona, 1972.

865.   Kealy, Kieran. "The Ballad Heroine." Come All Ye 4, no. 1 (1975): 5-12.

866.   Kearney, Michael. "La Llorona as a Social Symbol." Western Folklore 28 (1969): 199-206.

867.   ----------. The Winds of Ixtepeji: World View and Society in a Zapotec Town. New York: Holt, Rinehart and Winston, 1972.

868.   Kekis, Lisa. Obituary for Maria Cadilla de Marinez. Journal of American Folklore 65 (1952): 216.

869.   Kelley, Jane Holden. Yaqui Women: Contemporary Life Histories. Lincoln: University of Nebraska Press, 1978.

870.   Kelly-Gadol, Joan, Engel, Barbara Alpern, and Casey, Kathleen. Bibliography in the History of European Women. Bronxville, N.Y.: Sarah Lawrence College Women's Studies, 1976.

871.   Kelsey, N.G.N. "When They Were Young Girls: A Singing Game through the Century." Folklore 92 (1981): 104-109.

872.   Kennedy, D.N. "Violet Alford: An Appreciation." Folklore 82 (1971): 344-350.

873.   Kennedy, H.E. and Uminska, Zofia. "Polish Peasant Courtship and Wedding Customs." Folklore 36 (1925): 48-68.

874.   Kent, Kate P. Introducing West African Cloth. Denver: Museum of Natural History, 1971.

875.   Kerényi, Karl. "A Mythological Image of Girlhood: Artemis." In no. 733, pp. 39-45.

876.   ----------. Goddesses of Sun and Moon: Circe, Aphrodite, Medea, Niobe, trans. Murray Stein. Irving, Tx.: Spring, 1979.

877.   Kerns, Virginia. "Black Carib Women and Rites of Death." In no. 494, pp. 127-140.

878.   Kessler, Evelyn S. Women: An Anthropological View. New York: Holt, Rinehart and Winston, 1976.

879.   Key, Mary Ritchie. Male / Female Language, with a Comprehensive Bibliograhy. Metuchen, N.J.: Scarecrow Press, 1975.

880.   ----------. Nonverbal Communication: A Research Guide and Bibliography. Metuchen, N.J.: Scarecrow Press, 1977.

881.   Khattab, Hind Abou Seoud. "Current Roles of Ramah Navajo Women and their Natality Behavior." Ph.D. dissertation, University of North Carolina, 1975.

882.   Khayyat, Shimon L. "Lullabies of Iraqi Jews." Folklore 89 (1978): 13-22.

883.   Kimball, Solon T., and Watson, James B. Crossing Cultural Boundaries: The Anthropological Experience. San Francisco: Chandler, 1972.

884.   Kingsbury, J.B. "The Last Witch of England." Folklore 61 (1950): 134-145.

885.   Kingston, Maxine Hong. The Woman Warrior: Memoirs of a Girlhood among Ghosts. New York: Knopf, 1977.

886.   Kinsey, Alfred C., and others. Sexual Behavior in the Human Female. New York: Pocket Books, 1965.

887.   Kirkland, Winifred. "Say It with Quilts." Harper's Monthly January, 1923: 258-260.

888.   Kirksey, Barbara. "Hestia: A Background of Psychological Focusing." In no. 733, pp.101-113.

889.   Kirshenblatt-Gimblett, Barbara. "Research in Progress [on East European, female, Jewish traditional singers]." Folklore Feminists Communication 1 (1973): 3.

890.   ----------. "A Note on Female Narrators." Folklore Feminists Communication 3 (1974)): 11.

891.   ----------. "Jewish Childbed Amulets." Folklore Feminists Communication 5 (1975): 6-7.

892.   ----------. "A Parable in Context: A Social Interactional Analysis of Storytelling Performance." In Folklore: Performance and Context, ed. Dan Ben-Amos and Kenneth S. Goldstein, pp. 105-130. The Hague: Mouton, 1975.

893.   Kirshenblatt-Gimblett, Barbara, and Bromberg-Ross, JoAnn. "Folklore Courses." Folklore Feminists Communication 6 (1975): 14, 19-24.

894.   Kirtley, Bacil F. "La Llorona and Related Themes." Western Folklore 19 (1960): 155-168.

895.   Kitteringham, Jennie. Country Girls in 19th Century England. History Workshop Pamphlets, No. 11. Oxford: History Workshop, 1973.

896.   Kittredge, George Lyman. "English Folk-Tales in America." Journal of American Folklore 3 (1890): 291-292.

897.   Klein, Laura Frances. "Tlingit Women and Town Politics." Ph.D. dissertation, New York University, 1975.

898.   Klein, Viola. The Feminine Character: History of an Ideology. Urbana: University of Illinois Press, 1971.

899.   Kline, Elmer L. "Two-Headed Woman." Journal of American Folklore 60 (1947): 423.

900.   Kline, Rufus Orville. "Women in the Bar: Norm and Situation in a Northern Italian Hamlet." Ph.D. dissertation, University of California, Davis, 1976.

901.   Kloos, Peter. "Female Initiation among the Maroni

River Caribs." American Anthropologist 71 (1969): 898-905.

902.   Kluckhohn, Clyde. "Navajo Women's Knowledge of Their Song Ceremonials." In Culture and Behavior: Collected Essays, ed. Richard Kluckhohn, pp. 92-96. New York: Free Press, 1962.

903.   Knaster, Meri. Women in Spanish America: An Annotated Bibliography from Pre-Conquest to Contemporary Times. Boston: G.K. Hall, 1977.

904.   Knight, Lee. "A Remembrance of Marjorie Lansing Porter, 1891-1973." New York Folklore Quarterly 30 (1974): 77-80.

905.   Kobler, Turner S. Alice Marriott. Southwest Writers Series, No. 27. Austin: Steck-Vaughn, 1969.

906.   Koh, Hesung Chun, ed. Korean and Japanese Women: An Analytic Bibliographical Guide. Westport, Ct.: Greenwood Press, 1982.

907.   Koke, R.J. "American Quilts: An Exhibition." New York Historical Society Quarterly 32 (1948): 114-117.

908.   Kolodny, Annette. "Review Essay: Literary Criticism." Signs: Journal of Women in Culture and Society 2 (1976): 404-421.

909.   Komarovsky, Mirra. "Cultural Contradictions and Sex Roles." American Journal of Sociology 52 (1946): 184-189.

910.   ----------. "Functional Analysis of Sex Roles." American Sociological Review 15 (1950): 508-516.

911.   ----------. Women in the Modern World. Boston: Little, Brown, 1953.

912.   ----------. Blue-Collar Marriage. New York: Random House, 1962.

913.   Köngäs-Maranda, Elli. "The Carriers of Folklore and the Careers in Folklore." Folklore Women's Communication 27 and 28 (1982): 6-15.

914.   Kopp, Joel, and Kopp, Kate. American Hooked and Sewn Rugs: Folk Art Underfoot. New York: E.P. Dutton, 1975.

915.   Kotkin, Amy J., and Cutting-Baker, Holly. "Model Course Outline: Family Folklore." Baltimore: Maryland Arts Council Folklife Program, 1977.

916.   Kraemer, Ross S. "Ecstasy and Possession: Women of Ancient Greece and the Cult of Dionysus." In no. 494, pp. 53-69.

917.   Kramer, Cheris. "Women's Speech: Separate but Un-equal?" Quarterly Journal of Speech 60 (1974): 14-24.

918.   Kramer, Janet. "Anthropology: Rooting for Cultural Truffles." Ms. June, 1975: 44-46.

919.   Kramer, Sydelle, and Masur, Jenny. Jewish Grand-mothers. Boston: Beacon Press, 1976.

920.   Krauss, Joanne. "Love and Death in the American Ballad: A Morphology of 'Ballads of Family Opposition to Lovers.'" Folklore Annual 4 and 5 (1972-1973): 91-100.

921.   Krefting, Clara E. "Objective Studies in the Oral Style of American Women Speakers." Ph.D. dissertation, Louisiana State University, 1977.

922.   Kruckman, Lawrence Dean. "Women in Clay: The Pattern of La Chamba." Ph.D. dissertation, Southern Illinois University, 1977.

923.   Krueger, Glee. A Gallery of American Samplers. New York: Dutton, 1978.

924.   Krzyzanowski, Julian. "'We Rule the World and We Are Ruled by Women': A Turkish Story on Polish Soil." Fabula 3 (1959): 270-274.

925.   Kunzle, David. "Dress Reform as Antifeminism: A Response to Helene E. Roberts's 'The Exquisite Slave: The Role of Clothes in the Making of the Victorian Woman.'" Signs: Journal of Women in Culture and Society 2 (1977): 570-579.

926.   Kurath, Gertrude P. "Puberty Dances." In no. 957, pp. 908-909.

927.   Kurian, George, ed. Cross-Cultural Perspectives of Mate-Selection and Marriage. Contributions to Family Studies, no. 3. Westport, Ct.: Greenwood Press, 1979.

928.   Kurian, George, and John, Mariam. "Women and Social Customs within the Family: A Case Study of Attitudes in Kerala, India." In no. 1267, pp. 255-265.

929.   L., E.M. "Folklore of London Dressmakers." Folk-Lore 25 (1914): 371.

930.   La Barbera, Michael. "An Ounce of Prevention, and Grandma Tried Them All." New York Folklore Quarterly 20 (1964): 126-129..

931.   Ladden, Arlene. "The Martyr Arts." Heresies 4 (1978): 16-19.

932.   La Flesche, Francis. "Osage Marriage Customs."

American Anthropologist 14 (1912): 127-130.

933.   La Fontaine, J.S. "Ritualization of Women's Life-Crises in Bugisu." In *The Interpretation of Ritual: Essays in Honor of A.I. Richards*, ed. J.S. La Fontaine, pp. 159-186. London: Tavistock, 1972.

934.   Lakoff, Robin. *Language and Woman's Place*. New York: Harper, 1975.

935.   Lambrecht, Francis. "The Hudhúd of Dinulawan and Bugan at Gonhadan." *St. Louis Quarterly* 5 (1967): 267-713.

936.   Lamphere, Louise. "Review Essay: Anthropology." *Signs: Journal of Women in Culture and Society* 2 (1977): 612-627.

937.   Lancaster, J.C. *Godiva of Coventry*. Coventry: Coventry Corporation, 1967.

938.   Landes, Ruth. *The Ojibwa Woman*. Columbia University Contributions to Anthropoplogy, No. 31. New York: Columbia University Press, 1938.

939.   ----------. *The City of Women*. New York: Macmillan, 1947.

940.   ----------. "A Woman Anthropologist in Brazil." In no. 604, pp. 119-139.

941.   Lange, Yvonne. "Occupational Alternatives to Teaching for Women." *Folklore Feminists Communication* 11 (1977): 10-12.

942.   Langlois, Janet Louise. "Belle Gunness, The Lady Bluebeard: Community Legend as Metaphor." Ph.D. dissertation, Indiana University, 1977.

943.   ----------. "Belle Gunness, the Lady Bluebeard: Community Legend as Metaphor." *Journal of the Folklore Institute* 15 (1978): 147-160.

944.   ----------. "English 0328: Folklore of Women Syllabus." *Folklore Women's Communication* 20 (1980): 25-31.

945.   ----------. "The Lady Bluebeard: Narrative Use of a Deviant Woman." In no. 835.

946.   Langness, L.L. *The Life History in Anthropological Science*. New York: Holt, Rinehart and Winston, 1965.

947.   Larsen, Jack Lenor, Buhler, Alfred, Solyom, Bronwen, and Solyom, Garrett. *The Dyer's Art: Ikat, Batik, Plangi*. New York: Van Nostrand Reinhold, 1976.

948.   Laury, Jean Ray. Quilts and Coverlets: A Contemporary Approach. New York: Van Nostrand Reinhold, 1970.

949.   Lavrin, Asunción Irigoyen. "Religious Life of Mexican Women in the XVIII Century." Ph. D. dissertation, Howard University, 1963.

950.   ----------. Latin American Women: Historical Perspectives. Contributions to Women's Studies, No. 3. Westport, Ct.: Greenwood Press, 1978.

951.   Lawson, Joan. European Folk Dance: Its National and Musical Characteristics. London. Sir Isaac Pitman and Sons, 1953.

952.   Lawson, Sarah Ann., "Cutting the Fool: Women in the School Lunch Program." Ph.D. dissertation, University of Florida, 1976.

953.   Layard, John. "Labyrinth Ritual in South India: Threshold and Tattoo Designs." Folk-Lore 48 (1937): 115-182.

954.   Leach, MacEdward. Obituary for Grace Partridge Smith. Journal of American Folklore 73 (1960): 154.

955.   ----------. "Chastity." In no. 957, p. 213-214.

956.   ----------. "Chastity Test." In no. 957, p. 214.

957.   Leach, Maria, ed. Standard Dictionary of Folklore, Mythology and Legend. New York: Funk and Wagnalls, 1972.

958.   Leacock, Eleanor, and others. "Women's Status in Egalitarian Society." Current Anthropology 19 (1978): 247-275.

959.   Leavitt, Ruby R. "Women in Other Cultures." In no. 623, pp. 393-427.

960.   Leddy, Betty. "La Llorona in Southern Arizona." Western Folklore 7 (1948): 272-277.

961.   ----------. "La Llorona Again." Western Folklore 9 (1950): 363-365.

962.   Lederer, Wolfgang. The Fear of Women. New York: Harvest, 1968.

963.   Lee, Dorothy. "Folklore of the Greeks in America." Folk-Lore 47 (1936): 294-310.

964.   ----------. Obituary for Ruth Fulton Benedict. Journal of American Folklore 62 (1949): 345-347.

965.   Leechman, Douglas. "Loucheux Tales." Journal of American Folklore 63 (1950): 158-162.

966.   Leeming, David A. Mythology: The Voyage of the Hero. 2nd ed. New York: Harper and Row, 1981.

967.   Lefkowitz, Mary. "Classical Mythology and the Role of Women in Modern Literature." In A Sampler of Women's Studies, ed. Dorothy Gies McGuigan, pp. 77-84. Ann Arbor: University of Michigan Center for Continuing Education, 1973.

968.   Legman, G. The Horn Book: Studies in Erotic Folklore and Bibliography. New Hyde Park, N.Y.: University Books, 1964.

969.   ----------. Rationale of the Dirty Joke: An Analysis of Sexual Humor. New York: Grove Press, 1968.

970.   ----------. No Laughing Matter: Rationale of the Dirty Joke: 2nd Series. New York: Breaking Point, 1975.

971.   Leino, Pentti. "The Language of Laments: The Role of Phonological and Semantic Features in Word Choice." Studia Fennica 17 (1974): 92-131.

972.   Lemaire, Ria. "The Woman-Song Tradition in West-European Tradition." Folklore Women's Communication 25 (1981): 14-15.

973.   Lerner, Gerda, ed. The Female Experience: An American Documentary. Indianapolis: Bobbs-Merrill, 1977.

974.   Leslau, Wolf. "Mother's Day in Ethiopia." Journal of American Folklore 61 (1948): 394-395.

975.   Lever, Janet Rae. "Games Children Play: Sex Differences and the Development of Role Skills." Ph.D. dissertation, Yale University, 1974.

976.   Levine, Joan B. "The Feminine Routine." Journal of Communication 26, no. 3 (1976): 173-175.

977.   LeVine, Sarah, and LeVine, Robert A. Mothers and Wives: Gusii Women of East Africa. Chicago: University of Chicago Press, 1979.

978.   Lewis, Alfred Allan. The Mountain Artisan Quilting Book. New York: Macmillan, 1973.

979.   Lewis, I.M. Ecstatic Religion. Harmondsworth: Penguin, 1971.

980.   Lewis, Mary Ellen B. "The Feminists Have Done It: Applied Folklore." Journal of American Folklore 87 (1974): 85-87.

981. Lewis, Oscar. "Manly Hearted Women among the North Piegan." American Anthropologist 43 (1941): 173-187.

982. Li, Lillian. "Two Chinese Ghosts." California Folklore Quarterly 4 (1945): 278-280.

983. Lieberman, Marcia R. "'Some Day My Prince Will Come': Female Acculturation through the Fairy Tale." College English 34 (1972): 383-395.

984. Lifton, Robert, ed. The Woman in America. Boston: Houghton Mifflin, 1967.

985. Lippard, Lucy R. "Making Something from Nothing (Toward a Definition of Women's 'Hobby Art')." Heresies 4 (1978): 62-65.

986. Lipshitz, Susan. "The Witch and Her Devils: An Exploration of the Relationship between Femininity and Illness." In Tearing the Veil: Essays on Femininity, ed. Susan Lipshitz, pp. 39-53. London: Routledge and Kegan Paul, 1978.

987. List, Edgar A. "Holda and the Venusberg." Journal of American Folklore 73 (1960): 307-311.

988. Lithgow, Marilyn. Quiltmaking and Quiltmakers. New York: Funk and Wagnalls, 1974.

989. Litoff, Judy Barrett. American Midwives: 1860 to the Present. Contributions to Medical History, No. 1. Westport, Ct.: Greenwood Press, 1978.

990. Little, Nina Fletcher. Country Arts in Early American Homes. New York: E.P. Dutton, 1975.

991. Litto, Gertrude. South American Folk Pottery. New York: Watson-Guptill, 1976.

992. Loeb, Edwin M., Loch, Carl, and Loeb, Ella-Marie K. "Kuanyama Ambo Magic." Journal of American Folklore 69 (1956): 147-174.

993. Lomax, Alan. "Folk Song Style." American Anthropologist 61 (1959): 927-954.

994. ----------. The Rainbow Sign. New York: Duell, Sloan and Pearce, 1959.

995. ----------. "Zora Neale Hurston--A Life of Negro Folklore." Sing Out! 10 (1960): 12-13.

996. ----------. "The Good and the Beautiful in Folksong." Journal of American Folklore 80 (1967): 213-235.

997.   ----------. Folk Song Style and Culture. American Association for the Advancement of Science Publications, No. 88. Washington: American Association of the Advancement of Science, 1968.

998.   ----------. "A Note on a Feminine Factor in Cultural History." In no. 1267, pp. 131-137.

999.   Long, Eleanor. "Aphrodisiacs, Charms and Philters." Western Folklore 32 (1973): 153-163.

1000.   Lopata, Helen Znaniecki. Occupation: Housewife. New York: Oxford University Press, 1971.

1001.   ----------. "Review Essay: Sociology." Signs: Journal of Women in Culture and Society 2 (1976): 165-176.

1002.   Lopez, Griselda Maria, and Joly, Luz Graciela. "Singing a Lullaby in Kuna: A Female Verbal Art." Journal of American Folklore 94 (1981): 351-358.

1003.   Lowie, Robert H., and Hollingworth, Leta. "Science and Feminism." Scientific Monthly 3 (1916): 277-284.

1004.   Lowrimore, Burton. "Six California Tales." California Folklore Quarterly 4 (1945): 154-157.

1005.   Lunt, C. Richard K. "The Laughing Woman." Indiana Folklore 1 (1969): 78-81.

1006.   Luomala, Katherine. "Martha Warren Beckwith: A Commemorative Essay." Journal of American Folklore 75 (1962): 341-353.

1007.   ----------. "Disintegration and Regeneration, the Hawaiian Phantom Hitchhiker Legend." Fabula 13 (1972): 20-59.

1008.   Lupton, Mary Jane, Toth, Emily, and Delaney, Janice. The Curse: A Cultural History of Menstruation. New York: Dutton, 1976.

1009.   Luria, Gina, and Tiger, Virginia. Everywoman. New York: Random House, 1976.

1010.   Lurie, Nancy O., ed. Mountain Wolf Woman, Sister of Crashing Thunder: The Autobiography of a Winnebago Indian. Ann Arbor: University of Michigan Press, 1961.

1011.   ----------. "Women in Early American Anthropology." In Pioneers of American Anthropology: The Uses of Biography, ed. June Helm, pp. 29-81. Seattle: University of Washington Press, 1966.

1012.   Lüthi, Max. Once Upon a Time: On the Nature of

Fairy Tales, trans. Lee Chadeayne and Paul Gottwald. Bloomington and London: Indiana University Press, 1976.

1013.   Lyford, Carrie A. Quill and Beadwork of the Western Sioux. Washington: Education Division, U.S. Office of Indian Affairs, 1940.

1014.   MacCurtain, Margaret, and Ó Corráin, Donncha, eds. Women in Irish Society: The Historical Dimension. Contributions to Women's Studies, No. 11. Westport, Ct.: Greenwood Press, 1979.

1015.   MacGaffey, Janet. "Two Kongo Potters." African Arts 9 (1975): 28-31, 92.

1016.   ----------. "Kongo Pottery: Woman's Art from Zaire." Heresies 4 (1978): 116-117.

1017.   Maclagan, R.C. "'The Keener' in the Scottish Highlands and Islands." Folk-Lore 25 (1914): 84-91.

1018.   MacLaughlin, E. Jean M. "More about the Stuck Tampax." Folklore Feminists Communication 4 (1974): 12.

1019.   ----------. "Query: Scare-Warning Legends for New Mothers?" Folklore Feminists Communication 4 (1974): 13.

1020.   Maclean, Calum I. "Traditional Beliefs in Scotland." Scottish Studies 3 (1959): 189-200.

1021.   MacNeish, June Helm. "Contemporary Folk Beliefs of a Slave Indian Band." Journal of American Folklore 67 (1954): 185-198.

1022.   Madsen, William, and Madsen, Claudia. "Witchcraft in Tecospa and Tepepan." In Systems of North American Witchcraft and Sorcery, ed. D.E. Walker, Jr., pp. 73-94. University of Idaho Anthropological Monographs, No. 1. Moscow, Idaho: University of Idaho, 1970.

1023.   Mainardi, Patricia. "Quilts: A Great American Art." Ms. December, 1973: 58-62.

1024.   ----------. "Quilts: The Great American Art." Feminist Art Journal 2, no. 1 (1973): 18-23.

1025.   Maines, Rachel. "Is Your Quilt Trying to Tell You Something?" Majority Report June, 1975: 6; reprinted Folklore Feminists Communication 7: 18-19.

1026.   Mair, Lucy. Witchcraft. New York: McGraw-Hill, 1969.

1027.   ----------. Marriage. New York: Pica Press, 1971.

1028.   Makhlouf, Carla. Changing Veils: Women and Modernisation in North Yemen. Austin: University of Texas Press, 1978.

1029.   Maksymowicz, Virginia. "Myth and the Sexual Division of Labor." Heresies 4 (1978): 116-117.

1030.   Malamud, Rene. "The Amazon Problem." In no. 733, pp. 47-66.

1031.   Malone, Bill C. Country Music, U.S.A.: A Fifty Year History. American Folklore Society Memoirs, No. 54. Austin and London: University of Texas Press, 1968.

1032.   Malone, Bill, and McCulloh, Judith. Stars of Country Music: Uncle Dave Macon to Johnny Rodriguez. Urbana: University of Illinois Press, 1975.

1033.   Mancuso, Arlene. "Women of Old Town." Ph.D. dissertation, Columbia University Teacher's College, 1977.

1034.   Manges, Frances May. "Women Shopkeepers, Tavern-keepers, and Artisans in Colonial Philadelphia." Ph.D. dissertation, University of Pennsylvania, 1958.

1035.   Marein, Shirley. Stitchery, Needlepoint, Applique, and Patchwork. New York: Viking Press, 1974.

1036.   Marett, R.R. Obituary for Eleanor Hull. Folklore 46 (1935): 76-77.

1037.   ----------. Obituary for Edith Carey. Folk-Lore 47 (1936): 230-231.

1038.   Marlin, Abbe. "Query: The Stuck Tampax." Folklore Feminists Communiucation 3 (1974): 12.

1039.   Marriott, Alice Lee. Maria: The Potter of San Ildefonso. Norman: University of Oklahoma Press, 1948.

1040.   Marston, Doris E. Exploring Patchwork. Newton Centre, Mass.: Charles Branford, 1972.

1041.   Martin, M. Kay, and Voorhies, Barbara. Female of the Species. New York and London: Columbia University Press, 1975.

1042.   Martin, Mary A. "Turkmen Women, Weaving and Cultural Change." Heresies 4 (1978): 114-115.

1043.   Martin, Wendy. "Seduced and Abandoned in the New World." In no. 623, pp. 329-346.

1044.   Mason, Otis T. Woman's Share in Primitive Culture. New York: Appleton, 1895.

1045.   ----------. Aboriginal Indian Basketry. Glorieta,

N.M.: Rio Grande Press, 1970.

1046.   Matalene, Carolyn. "Women as Witches." International Journal of Women's Studies 1 (1978): 473-587.

1047.   Mathias, Elizabeth. "Sardianan Emigration and Bread:
Changes in the Form and Social Uses of a Female Plastic
Art." Folklore Women's Communication 27 and 28 (1982): 15.

1048.   Matossian, Mary Kilbourne. "In the Beginning, God
Was a Woman." Journal of Social History 6 (1973): 325-343.

1049.   Matthews, Thomas. "Mural Painting in South Africa."
African Arts January, 1977: 28-33.

1050.   Maurer, David W. "Prostitutes and Criminal Argots."
American Journal of Sociology 44 (1939): 546-550.

1051.   May, Florence Lewis. Hispanic Lace and Lace
Making. New York: Hispanic Society of America, 1939.

1052.   Mayo, Edith. "Ladies and Liberation: Icon and
Iconoclast in the Women's Movement." In Icons of America,
ed. Ray B. Browne and Marshall Fishwick, pp. 208-227.
Bowling Green: Popular Press, 1978.

1053.   Mayotte, Denise. "An Interview with Jennie Smith--
Quilter." Folklore Women's Communication 19 (1979): 11-14.

1054.   McCarthy, William B. "Creativity, Tradition and History: The Ballad Repertoire of Agnes Lyle of Kilbarchan."
Ph.D. dissertation, Indiana University, 1978.

1055.   McCrindle, Jean, and Rowbotham, Sheila, eds. Duti-
ful Daughters: Women Talk about their Lives. Austin:
University of Texas Press, 1977.

1056.   McDowell, Margaret B. "Folk Lullabies: Songs of
Anger, Love and Fear." Feminist Studies 5 (1977): 205-218.

1057.   McElwain, Mary A. The Romance of the Village
Quilts. Walsworth, Wis.: n.p., 1936.

1058.   ----------. Notes on Appliqued Work and Patchwork.
London: Victoria and Albert Museum, 1949.

1059.   McGinty, Sue Simmons. "Honky Tonk Angels." In no. 2,
pp. 202-210.

1060.   McIntosh, Karyl. "Folk Obstetrics, Gynecology, and
Pediatrics in Utica, New York." New York Folklore 4
(1978): 49-59.

1061.   McKay, J.G. "The Deer-Cult and the Deer-Goddess Cult
of the Ancient Caledonians." Folklore 43 (1932): 144-174.

1062.   McKim, Ruby Short. One Hundred and One Patchwork Patterns. New York: Dover, 1962.

1063.   McLeod, Norma, and Herndon, Marcia. "The Bormliza: Maltese Folksong Style and Women." Journal of American Folklore 88 (1975): 81-100.

1064.   McMurray, Martha Jean. "Religion and Women's Sex-Role Traditionalism." Ph.D. dissertation, Indiana University, 1975.

1065.   McMurtie, Douglas. "A Legend of Lesbian Love among North American Indians." Urologic and Cultaneous Review April, 1914: 192-193.

1066.   McNeil, W.K. "Mary Henderson Eastman: Pioneer Collector of American Folklore." Southern Folklore Quarterly 39 (1975): 271-289.

1067.   Mead, Margaret. Sex and Temperment in Three Societies. New York: Morrow, 1935.

1068.   ----------. Male and Female: A Study of the Sexes in a Changing World. New York: Morrow, 1950.

1069.   ----------. Blackberry Winter: My Earlier Years. New York: Morrow, 1973.

1070.   Mead, Sidney M. The Art of Taaniko Weaving. Wellington: Reed, 1968.

1071.   Meade, Florence O. "Folk Tales from the Virgin Islands." Journal of American Folklore 45 (1932): 363-371.

1072.   Medicine, Beatrice. "The Role of Women in Native American Societies: A Bibliography." Indian Historian 8, no. 3 (1975): 50-53.

1073.   ----------. The Native American Woman: A Perspective. Albuquerque: Eric/Cress, 1978.

1074.   Meese, Elizabeth A. "Telling It All: Literary Standards and Narratives by Southern Women." Frontiers 2, no. 2 (1977): 63-67.

1075.   Mellen, Joan. Women and their Sexuality in the New Film. New York: Horizon Press, 1973.

1076.   Messenger, Betty. "Picking Up the Linen Threads: Some Folklore of the Northern Irish Linen Industry." Journal of the Folklore Institute 9 (1972): 18-27.

1077.   ----------. Picking Up the Linen Threads: A Study in Industrial Folklore. Austin: University of Texas Press, 1978.

1078.   Metraux, Alfred, Luomala, Katharine, and Anonymous. "Initiation." In no. 957, p. 525.

1079.   Metraux, Alfred, and Voeglin, Erminie W. "Vagina Dentata." In no. 957, p. 1152.

1080.   Meyer, Melissa, and Schapiro, Miriam. "Waste Not, Want Not: An Inquiry into What Women Saved and Assembled. Femmage." Heresies 4 (1978): 66-69.

1081.   Meyerhoff, Barbara. "The Older Woman as Androgyne." Parabola: Myth and the Quest for Meaning 3 (1978): 75-89.

1082.   Miles, Emma Bell. The Spirit of the Mountains. Intro. David E. Whisnant, foreword Roger D. Abrahams. Facsimilie ed. Knoxville: University of Tennesse Press, 1975.

1083.   Miller, David L. "Red Riding Hood and Grand Mother Rhea: Images in a Psychology of Inflation." In no. 733, pp. 87-99.

1084.   Miller, Jean Baker, ed. Psycholanalysis and Women. Baltimore: Penguin, 1973.

1085.   Miller, Jennifer. "Quilting Women: 'Rather Quilt Than Eat Almost.'" Southern Exposure 4 (1977): 24-28.

1086.   Millman, Marcia, and Kanter, Rosabeth Moss. Another Voice: Feminist Perspectives on Social Life and Social Science. Garden City: Anchor Press/Doubleday, 1975.

1087.   Mills, George. Navaho Art and Culture. Colorado Springs: Taylor Museum, 1959.

1088.   Mills, Margaret. "Sex Role Reversals, Sex Changes and Transvestite Disguise in the Oral Tradition of a Conservative Muslim Community." In no. 835.

1089.   Millstein, Beth, and Bodin, Jeanne, eds. We, the American Women: A Documentary History. N.p.: Jerome S. Ozer, 1977.

1090.   Milspaw, Yvonne J. "Applachian Crafts in Transition." Goldenseal 2 (1976): 14-16.

1091.   ----------. "Gossip over the Frames: The Social Function That Wasn't There." Folklore Feminsits Communication 13 (1977): 13-14.

1092.   Minard, Rosemary, ed. Womenfolk and Fairy Tales. Boston: Houghton Mifflin, 1975.

1093.   Misra, Rekha. Women in Mughal India, 1526-1748 A.D. Delhi: Munshiram Manoharlal, 1967.

1094.   Mitchell, Arlene Edith. "Informal Inmate Social Structure in Prisons for Women: A Comparative Study." Ph.D. dissertation, University of Washingon, 1969.

1095.   Mitchell, Carol. "Query [on narratives told by women about rape]." Folklore Feminists Communication 1 (1973): 4.

1096.   ----------. "The Difference between Male and Female Joke Telling as Exemplified in a College Community." 2 vols. Ph.D. dissertation, Indiana University, 1976.

1097.   ----------. "Bawdy Folklore." Folklore Feminists Communication 13 (1977): 9-10.

1098.   ----------. "The Sexual Perspective in the Appreciation of Jokes." Western Folklore 26 (1977): 303-329.

1099.   ----------. "Hostility and Aggression toward Males in Female Joke Telling." Frontiers 3, no. 3 (1978): 19-23.

1100.   ----------. "Bless Me, Ultima and Other Ethnographic Novels for the Folklore Class." Folklore Women's Communication 17 (1979): 22-23.

1101.   ----------. "Jokes Collected from Women." Folklore Women's Communication 22 (1980): 25-28.

1102.   ----------. "To Pregnant Women." Folklore Women's Communication 25 (1981): 20-22.

1103.   ----------. "Some Differences in Male and Female Joke Telling." In no. 835.

1104.   Mitchell, Carol, and Manley, Kathleen. "Survey." Folklore Women's Communication 21 (1980): 19-22.

1105.   Mitchell, Juliet. Psychoanalysis and Feminism. New York: Pantheon, 1974.

1106.   Mitchell-Kernan, Claudia. "Signifying and Marking: Two Afro-American Speech Acts." In Directions in Sociolinguistics: The Ethnography of Communication, ed. John J. Gumperz and Dell Hymes, pp. 161-167. New York: Holt, Rinehart and Winston, 1972.

1107.   ----------. "Signifying." In Mother Wit from the Laughing Barrel: Readings in the Interpretation of Afro-American Folklore, ed. Alan Dundes, pp. 310-328. Englewood Cliffs, N.J.: Prentice Hall, 1973.

1108.   Modell, Judith. "A Biographical Study of Ruth Fulton Benedict." Ph.D. dissertation, University of Minnesota, 1978.

1109. Modi, Jivanji Jamshedji. "The Vish-Kanya or Poison
Damsels of Ancient India, Illustrated by the Story of Susan
Ramashgar in the Persian Burzo-Nameh." Folklore 38 (1927):
324-337.

1110. Molloy, John T. The Woman's Dress for Success
Book. Chicago: Follett, 1977.

1111. Monaghan Patricia. The Book of Goddesses and Heroines. New York: Dutton, 1981.

1112. Monteiro, Lois. "Nursing-Lore," New York Folklore
Quarterly 29 (1973): 95-104.

1113. Montemayor, Raymond. "Children's Performance in a
Game and Their Attraction to It as a Function of Sex-typed
Labels." Child Development 45 (1974): 152-156.

1114. Monter, E. William. "The Pedestal and the Stake:
Courtly Love and Witchcraft." In no. 210, pp. 120-136.

1115. Mooney, James. "Folk-Lore of the Carolina Mountains." Journal of American Folklore 2 (1889): 95-104.

1116. Moore, Arthur K. "The Types of the Folk Song 'Father
Grumble.'" Journal of American Folklore 64 (1951): 89-94.

1117. Moore, Carmen. Somebody's Angel Child: The Story of
Bessie Smith. New York: Crowell, 1969.

1118. Moore, Ruby Andrews. "Superstitions in Georgia."
Journal of American Folklore 5 (1892): 230-231.

1119. Morewedge, Rosemarie Thee, ed. The Role of Woman in
the Middle Ages. Albany: State University of New York
Press, 1975.

1120. Morgan, Kathryn L. "Caddy Buffers: Legends of a
Middle-Class Negro Family in Philadelphia." Keystone
Folklore Quarterly 11 (1966): 67-88; reprinted in Mother
Wit from the Laughing Barrel: Readings in the Interpretation
of Afro-American Folklore, ed. Alan Dundes, pp. 595-610.
Englewood Cliffs, N.J.: Prentice-Hall, 1973.

1121. ----------. Children of Strangers: The Stories of a
Black Family. Philadelphia: Temple University Press, 1980.

1122. Morris, Alton C. "Mrs. Griffin of Newberry." Southern Folklore Quarterly 8 (1944): 133-198.

1123. Morris, Barbara. Victorian Embroidery. New York:
Thomas Nelson and Sons, 1962.

1124. Moses, Yolanda Theresa. "Female Status and Male
Dominance in Montserat, West Indies." Ph.D. dissertation,
University of California, Riverside, 1976.

1125.   Mulhare, Mirta de la Torre. "Sexual Ideology in Pre-Castro Cuba: A Cultural Analysis." Ph.D. dissertation, University of Pittsburgh, 1969.

1126.   Muncy, Elizabeth R. "Dorothy Scarborough: A Literary Pioneer." M.A. thesis, Baylor University, 1940.

1127.   Munro, Ailie. "Lizzie Higgins and the Transmission of Ten Child Ballads." Scottish Studies 14 (1970): 155-188.

1128.   ----------. "'Abbotsford Collection of Border Ballads': Sophia Scott's Manuscript Book with Airs." Scottish Studies 20 (1976): 91-108.

1129.   Murphy, Yolanda, and Murphy, Robert F. Women of the Forest. New York: Columbia University Press, 1974.

1130.   Murray, Margaret. My First Hundred Years. London. W. Kimber, 1963.

1131.   Myers, Elizabeth Lehman. A Century of Moravian Sisters: The Record of Community Life. New York: Revell, 1918.

1132.   Myrdal, Alva, and Klein, Viola. Women's Two Roles. New York: Humanities Press, 1968.

1133.   Nabokov, Peter. Adobe: Pueblo and Hispanic Folk Traditions of the Southwest. Washington: Smithsonian Institution and Department of Energy, 1981.

1134.   Nagorka, Suzanne. "The Life of Felicia Nagorka." New York Folklore Quarterly 28 (1972): 286-292.

1135.   Nagy, Olga. "Personality and Community as Mirrored in the Formation of Klára Györi's Repertoire." In Studies in East European Folk Narrative, ed. Linda Degh, pp. 473-557. Publications of the American Folklore Society, Bibliographical and Special Series, No. 30; Indiana University Folklore Monograph Series, No. 25. Bloomington: American Folklore Society and Indiana University, 1978.

1136.   Neatherlin, James W. "Dorothy Scarborough: Form and Milieu in the Work of a Texas Writer." Ph.D. dissertation, University of Iowa, 1973.

1137.   Needham, Gwedolyn B. "New Light on Maids' 'Leading Apes in Hell.'" Journal of American Folklore 75 (1962): 106-119.

1138.   Nenola-Kallio, Aili. "Lucky Shoes or Weeping Shoes: Structural Analysis of Ingrian Shoeing Laments." Studia Fennica 17 (1974): 62-91.

1139.   Neumann, Erich. The Great Mother: An Analysis of the Archetype, trans. Ralph Manheim. Bolligen Series, No. 47. Princeton: Princeton University Press, 1953.

1140.   Nevadomsky, Joseph. "Wedding Rituals and Women's Rights among the East Indians in Rural Trinidad." International Journal of Women's Studies 4 (1981): 484-496.

1141.   Newall, Venetia, ed. The Witch Figure. London and Boston: Routledge and Kegan Paul, 1973.

1142.   ----------. The Encyclopedia of Witchcraft and Magic. New York: Dial, 1974.

1143.   ----------. "Narrative as a Means of Communication." Fabula 22 (1981): 84-89.

1144.   ----------. Obituary for Katharine M. Briggs. Journal of American Folklore 94 (1981): 228.

1145.   Newell, Jane H. "Superstitions of Irish Origin in Boston, Mass." Journal of American Folklore 5 (1892): 242-243.

1146.   Newell, W.W. "Primitive Marriage Customs as Preserved in the Games of Children." Journal of American Folklore 5 (1892): 70-71.

1147.   ----------. "Custom of Wearing Gold Beads." Journal of American Folklore 8 (1895): 85.

1148.   Newman, L.F. "Some References to the Couvade in Literature." Folk-Lore 53 (1942): 148-157.

1149.   Newman, Lucille F. "Folklore of Pregnancy: Wives' Tales in Contra Costa County, California." Western Folklore 28 (1969): 112-135.

1150.   Newton, Esther, and Webster, Paula. "Matriarchy: As Women See It." Aphra 4, no. 3 (1973): 6-22.

1151.   Newton, Niles. "Birth Rituals in Cross-Cultural Perspective: Some Practical Applications." In no. 1267, pp. 37-41.

1152.   Nichols, Olivia M. "Curses--The Curse! Euphemisms for Menstruation." Midwestern Journal of Language and Folklore 4 (1978): 37-38.

1153.   Nicklin, Keith. "Ibibio Musical Pots." African Arts Autumn, 1975: 50-55.

1154.   Nielsen, Edith. Scandinavian Embroidery, Past and Present. New York: Scribner, 1978.

1155.   Niethammer, Carolyn. Daughters of the Earth: The

Lives and Legends of American Indian Women. New York:
Collier, 1977.

1156.   Nilsen, Alleen Pace, Bosmajian, Haig, Gershuny, H.
Lee, and Stanley, Julia P. Sexism and Language. Urbana:
National Council of Teachers of English, 1977.

1157.   Nilsson, Martin P. Greek Popular Religion. New
York: Columbia University Press, 1940.

1158.   Noall, Claire. "Superstitions, Customs, and Pre-
scriptions of Mormon Midwives." California Folklore
Quarterly 3 (1944): 102-114.

1159.   Norlin, Ethel Todd. "Present-Day Superstitions at La
Harpe, Ill.: Survivals in a Community of English Origin."
Journal of American Folklore 31 (1918): 202-215.

1160.   Nwoga, D. Ibe. "Mma Nwany Wu Nwa: Poetic Images of
Childbirth among the Igbo." Folklore 84 (1973): 142-156.

1161.   Nylén, Anna-Maja. Swedish Handcraft, trans. Anne-
Charlotte Hanes Harvey. New York: Van Nostrand Reinhold,
1977.

1162.   Oakley, Ann. Sex, Gender, and Society. New York:
Harper and Row, 1973.

1163.   Oaks, Priscilla. "Query [on women in American
folksong]." Folklore Feminists Communication 9 (1976): 5.

1164.   Obbo, Christine Sally. "Town Migration Is Not for
Women." Ph.D. dissertation, University of Wisconsin, 1977.

1165.   Oermann, Robert K., and Bufwack, Mary A. "Rockabilly
Women." Journal of Country Music 8 (1979): 65-94.

1166.   Oetzel, Roberta M. "Annotated Bibliography." In The
Development of Sex Differences, ed. Eleanor E. Maccoby, pp.
223-321. Stanford: Stanford University Press, 1966.

1167.   O'Faolain, Julia, and Martines, Lauro. Not in God's
Image: Women in History from the Greeks to the Victorians.
New York: Harper and Row, 1973.

1168.   O'Flaherty, Wendy Doniger. Women, Androgynes, and
Other Mythical Beasts. Chicago: University of Chicago
Press, 1980.

1169.   Okely, Judith. "Gypsy Women: Models in Conflict." In
no. 64, pp. 55-86.

1170.   Okpewh, Isidore. "Poetry and Pattern: Structural
Analysis of an Ijo Creation Myth." Journal of American
Folklore 92 (1979): 302-325.

1171.   Olajubu, Oludare. "References to Sex in Yoruba Oral Literature." _Journal of American Folklore_ 85 (1972): 152-166.

1172.   Oliver, Caroline. _Western Women in Colonial Africa_. Contributions in Comparative Colonial Studies, no. 12. Westport, Ct.: Greenwood Press, 1982.

1173.   Oliver, Paul. _Kings of Jazz: Bessie Smith_. New York: A.S. Barnes, 1981.

1174.   Oliver, Rose. "Whatever Became of Goldilocks?" _Frontiers_ 2, no. 3 (1977): 85-93.

1175.   Olsen, Louise. P. "Tomte." _Journal of American Folklore_ 63 (1950): 97-98.

1176.   O'Meara, Walter. _Daughters of the Country: The Women of the Fur Traders and Mountain Men_. New York: Harcourt, Brace and World, 1968.

1177.   Ominde, S.H.   _The Luo Girl: From Infancy to Marriage_. London: Macmillan, 1970.

1178.   O'Nell, Carl W., and Selby, Henry A. "Sex Differences in the Incidence of _Susto_ in Two Zapotec Pueblos: An Analysis of the Relationship between Sex Role Expectations and a Folk Illness." _Ethnology_ 7 (1969): 95-105.

1179.   Opler, Marvin K. "Japanese Folk Beliefs and Practices, Tule Lake, California." _Journal of American Folklore_ 63 (1950): 385-397.

1180.   Opler, Morris E. "Cause and Effect in Apachean Agricultural Division of Labor and Girls' Puberty Rites." _American Anthropologist_ 74 (1972): 1133-1146.

1181.   Orasanu, Judith, Slater, Miriam K., and Adler, Leonore Loeb. _Language, Sex and Gender_. New York: New York Academy of Sciences, 1979.

1182.   Orchard, William C. _The Technique of Porcupine Quill Decoration among the Indians of North America_. Museum of the American Indian, Heye Foundation, Contributions 4, no. 1. New York: Heye Foundation, 1916.

1183.   Orlofsky, Patsy, and Orlofsky, Myron. _Quilts in America_. New York: McGraw-Hill, 1974.

1184.   ----------. "The Quilting Bee." _Harvard Magazine_ September, 1975: 28-37.

1185.   Ortner, Sherry B. "Is Female to Male as Nature Is to Culture?" In no. 1332, pp. 67-87.

1186.   Osborne, Lilly de Jongh. Indian Crafts of Guatemala and El Salvador. Norman: University of Oklahoma Press, 1975.

1187.   Oswalt, Wendell H. "Traditional Storyknife Tales of Yuk Girls." Proceedings of the American Philosophical Society 108 (1964): 310-336.

1188.   Oubouzar, Sharon Overton. "Dazir: Kabyle Mothers, Daughters and Granddaughters in the Urban Environment of Algiers." Ph.D. dissertation, University of Kansas, 1974.

1189.   Owens, William A. Swing and Turn: Texas Play-Party Games. Dallas: Tardy, 1936.

1190.   Paddon, M.C. "The Taboo of Iron in Childbirth." Folklore 32 (1921): 211.

1191.   Page-Hollander, Linda Jewel. "Sex Role, Speech and Status: An Analysis of Public Telephone Conversations." Ph.D. dissertation, Princeton University, 1973.

1192.   Palliser, Mrs. Bury. A History of Lace. London: Marston, Low, and Searle, 1875.

1193.   Pan, Margaret Tai-Li. "The Attitudes of Taiwan Businessmen toward the Entertaining Girls of the City of Taipei." Ph.D. dissertation, New York University, 1973.

1194.   Papanek, Hanna. "Purdah: Separate Worlds and Symbolic Shelter." Comparative Studies in Society and History 15 (1973): 289-325.

1195.   Parker, Ann, and Neal, Aron. Molas. Barre, Mass.: Barre, 1977.

1196.   Parker, Anne. "Lonely Lucy of Frost Town." New York Folklore Quarterly 11 (1955): 292-295.

1197.   Parker, Cherry. "Mother-in-Law Lore." North Carolina Folklore 5, no. 2 (1957): 22.

1198.   Parker, Harbison. "The Scobs Was in her Lovely Mouth." Journal of American Folklore 71 (1958): 532-540.

1199.   Parlee, Mary Brown. "Review Essay: Psychology." Signs: Journal of Women in Culture and Society 1 (1975): 119-138.

1200.   Parrinder, Geoffrey. Witchcraft: European and African. London: Faber and Faber, 1963.

1201.   Parsons, Elsie Clews. "Zuñi Conception and Pregnancy Beliefs." In Proceedings of the 19th International Congress of Americanists, pp. 379-383. Washington: International Congress of Americanists, 1915.

1202. ----------. "Tales from Guilford County, North Carolina." Journal of American Folklore 30 (1917): 168-208.

1203. ----------. "Tales from Maryland and Pennsylvania." Journal of American Folklore 30 (1917): 209-217.

1204. ----------. "Folk-Lore of the Cherokee of Robeson County, North Carolina." Journal of American Folklore 32 (1919): 384-393.

1205. ----------. "Mothers and Children at Zuñi." Man 19 (1919): 168-173.

1206. ----------. "Waiyautitsa of Zuñi, New Mexico." Scientific Monthly 9 (1919): 443-457.

1207. ----------. "Zuñi Names and Naming Practices." Journal of American Folklore 36 (1923): 171-176.

1208. Parsons, Gerald E., comp. "A Brief List of Works Concerning Aunt Molly Jackson." Washington: Library of Congress Archive of Folk Song (pamphlet), 1975.

1209. Parsons, Talcott. "Age and Sex in the United States Social Structure." American Sociological Review 7 (1942): 604-616.

1210. Patai, Raphael. "Jewish Folk-Cures for Barrenness." Folk-Lore 55 (1944): 117-124.

1211. ----------. "Jewish Folk-Cures for Barrenness." Folk-Lore 56 (1945): 208-218.

1212. ----------. "Lilith." Journal of American Folklore 77 (1964): 295-314.

1213. ----------. The Hebrew Goddess. New York: Ktav, 1967.

1214. ----------, ed. Women in the Modern World. New York: Free Press, 1967.

1215. Patterson, Daniel W. "A Woman of the Hills: The Work of Maude Minish Sutton." Southern Exposure 5, nos. 2-3 (1977): 105-113.

1216. Patterson, Patricia. "Aran Kitchens, Aran Sweaters." Heresies 4 (1978): 89-92.

1217. Paulme, Denise, ed. Women of Tropical Africa, trans. H.M. Wright. Berkeley and Los Angeles: University of California Press, 1963.

1218.   Pebworth, Ted-Larry. "Aunt Loda's Legacy." Louisiana Folklore Miscellany 2, no. 4 (1968): 24-33.

1219.   Pellman, Rachel T., and Rauch, Joanne. Quilts among the Plain People. Lancaster, Pa.: Good Books, 1981.

1220.   Pentikäinen, Juha. "On the Study of Rhythm in Storytelling." Studia Fennica 17 (1974): 132-177.

1221.   ----------. Oral Repertoire and World View: An Anthropological Study of Marina Tokalo's Life History. FF Communications, No. 219. Helsinki: Academia Scientarum Fennica, 1978.

1222.   Percival, A.C. Obituary for B.M. Blackwood. Folklore 87 (1976): 113-114.

1223.   Perez, Soledad. "Mexican Folklore from Austin, Texas." Publications of the Texas Folklore Society 24 (1951): 71-127.

1224.   Peterson, Susan. The Living Traditions of Maria Martinez. Tokyo: Kodansha International, 1977.

1225.   Peterson, Tracey. "The Witch of Franklin." Southern Folklore Quarterly 33 (1969): 297-312.

1226.   Peto, Florence. "Patch Quilt as a Document." Hobbies January, 1942: 44-46.

1227.   Pettas, Mary. "An Exploratory Study of Oral Communication Characteristics in a Population of Aged Women." Ph.D. dissertation, University of Florida, 1963.

1228.   Pettigrew, Joyce. "Reminiscences of Fieldwork among the Sikhs." In Doing Feminist Research, ed. Helen Roberts, pp. 62-63. London and Boston: Routledge and Kegan Paul, 1981.

1229.   Pfarr, Effie Chalmers. Award Winning Quilts. Birmingham: Oxmoor House, 1974.

1230.   Phelps, Ethel Johnston. Tatterhood and Other Tales. Old Westbury, N.Y.: Feminist Press, 1978.

1231.   ----------, ed. The Maid of the North: Feminist Folk Tales from Around the World. New York: Holt, Rinehart and Winston, 1981.

1232.   Phillips, George L. "The Chimney-Sweepers' Assimilation of the Milkmaids' Garland." Folk-Lore 62 (1951): 383-387.

1233.   Pietropaoli, Lydia Q. "Folklore from the Heart of Italy." New York Folklore Quarterly 19 (1963): 163-182, 282-295.

1234.   Pike, Robert E. "The Female Hermit." New York Folklore Quarterly 23 (1967): 133-135.

1235.   Pindell, Howardena. "Afro-Carolinian 'Gullah' Baskets." Heresies 4 (1978): 22.

1236.   Pitseolak, and Eber, Dorothy. Pictures Out of My Life. Seattle: University of Washington Press, 1971.

1237.   Pocius, Gerald L. "'The First Day that I Thought of It Since I Got Wed': Role Expectations and Singer Status in a Newfoundland Outport." Western Folklore 35 (1976): 109-122.

1238.   ----------. "Hooked Rugs in Newfoundland: The Representation of Social Structure in Design." Journal of American Folklore (1979): 273-284.

1239.   Pomeroy, Sarah B. Goddesses, Whores, Wives, and Slaves: Women in Classical Antiquity. New York: Schoken, 1975.

1240.   ----------. "A Classical Scholar's Perspective on Matriarchy." In no. 236, pp. 217-223.

1241.   Poole, Robert U. "Women in Early Spanish Literature with Special Emphasis on the Women in the Medieval Spanish Ballad." Ph.D. dissertation, Stanford University, 1950.

1242.   Porter, J. Hampden. "Folk-Lore of the Mountain Whites of the Alleghenies." Journal of American Folklore 7 (1894): 105-117.

1243.   Porter, James. "Jeannie Robertson's 'My Son David': A Conceptual Performance Model." Journal of American Folklore 89 (1976): 7-26.

1244.   Porter, Kenneth Wiggins, and McCollum, Catharine Ann. "Winter Evenings in Iowa, 1873-1880." Journal of American Folklore 56 (1943): 97-112.

1245.   Post, Lauren C. Cajun Sketches from the Prairies of Southwest Louisiana. Baton Rouge: Louisiana State University Press, 1962.

1246.   Potter, Charles Francis. "Mother-Worship, Mariology." In no. 957, pp. 752-753.

1247.   Potter, Charles Francis, and Foster, George M. "Childbirth." In no. 957, pp. 217-218.

1248.   Potts, William John. "The Evil Eye." Journal of American Folklore 3 (1890): 70.

1249.   Powdermaker, Hortense. Stranger and Friend: The

Way of an Anthropologist. New York: Norton, 1966.

1250.   ----------. "Fieldwork." In International Encyclopedia of the Social Sciences, ed. David L. Sills. 5:
418-424. New York: Macmillan, 1968.

1251.   Powys, Marian. Lace and Lace-making. Boston:
Charles T. Branford, 1953.

1252.   Prendergast, Shirley. "Stoolball--the Pursuit of
Vertigo?" Women's Studies International Quarterly 1
(1978): 15-26.

1253.   Preussner, Alanna. Review of The Quilters: Women
and Domestic Art, by Patricia Cooper and Norma Bradley
Buferd. Frontiers 2, no. 2 (1977): 107-109.

1254.   Pruitt, Ida. A Daughter of Han: The Autobiography
of a Chinese Working Woman. New Haven: Yale University
Press, 1945.

1255.   Rabuzzi, Kathryn Allen. The Sacred and the Feminine: Toward a Theology of Housework. New York: Seabury,
1982.

1256.   Raccagni, Michelle. The Modern Arab Woman: A Bibliography. Metuchen, N.J., and London: Scarecrow, 1978.

1257.   Raglan, Lord. The Hero: A Study in Tradition, Myth,
and Drama. London: Watts, 1949.

1258.   Ramanujan, A.K. "The Clay Mother-in-Law: A South
Indian Folktale." Southern Folklore Quarterly 20 (1956):
130-135.

1259.   Ramaswami, Meenakshi. "Threshold Designs." Folk-
Lore 49 (1938): 181.

1260.   Randle, Martha Champion. "Iroquis Women, Then and
Now." In Symposium on Local Diversity in Iroquis Culture,
ed. William N. Fenton, pp. 167-180. Bulletin of the Bureau
of American Ethnology, No. 149. Washington: Bureau of
American Ethnology, 1951.

1261.   Randolph, Mary Claire. "Female Satirists of Ancient
Ireland." Southern Folklore Quarterly 6 (1942): 75-87.

1262.   Randolph, Vance. "Nakedness in Ozark Folk Belief."
Journal of American Folklore 66 (1953): 333-339.

1263.   ----------. Sticks in the Knapsack and Other Ozark
Folk Tales. New York: Columbia University Press, 1958.

1264.   ----------. Pissing in the Snow and Other Ozark
Folktales. Intro. Rayna Green, annotations Frank Hoffman,
Urbana: University of Illinois Press, 1976.

1265.   Rank, Otto. The Myth of the Birth of the Hero: A Psychological Interpretation of Mythology, trans. F. Robbins and S.E. Jelliffe. New York: R. Brunner, 1952.

1266.   Ranum, Orest, and Ranum, Patricia, eds. Popular Attitudes toward Birth Control in Pre-Industrial France and England. New York: Harper and Row, 1972.

1267.   Raphael, Dana, ed. Being Female: Reproduction, Power and Change. The Hague: Mouton; Chicago: Aldine, 1975.

1268.   ----------. "Matrescence, Becoming a Mother, A 'New/Old' Rite de Passage." In no. 1267, pp. 65-71.

1269.   Rapp, Rayna. "Review Essay: Anthropology." Signs: Journal Of Women in Culture and Society 4 (1979): 497-513.

1270.   Rattray, Jeannette Edwards. "Long Island Women and Whaling." New York Folklore Quarterly 10 (1954): 95-102.

1271.   Reaver, J. Russell. "Four Lithuanian-American Folk Tales." Southern Folklore Quarterly 12 (1948): 259-265.

1272.   ----------. "Lithuainian Tales from Illinois." Southern Folklore Quarterly 14 (1950): 160-168.

1273.   Redfield, Margaret Park. "Notes on the Cookery of Tepoztlan, Morelos." Journal of American Folklore 42 (1929): 167-196.

1274.   Reed, Evelyn. Woman's Evolution from Matriarchal Clan to Patriarchal Family. New York: Pathfinder Press, 1975.

1275.   Reeves, Nancy. Womankind: Beyond the Stereotypes. Chicago and New York: Aldine, Atherton, 1971.

1276.   Register, Cheri. "American Feminist Literary Criticism: A Bibliographical Introduction." In Feminist Literary Criticism: Explorations in Theory, ed. Josephine Donovan, pp. 1-28. Lexington: University of Kentucky Press, 1975.

1277.   Reich, Wendy, Buss, Rosalie, Fein, Ellen, and Kurtz, Terry. "Notes on Women's Graffiti." Journal of American Folklore 90 (1977): 188-191.

1278.   Reichard, Gladys A. Navajo Shepherd and Weaver. New York: J.J. Augustin, 1936.

1279.   ----------. Dezba: Woman of the Desert. New York: J.J. Augustin, 1939.

1280.   ----------. Obituary for Elsie Clews Parsons. Journal of American Folklore 56 (1943): 45-56.

1281.   ----------. Spider Woman: A Story of Navajo Weavers and Chanters. Glorieta, N.M.: Rio Grande Press, 1968.

1282.   ----------. Weaving a Navajo Blanket. New York: Dover, 1974.

1283.   Reichel-Dolmatoff, Gerardo. Amazonian Cosmos: The Sexual and Religious Symbolisim of the Tukano Indians Chicago: University of Chicago Press, 1971.

1284.   Reik, Theodor. The Creation of Woman: A Psycho-analytic Inquiry into the Myth of Eve. New York: McGraw-Hill, 1960.

1285.   Reimensnyder, Barbara. "Women and Folklore Conference Report." Folklore Women's Communication 18 (1979): n.p.

1286.   Reiter, Rayna R., ed. Toward an Anthropology of Women. New York and London: Monthly Review Press, 1975.

1287.   Reminick, Ronald A. "The Symbolic Significance of Ceremonial Defloration among the Amhara of Ethiopia." American Ethnologist 3 (1976): 751-763.

1288.   Reuss, Richard A. "On Folklore and Women Folklorists." Folklore Feminists Communication 3 (1974): 4, 29-37.

1289.   ----------. "'That Can't Be Alan Dundes! Alan Dundes is Taller Than That!': The Folklore of Folklorists." Journal of American Folklore 87 (1974): 303-317.

1290.   Reuss, Richard A., and Lund, Jens. Roads into Folklore: Festchrift in Honor of Richard M. Dorson. Folklore Forum Bibliographic and Special Series, No. 14. Bloomington: Folklore Forum, 1975.

1291.   Reynolds, Emily K. "The Dumb Wife." Journal of American Folklore 62 (1949): 62.

1292.   Rhodes, Willard. "Maud Karpeles 1885-1976." Ethnomusicology 21 (1977): 283-288.

1293.   Rice, Timothy. "A Macedonian Sobor: Anatomy of a Celebration." Journal of American Folklore 93 (1980): 113-128.

1294.   Rich, Carroll L. "Born with the Veil: Black Folklore in Louisiana." Journal of American Folklore 89 (1976): 328-331.

1295.   Richards, Audrey I. Chisungu: A Girl's Initiation Ceremony among the Bemba of Northern Rhodesia. New York: Grove, 1956.

1296.   Riddle, Almeda. A Singer and Her Songs: Almeda Riddle's Book of Ballads, ed. Roger D. Abrahams, music ed. George Foss. Baton Rouge: Louisiana State University Press, 1970.

1297.   Riesenberg, Saul H. "Ponapean Omens." Journal of American Folklore 65 (1952): 351-352.

1298.   Riesenberg, Saul H., and Fischer, J.L. "Some Ponapean Proverbs." Journal of American Folklore 68 (1955): 9-18.

1299.   Rigby, Peter. "The Structural Context of Girls' Puberty Rites." Man 2 (1970): 434-444.

1300.   Ring, Elizabeth. "Fannie Hardy Eckstorm: Maine Woods Historian." New England Quarterly 26 (1953): 45-64.

1301.   Ripps, Sharon. "Query [on folklore aspects of Jewish American Princess stereotype]." Folklore Women's Communication 26 (1982): 10.

1302.   Ritchie, Jean. Singing Family of the Cumberlands. New York: Oxford University Press, 1955.

1303.   Rivlin, Lilly. "Lilith." Ms. December, 1972: 114-115.

1304.   Roach, Susan, and Weidlich, Lorre. "Quilt Making in America: A Selected Bibliography." Folklore Feminists Communication 3 (1974): 17-28.

1305.   Roach Lankford, Susan. Patchwork Quilts: Deep South Traditions. Alexandria, La.: Alexandria Museum, 1980.

1306.   ----------. "The 'Kinship Quilt': An Ethnographic Semiotic Analysis of a Quilting Bee." In no. 835.

1307.   Robacker, Earl F., and Robacker, Ada F. "Quilting Traditions of the Dutch Country." Pennsylvania Folklife 21, supplement (1972): 31-38.

1308.   Robbins, Rossell Hope. Witchcraft: An Introduction to the Literature of Witchcraft. Millwood, N.Y.: KTO Press, 1978.

1309.   Robert, Ellen Ruth. "Women's Roles: A Marxist-Existentialist Analysis." Ph.D. dissertation, Western Michigan University, 1973.

1310.   Roberts, Helene E. "The Exquisite Slave: The Role of Clothes in the Making of the Victorian Woman." Signs: Journal of Women in Culture and Society 2 (1977): 554-569.

1311.   Roberts, Hilda. "Louisiana Superstitions." Journal

of American Folklore 40 (1927): 144-208.

1312.   Roberts, John M., and Sutton-Smith, Brian. "Child Training and Game Involvement." _Ethnology_ 1 (1962): 166-185.

1313.   Roberts, Leonard. _Sang Branch Settlers: Folksongs and Tales of a Kentucky Mountain Family_. American Folklore Society Memoirs, No. 61. Austin: University of Texas Press, 1974.

1314.   Robertson, Elizabeth Wells. _American Quilts_. New York: Studio, 1948.

1315.   Robinson, Beverly J. "The Ekonda: A Legend of Women through Song and Dance." _Folklore Feminists Communication_ 10 (1976): 10.

1316.   Robinson, Christine. "Research in Progress [on Snow White, Disney, and female roles]." _Folklore Feminists Communication_ 2 (1974): 12.

1317.   Robinson, Lillian S. _Sex, Class, and Culture_. Bloomington: Indiana University Press, 1978.

1318.   Rodríguez Rivera, Virginia. _Mujeres Folkloristas_. Estudio de Folklore, No. 3. Mexico City: Instituto de Investigaciones Esteticas, Universidad Nacional Autonoma de Mexico, 1967.

1319.   Roemer, Danielle. "Scary Story Legends." _Folklore Annual_ 3 (1971): 1-16.

1320.   ----------. "Children's Indiscretions and Women's Narratives." _Folklore Women's Communication_ 27 & 28 (1982): 3-5.

1321.   Rogers, Abby, and Lyons, Joan. _Abby Rogers to her Grand-daughter_. Rochester, N.Y.: Visual Studies Workshop, 1976.

1322.   Rogers, Edith. "Clothing as a Multifarious Ballad Symbol." _Western Folklore_ 34 (1975): 261-297.

1323.   Rogers, Kathrine M. _The Troublesome Helpmate: A History of Misogyny in Literature_. Seattle: University of Washington Press, 1976.

1324.   Rohrlich-Leavitt, Ruby, ed. _Women Cross-Culturally: Change and Challenge_. Mouton: The Hague, 1975.

1325.   Rohrmann, G.T. "South African House Painting." _African Arts_ Spring, 1974: 18-21.

1326.   Romero, Myrtle White. _Housewife by the Rio Grande_. Espanola, N.M." Las Trampas, 1971.

1327.   Rooth, Anna Birgitta. The Cinderella Cycle. Lund: C.W.K. Gleerup, 1951.

1328.   Roper, Joyce. The Women of Nar. London: Faber and Faber, 1974.

1329.   Rorie, David. "Pregnant Women as Pall Bearers." Folk-Lore 47 (1936): 230.

1330.   Rosaldo, Michelle Zimbalist. "Woman, Culture, and Society: A Theoretical Overview." In no. 1332, pp. 17-42.

1331.   Rosaldo, Michelle Zimbalist, and Atkinson, Jane Monnig. "Man the Hunter and Woman: Metaphors for the Sexes in Ilongot Magical Spells." In The Interpretation of Symbolism, ed. Roy Willis, pp. 43-75. New York: Halsted Press, John Wiley and Sons, 1975.

1332.   Rosalso, Michelle Zimbalist, and Lamphere, Louise, eds. Women, Culture, and Society. Stanford: Stanford University Press, 1974.

1333.   Rose, H.A. "Customary Restraints on Celibacy." Folklore 30 (1919): 63-70.

1334.   ----------. "The Development of Bride-Price and of Dowry." Folklore 36 (1925): 189-193.

1335.   Rose, H.J. "On the Alleged Evidence for Mother-Right in Early Greece." Folk-Lore 22 (1911): 277-291.

1336.   ----------. "Mother-Right in Ancient Italy." Folk-lore 31 (1920): 93-108.

1337.   ----------. "Christening Custom (Angus)." Folk-Lore 54 (1943): 308.

1338.   Rosell, Lauro E. México y la guadalupana: Cuarto siglos de culto a la patrona de America. Mexico: La Enseñanza Objectiva Mexicana, 1931.

1339.   Rosenberg, Bruce G., and Sutton-Smith, Brian. "A Revised Conception of Masculine-Feminine Differences in Play Activities." Journal of Genetic Psychology 96 (1960): 165-170.

1340.   Rosenberg, Marie Barovic, and Bergstrom, Len V. Women and Society: A Critical Review of the Literature with a Selected Annotated Bibliography. Beverly Hills and London: Sage Publications, 1975.

1341.   Rosnow, Ralph L., and Fine, Gary Alan. Rumors and Gossip: The Social Psychology of Hearsay. New York: Elsevier, 1976.

1342.   Ross, James. "Folk Song and Social Environment: A Study of the Repertoire of Nan MacKinnon of Vatersay." Scottish Studies 5 (1961): 18-39.

1343.   Ross, Joe. "Hags Out of Their Skins." Journal of American Folklore 93 (1980): 183-186.

1344.   Rossi, Alice S. "Naming Children in Middle-Class Families." American Sociological Review 30 (1965): 499-513.

1345.   Rowe, Karen E. "Feminism and Fairy Tales." Feminist Studies 6 (1979): 237-257.

1346.   Roy, Manisha. Bengali Women. Chicago: University of Chicago Press, 1975.

1347.   Rubin, Barbara. "Calabash Decoration in North East State, Nigeria." African Arts Autumn, 1970: 20-25.

1348.   Rubin, Ruth. "Nineteenth-century Yiddish Folksongs of Children in Eastern Europe." Journal of American Folklore 65 (1952): 227-254.

1349.   Rufty, Ruby. "Query [on narratives about a single woman in a close-knit community]." Folklore Women's Communication 17 (1979): 15.

1350.   Ruiz Perez, Sonia. "Beyond Poverty: A Study of Begging in a Mexican City." Ph.D. dissertation, Michigan State University, 1975.

1351.   Rumpf, Marianne. "The Legends of Bertha in Switzerland." Journal of the Folklore Institute 14 (1977): 181-195.

1352.   Russel, Louise. "Conversation with a Curandera." Folklore Women's Communication 21 (1980): 11-12.

1353.   Russell, W.M.S., and Henriques, M. "Christina Hole: A Select Bibliography to 1978." Folklore 90 (1979): 9-10.

1354.   Ryan, Lawrence. "Some Czech-American Forms of Divination and Supplication." Journal of American Folklore 69 (1956): 281-285.

1355.   Ryesky, Diana. "World of the Weaver: An Ethnographic Study of Textile Production in a Mexican Village." Ph.D. dissertation, New School for Social Research, 1977.

1356.   Sackett, Marjorie. "Kansas Pioneer Recipes." Western Folklore 22 (1963): 103-106.

1357.   ----------. "Folk Recipes as a Measure of Intercultural Penetration." Journal of American Folklore 85 (1972): 77-81.

1358.   Safford, Carleton L., and Bishop, Robert. America's Quilts and Coverlets. New York: Dutton, 1972.

1359.   Safilios-Rothschild, Constantina, ed. Toward A Sociology of Women. Lexington, Mass., and Toronto: Xerox College Publishing, 1972.

1360.   St. John, Jacquelin D. "Sex Role Stereotyping in Early Broadcast History: The Career of Mary Margaret McBride." Frontiers 3, no. 3 (1978): 31-38.

1361.   Salvador, Mari Lyn Catherin. "Molas of the Cuna Indians: A Case Study of Artistic Criticism and Ethno-Aesthetics." Ph.D. dissertation, University of California, Berkeley, 1976.

1362.   ----------. Yer Dailege! Kuna Women's Art. Albuquerque: University of New Mexico Press, 1978.

1363.   ----------. "Bird Design from San Blas Kuna Woman's Mola." Folklore Women's Communication 18 (1979): inside cover.

1364.   ----------. "Kuna Women's Art: Research Methods and Some Results." Folklore Women's Communication 18 (1979): 17-20.

1365.   ----------. "Mosquito Evangelita: Possible Insect Repellant Mola Design." Folklore Women's Communication 18 (1979): 21.

1366.   Sanchez, Julio A. "The Community of Love: A Study of the Process of Change in a Congregation of Nuns in Puerto Rico." Ph.D. dissertation, Tulane University, 1975.

1367.   Sanday, Peggy R. "Toward a Theory of the Status of Women." American Anthropologist 75 (1973): 1682-1700.

1368.   Sanderson, Stewart T. Obituary for Mary Williams. Folklore 90 (1979): 9-10.

1369.   Sayers, Peig. An Old Woman's Reflections, trans. Seamus Ennis. Oxford: Oxford University press, 1962.

1370.   ----------. Peig: The Autobiography of Peig Sayers of the Great Blasket Island, trans. Bryan MacMahon. Syracuse: Syracuse University Press, 1974.

1371.   Scarborough, Dorothy. On the Trail of Negro Folk-Songs. Cambridge: Harvard University press, 1925.

1372.   ----------. A Song Catcher in the Southern Mountains: American Folk Songs of British Ancestry. New York: Columbia University Press, 1937.

1373.   Scheub, Harold Ernest. "The Ntsomi: A Xhosa Performing Art." Ph.D. dissertation, University of Wisconsin,
1969.

1374.   ----------. "The Art of Nongenile Mazithathu Zenani,
A Gcaleka Ntsomi Performer." In African Folklore, ed.
Richard M. Dorson, pp. 115-142. Garden City: Anchor Books,
1972.

1375.   Schiffer, Margaret B. Historical Needlework of
Pennsylvania. New York: Charles Scribner's Sons, 1968.

1376.   Schlachter, Gail Ann, and Belli, Donna. Minorities
and Women: A Guide to Reference Literature in the Social
Sciences. Los Angeles: Reference Service Press, 1977.

1377.   Schlauch, Margaret. Chaucer's Constance and Accused
Queens. New York: New York University Press, 1927.

1378.   Schlegel, Alice. Male Dominance and Female Auto-
nomy: Domestic Authority in Matrilineal Societies. New
Haven: HRAF Press, 1972.

1379.   Schlegel, Alice, and Barry, Herbert, III. "Adoles-
cent Initiation Ceremonies: A Cross-Cultural Code."
Ethnology 18 (1979): 199-210.

1380.   Schmitz, Nancy. "An Irish Wise Woman--Fact and
Legend." Journal of the Folklore Institute 14 (1977):
169-179.

1381.   Schoenfeld, Susan. Pattern Design for Needlework
and Patchwork. New York: Van Nostrand Reinhold, 1975.

1382.   Schwartz, Gary, and Merten, Don. "Social Identity
and Expressive Symbols: The Meaning of an Initiation
Ritual." American Anthropologist 70 (1968): 1117-1131.

1383.   Schweizer, Eva Julia. "Woman in North Germanic
Heroic Legend." Ph.D. dissertation, Yale University, 1965.

1384.   Scobie, Alastair. Women of Africa. London: Cassell, 1960.

1385.   Scott, Anne Firor. The Southern Lady: From Pedestal
to Politics, 1830-1930. Chicago and London: University of
Chicago Press, 1970.

1386.   Scott, George Ryley. Curious Customs of Sex and
Marriage. London: Torchstream, 1953.

1387.   Scott, John Finley. "The Role of Collegiate Sororities in Maintaining Class and Ethnic Endogamy." American
Sociological Review 30 (1965): 415-426.

1388.   Seckar, Alvena V. "Slovak Wedding Customs." New

York Folklore Quarterly 3 (1947): 189-205.

1389.   Seifer, Nancy. Nobody Speaks for Me: Self-Portraits of American Working Class Women. New York: Simon and Schuster, 1976.

1390.   Seip, Elisabeth Cloud. "Witch-Finding in Western Maryland." Journal of American Folklore 14 (1901): 39-44.

1391.   Selby, Lucy Garretson. "The Nature of American Woman: A Cultural Account." Ph.D. dissertation, University of Texas, 1972.

1392.   Sells, Lucy W. Sociologists for Women in Society: Current Research on Sex Roles. Berkeley: Sociologists for Women in Society, 1972.

1393.   Seltman, Charles. Women in Antiquity. New York: Collier, 1962.

1394.   Sengupta, S. Women in Indian Folklore: Linguistic and Religious Study: A Short Survey of this Social Status and Position. Calcutta: Indian Publications, 1969.

1395.   Shanklin, Eugenia. "A Tide in the Affairs of Women." American Anthropologist 78 (1976): 861-865.

1396.   Shapiro, Judith Rae. "Sex Roles and Social Structure among the Yanomama Indians of Northern Brazil." Ph.D. dissertation, Columbia University, 1972.

1397.   Shearman, Julia A. On the Psychology of Women: A Survey of Empirical Studies. Springfield, Ill.: Charles C. Thomas, 1971.

1398.   Shiloh, Ailon, ed. By Myself, I'm a Book! An Oral History of the Immigrant Jewish Experience in Pittsburgh. Waltham, Mass.: American Jewish Historical Society, 1972.

1399.   Shostak, Marjorie. "A !Kung Woman's Memories of Girlhood." In Kalahari Hunter-Gatherers: Studies of the !Kung San and Their Neighbors, ed. Richard B. Lee and Irven DeVore, pp. 246-278. Cambridge: Harvard University Press, 1976.

1400.   Shumsky, Ellen. "Women's Songs from the Balkans and Eastern Europe." Balkan Arts Traditions 3, no. 1 (1977): 14-24.

1401.   Sicherman, Barbara. "Review Essay: American History." Signs: Journal of Women in Culture and Society 1 (1975): 461-485.

1402.   Siclier, Jacques. Le mythe de la femme dans le cinema Américain: de "La Divine" à Balnche Dubois. Paris: Ducerf, 1956.

1403.   Sides, Dudie Duncan. "Women and Slaves: An Interpretation Based on the Writings of Southern Women." Ph.D. dissertation, University of North Carolina, 1969.

1404.   Sieber,   Roy.   African Textiles and Decorative Arts. New York: Museum of Modern Art, 1972.

1405.   Siefert, Susan. The Dilemma of the Talented Heroine: A Study in Nineteenth Century Fiction. St. Albans, Vt.: Eden Press, 1978.

1406.   Silverman, Eliane. "In Their Own Words: Mothers and Daughters on the Alberta Frontier, 1890-1929." Frontiers 2, no. 2 (1977): 37-44.

1407.   Silverman, Sydel F. "The Life Crisis as a Clue to Social Function: The Case of Italy." In no. 1286, pp. 309-321.

1408.   Simon, Gwladys Hughes. "Some Japanese Beliefs and Home Remedies." Journal of American Folklore 65 (1952): 281-293.

1409.   Simpson, Claude M., Jr. "The Dumb Wife." Journal of American Folklore 62 (1949): 424-426.

1410.   Sims, Barbara. "'She's Got to Be a Saint, Lord Knows I Ain't': Feminine Masochism in Country Music." Journal of Country Music 5, no. 1 (1974): 17-23.

1411.   ----------. "Facts in the Life of a Black Mississippi-Louisiana Healer." Mississippi Folklore Register 15, no. 2 (1981): 63-70.

1412.   Siskind, Elli. "The Apron...Status Symbol...or Stitchery Sample?" Heresies 4 (1978): 71.

1413.   Siskind, Janet. To Hunt in the Morning. New York: Oxford University Press, 1973.

1414.   Skoner, Martha M. "The Working World of Obstetrical Nurses: An Ethnographic Case Study." Ph.D. dissertation, University of Pittsburgh, 1975.

1415.   Skov, G.E. "The Priestess of Demeter and Kore and Her Role in the Initiation of Women at the Festival of the Haloa at Eleusis." Temenos 11 (1975): 136-147.

1416.   Skultans, Vieda. "The Symbolic Significance of Menstruation and Menopause." Man 5 (1970): 639-651.

1417.   Slater, Philip E. The Glory of Hera: Greek Mythology and the Greek Family. Boston: Beacon Press, 1968.

1418.   Smiley, Portia. "Folk-Lore from Virginia, South

Carolina, Georgia, Alabama, and Florida." <u>Journal of American Folklore</u> 32 (1919): 357-383.

1419.   Smith, Grace Partridge. "Churching of Women." In no. 957, p. 232.

1420.   Smith, Margo Lane. "Institutionalized Servitude: The Female Domestic Servant in Lima, Peru." Ph.D. dissertation, Indiana University, 1971.

1421.   Smith, Mary. <u>Baba of Karo: A Woman of the Muslim Hausa</u>. New York: Philosophical Library, 1955.

1422.   Smith-Rosenberg, Carroll. "The Female World of Love and Ritual: Relations between Women in Nineteenth Century America." <u>Signs: Journal of Women in Culture and Society</u> 1 (1975): 1-29.

1423.   Snow, Loudell F. "'I Was Born Just Exactly with the Gift': An Interview with a Voodoo Practitioner." <u>Journal of American Folklore</u> 86 (1973): 272-281.

1424.   ----------. "Old-Fashioned 'Medicine' Is Still with Us." <u>Osteopathic Physician</u> 43 (1976): 51-54.

1425.   Snow, Loudell F., and Johnson, Shirley M. "Modern Day Menstrual Folklore: Some Clinical Implications." <u>Journal of the American Medical Association</u> 237 (1977): 2736-2739.

1426.   ----------. "Myths about Menstruation: Victims of Our Own Folklore." <u>International Journal of Women's Studies</u> 1 (1978): 64-72.

1427.   Snow, Loudell F., Johnson, Shirley M., and Mayhew, Harry E. "The Behavioral Implications of Some Old Wives' Tales." <u>Obstetrics and Gynecology</u> 51 (1978): 727-732.

1428.   Snowden James. <u>The Folk Dress of Europe</u>. New York: Mayflower, 1979.

1429.   Sobol, Donald J. <u>The Amazons of Greek Mythology</u>. New York: A.S. Barnes, 1972.

1430.   Speck, Frank G. "A Pequot-Mohegan Witchcraft Tale." <u>Journal of American Folklore</u> 16 (1903): 104-106.

1431.   ----------. "Some Catawba Texts and Folk-Lore." <u>Journal of American Folklore</u> 26 (1913): 319-330.

1432.   ----------. "The Banished Wife and Maid without Hands." <u>New York Folklore Quarterly</u> 3 (1947): 312-319.

1433.   Speitel, Hans. "'Caller Ou!' An Edinburgh Fishwives' Cry and an Old Scottish Sound Change." <u>Scottish Studies</u> 19 (1975): 69-73.

1434.   Spender, Dale. Man Made Language. London and Boston: Routledge and Kegan Paul, 1980.

1435.   Speroni, Charles. "Some Rope-Skipping Rhymes from Southern California." California Folklore Quarterly 1 (1942): 245-252.

1436.   Spiegel, Jeanne. Sex Role Concepts: How Women and Men See Themselves and Each Other: A Selected Annotated Bibliography. Washington: Business and Professional Women's Foundation, 1969.

1437.   Spindler, George D., ed. Being an Anthropologist: Fieldwork in Eleven Cultures. New York: Holt, Rinehart and Winston, 1970.

1438.   Spindler, George, and Spindler, Louise. "Fieldwork among the Menomini." In no. 1437, pp. 267-301.

1439.   Spitzer, Nicholas. "'I Got the World in a Jug': Reputation and Respectability in the Classic Blues." Folklore Annual 7 and 8 (1977): 54-77.

1440.   ----------. "Queen of the Cajun Sound." Ms. October, 1977: 27-28.

1441.   Spivey, Richard. Maria. Flagstaff: Northland Press, 1979.

1442.   Spradley, James P., and Mann, Brenda J. The Cocktail Waitress: Woman's Work in a Man's World. New York: John Wiley, 1975.

1443.   Spreadbury, Constance Lizotte. "A Test of Three Theories of Dating Preference." Ph.D. dissertation, Texas A & M University, 1975.

1444.   Spretnak, Charlene. Lost Goddesses of Early Greece: A Collection of Pre-Hellenic Mythology. Berkeley: Moon, 1978.

1445.   ----------, ed. The Politics of Women's Spirituality: Essays on the Rise of Spiritual Power within the Feminist Movement. Garden City: Doubleday, 1982.

1446.   Spring, Anita. "Women's Rituals and Natality among the Luvale of Zambia." Ph.D. dissertation, Cornell University, 1976.

1447.   Spruill, Julia Cherry. Women's Life and Work in the Southern Colonies. Chapel Hill: University of North Carolina Press, 1938.

1448.   Stack, Carol B., Caulfield, Mina Davis, Estes, Valerie, Landes, Susan, Larson, Karen, Johnson, Pamela,

Rake, Juliet, and Shirek, Judith. "Review Essay: Anthropology." Signs: Journal of Women in Culture and Society 1 (1975): 147-159.

1449.   Stanley, Len. "Hazel and Alice: Custom Made Woman Blues." Southern Exposure 4, no. 4 (1977): 92-94.

1450.   Starr, Elizabeth. "On Sexism in Folklore Scholarship." Folklore Women's Communication 20 (1980): 16-22.

1451.   Stearns, Martha Genung. Homespun and Blue: A Study of American Crewel Embroidery. New York: Scribner's, 1963.

1452.   Steed, Daniel W., Jr. "The Dentata and Black Syphilis: Fear and Sex in Vietnam." Folklore Feminists Communication 4 (1974): 11.

1453.   Stein, Evelyn. "Pages from an Asian Notebook." Heresies 4 (1978): 108-111.

1454.   Stein, Hazel. "Fashion on the Frontier." Southern Folklore Quarterly 21 (1957): 160-164.

1455.   Stekert, Ellen J. "Focus for Conflict: Southern Mountain Medical Beliefs in Detroit." Journal of American Folklore 83 (1970): 115-156.

1456.   Stephens, William N. "A Cross-Cultural Study of Menstrual Taboos." Genetic Psychology Monographs 64 (1961): 385-416.

1457.   ----------. "A Cross-Cultural Study of Menstrual Taboos." In Cross-Cultural Approaches: Readings in Comparative Research, ed. Clellan S. Ford, pp. 67-94. New Haven: HRAF Press, 1967.

1458.   Stern, Theodore. "Some Sources of Variability in Klamath Mythology." Journal of American Folklore 69 (1956): 1-12.

1459.   ----------. "Klamath Myth Abstracts." Journal of American Folklore 76 (1963): 31-41.

1460.   Stevens, Evelyn P. "Marianismo: The Other Face of Machismo in Latin America." In Female and Male in Latin America, ed. Ann Pescatello, pp. 89-101. Pittsburgh: University of Pittsburgh Press, 1973.

1461.   Stewart, G.B. A New Mythos: The Novel of the Artist as Heroine, 1877-1977. St. Albans, Vt.: Eden Press, 1978.

1462.   Stewart, Susan. "Sociological Aspects of Quilting in Three Brethren Churches in South Central Pennsylvania." Pennsylvania Folklife 23, no. 3 (1974): 15-29.

1463.   ----------. "These Are the Quilts." Alcheringa: Ethnopoetics n.s. 3, no. 2 (1977): 142-144.

1464.   Stewart-Baxter, Derrick. Ma Rainey and the Classic Blues Singers. New York: Stein and Day, 1970.

1465.   Stiles, Henry Reed. Bundling: Its Origin, Progress and Decline in America. N.p.: privately published, 1871.

1466.   Stineman, Esther, Loeb, Catherine, and Walton, Whitney. "Recent Sources for the Study of the Culture of Women of Color." Concerns 9, no. 3 (1979): 15-24.

1467.   Stoddard, Karen M. "'Women Have No Sense of Humor' and Other Myths: A Consideration of Female Stand-Up Comics, 1960-1976." American Humor 4, no. 2 (1977): 11-14.

1468.   Stoeltje, Beverly. "'Bow-Legged Bastard: A Manner of Speaking.' Speech Behavior of a Black Woman." Folklore Anual 4 and 5: (1972-1973): 152-178.

1469.   ----------. "'A Helpmate for Man Indeed': The Image of the Frontier Woman." Journal of American Folklore 88 (1975): 25-41.

1470.   ----------. "Guest Editorial: Reflections on Ourselves as Folklorists." Folklore Feminists Communication 10 (1976): 4-6.

1471.   Stone, Kay F. "Teaching Activities and Research in Progress [on female figures in folk and popular literature]." Folklore Feminists Communication 1 (1973): 4.

1472.   ----------. "Interview: Eleanor Boyce, Quilt Maker." Folklore Feminists Communication 3 (1974): 9-10.

1473.   ----------. Review of The Classic Fairy Tales, by Iona Opie and Peter Opie. Folklore Feminists Communication 7 (1975): 22-23.

1474.   ----------. "Romantic Heroines in Anglo-American Folk and Popular Literature." Ph.D. dissertation, Indiana University, 1975.

1475.   ----------. "Things Walt Disney Never Told Us." Journal of American Folklore 88 (1975): 42-50.

1476.   ----------. "Baby Lore." Folklore Feminists Communication 10 (1976): 7.

1477.   ----------. "Eleonora Plutyńska, Polish Weaver." Folklore Feminists Communication 10 (1976): 8-9.

1478.   ----------. "More on Quilting." Folklore Feminists Communication 13 (1977): 11-12.

1479. ----------. "Query: Folktales by Children." Folk-lore Feminists Communication 12 (1977): 6.

1480. ----------. [Query.] Folklore Women's Communication 20 (1980): 15.

1481. ----------. "The Misuses of Enchantment: Contro-versies on the Significance of Fairy Tales." In no. 835.

1482. Stone, Merlin. When God Was a Woman. New York: Dial, 1976.

1483. ----------. Ancient Mirrors of Womanhood: Our Goddess and Heroine Heritage. New York: New Sibylline, 1979.

1484. ----------. "The Great Goddess: Who Was She?" In no. 1445, pp. 7-21.

1485. Strange, Heather. "The Weavers of Rusila: Working Women in a Malay Village." Ph.D. dissertation, New York University, 1971.

1486. Strathern, Marilyn. Women in Between. Female Roles in a Male World: Mount Hagen, New Guinea. London and New York: Seminar Press, 1972.

1487. Strobel, Margaret. "Doing Oral History as an Out-sider." Frontiers 2, no. 2 (1977): 68-72.

1488. Stroup, Thomas B. "Two Folk Tales from South-Central Georgia." Southern Folklore Quarterly 2 (1938): 207-212.

1489. Strouse, Jean. Women and Analysis: Dialogues on Psychoanalytic Views of Femininity. New York: Grossman Publishers, 1974.

1490. Stuard, Susan Mosher, ed. Women in Medieval Soci-ety. Philadelphia: University of Pennsylvania Press, 1976.

1491. Sugimoto, Etsu Inagaki. A Daughter of the Samurai. London: Hurst and Blackett, 1950.

1492. Suhr, Elmer G. "The Daughter of the Dragon." Folk-lore 80 (1969): 1-11.

1493. ----------. The Spinning Aphrodite: The Evolution of the Goddess from Earliest Pre-Hellenic Symbolism through Late Classical Times. New York: Helios, 1969.

1494. Suliteanau, Gisele. "The Traditional System of Melopeic Prose and the Funeral Songs Recited by the Jewish Women of the Socialist Republic of Rumania." Folklore

Research Center Studies 3 (1972): 291-349.

1495.   Sullerot, Evelyne. Woman, Society and Change. New York: McGraw-hill, 1971.

1496.   Sullivan, Elizabeth. Indian Legends of the Trail of Tears and Other Creek Stories as Told by Elizabeth Sullivan. Tulsa: Giant Services, 1974.

1497.   Sutton-Smith, Brian, ed. The Folkgames of Children. American Folklore Society Bibliographical and Special Series, No. 24. Austin: University of Texas Press, 1972.

1498.   Svartengren, T. Hilding. "The Feminine Gender for Inanimate Things in Anglo-American." American Speech 3 (1927): 83-113.

1499.   Swain, Margaret Byrne. "Aligandi Women: Continuity and Change in Cuna Female Identity." Ph.D. dissertation, University of Washington, 1978.

1500.   Swan, Susan Burrows. Plain and Fancy: American Women and Their Needlework, 1700-1850. New York: Holt, Rinehart and Winston, 1977.

1501.   Szöverffy, Joseph. "The Well of the Holy Women: Some St. Columba Traditions in the West of Ireland." Journal of American Folklore 68 (1955): 111-122.

1502.   Taggart, James M. "Men's Changing Image of Women in Nahuat Oral Tradition." American Ethnologist 6 (1979): 723-741.

1503.   Talbert, Carol Sullivan. "Ethnography of Poor Women: Family Design and Natality." Ph.D. dissertation, Washington University, 1976.

1504.   Tallman, Richard S. Review of People in the Tobacco Belt: Four Lives, by Linda Dégh. Journal of American Folklore 91 (1978): 590-592.

1505.   Taylor, Archer. "No House is Big Enough for Two Women." Western Folklore 16 (1957): 121-124.

1506.   Teilhet, Jehanne H. "The Equivocal Role of Women Artists in Non-Literate Culture." Heresies 4 (1978): 96-102.

1507.   Teleki, Gloria Roth. The Baskets of Rural America. New York: E.P. Dutton, 1975.

1508.   Terrell, John Upton, and Terrell, Donna M. Indian Women of the Western Morning: Their Life in Early America. New York: Dial, 1974.

1509.   Thatcher, George. "A Surrey Birch-Broom Custom."
Folk-Lore 21 (1910): 388.

1510.   Thiselton-Dyer, T.F. Folklore of Women. Chicago:
A.C. McClurg, 1906.

1511.   Thompson, Clara M. On Women. New York: Mentor,
1971.

1512.   Thompson, Ellen Powell. "Folk-Lore from Ireland."
Journal of American Folklore 6 (1893): 259-268.

1513.   ----------. "Folk-Lore from Ireland, II." Journal
of American Folklore 7 (1894): 224-227.

1514.   Thompson, J. Eric S. "The Moon Goddess in Middle
America, with Notes on Related Deities." Contributions to
American Anthropology and History, No. 29. Carnegie
Institution of Washington Publications, No. 509, pp.
121-173. Washington: Carnegie Institution, 1939.

1515.   Thompson, Stith. The Folktale. New York: Dryden
Press, 1946.

1516.   ----------. Motif-Index of Folk Literature. 6
vols. Bloomingotn: Indiana University Press, 1955-1958.

1517.   Tiffany, Sharon W., ed. Women and Society: An Anthropological Reader. St. Albans, Vt.: Eden Press, 1979.

1518.   Tiger, Lionel. Men in Groups. New York: Random
House, 1969.

1519.   Tiwary, K.M. "Tuneful Weeping: A Mode of Communication." Frontiers 3, no. 3 (1978): 24-27.

1520.   Toelken, Barre. The Dynamics of Folklore. Boston:
Houghton Mifflin, 1979.

1521.   Toeplitz, Martha. "Quilts: Handicraft of the Early
American Woman." Antiquarian July, 1930: 50-51, 76, 78.

1522.   Toor, Frances. A Treasury of Mexican Folkways. New
York: Crown, 1947.

1523.   Tracey, Hugh. "Tina's Lullaby." African Music 2,
no. 4 (1961): 99-101.

1524.   Traetteberg, Gunvor Ingstad. Folk-Costumes of
Norway. Oslo: Dreyers Forlag, 1966.

1525.   Travers, P.L. About the Sleeping Beauty. New York:
McGraw-Hill, 1975.

1526.   Travis, Kathryne Hall. "Quilts of the Ozarks."
Southwest Review 15 (1929): 236-244.

1527.   Tsung, Shiu-Kuen Fan. "Moms, Nuns, and Hookers: Extrafamilial Alternatives for Village Women in Taiwan." Ph.D. dissertation, University of California, San Diego, 1978.

1528.   Tuchman, Gaye. "Review Essay: Women's Depiction by the Mass Media." Signs: Journal of Women in Culture and Society 4 (1979): 528-542.

1529.   Tucker, Elizabeth Godfrey. "Tradition and Creativity in the Storytelling of Pre-Adolescent Girls." Ph.D. dissertation, Indiana University, 1977.

1530.   ----------. "Concepts of Space in Children's Narratives." In Folklore on Two Continents: Essays in Honor of Linda Dégh, ed. Nikolai Burlakoff and Carl Lindahl, pp. 19-25. Bloomington: Trickster Press, 1980.

1531.   ----------. "The Dramatization of Children's Narratives." Western Folklore 39 (1980): 184-197.

1532.   Tull, Marc. "Kosher Brownies for Passover." New York Folklore 4 (1978): 81-88.

1533.   Turner, E.S. A History of Courting. New York: Dutton, 1955.

1534.   Turner, Kay. "La Vela Prendida: Mexican-American Women's Home Altars." Folklore Women's Communication 25 (1981): 5-6.

1535.   ----------. "Contemporary Feminist Rituals." In no. 1445, pp. 219-233.

1536.   Twitty, Anne, comp. "Magic Songs." Heresies 1, no. 2 (1977): 42.

1537.   Underhill, Ruth. The Autobiography of a Papago Woman. Memoirs of the American Anthropological Association, No. 46. Menasha, Wis.: American Anthropological Association, 1936.

1538.   ----------. Papago Woman. New York: Holt, Rinehart and Winston, 1979.

1539.   Underwood, Marylyn. "The Ghost of Chipita: the Crying Woman of San Patricio." In no. 2, pp. 50-56.

1540.   Upadhyaya, Hari S. "Family Structure Depicted in Bhojpuri Folk-Songs." Folklore 78 (1967): 112-125.

1541.   ----------. "The Joint Family Structure and Familial Relationship Patterns in the Bhojpuri Folksongs." Ph.D. dissertation, Indiana University, 1967.

1542. ----------. "Mother-Daughter Relationship Patterns in the Hindu Joint Family: A Study Based on the Analysis of the Bhojpuri Folksongs of India." Folklore 79 (1968): 217-226.

1543. ----------. "Indian Family Structure and the Bhojpuri Riddles." Folklore 81 (1970): 115-131.

1544. Upadhyaya, K.D. "Society as Depicted in Indian Folk-Narratives." Fabula 9 (1967): 155-161.

1545. ----------. "Interaction among the Affinal Relatives in the Hindu Patrilocal Household as Manifested in the North Indian Folktales." Fabula 11 (1970): 271-274.

1546. Van der Meulen-Nulle, L.W. Lace London: Merlin, 1963.

1547. Van Vuren, Nancy. The Subversion of Women as Practiced by Churches, Witch-Hunters, and Other Sexists. Philadelphia: Westminster Press, 1973.

1548. Vatuk, Ved Prakash. "Craving for a Child in the Folksongs of East Indians in British Guiana." Journal of the Folklore Institute 2 (1965): 55-77.

1549. Vaughter, Reesa M. "Review Essay: Psychology." Signs: Journal Of Women in Culture and Society 2 (1976): 120-146.

1550. Vázsonyi, Andrew. "The Cicisbeo and the Magnificent Cuckold: Boardinghouse Life and Lore in Immigrant Communities." Journal of American Folklore 91 (1978): 641-656.

1551. Venkatasvami, M.N. "Two Hindu Singing Games." Folk-Lore 20 (1909): 337-340.

1552. Vequad, Yves. The Women Painters of Mithila. London: Thames and Hudson, 1976.

1553. Vicinus, Martha, ed. Suffer and Be Still: Women in the Victorian Age. Bloomington: Indiana University Press, 1972.

1554. Virtanen, Leea. "Boys and Girls in a Game-Starting Situation." Studia Fennica 18 (1974): 139-167.

1555. Vlach, John M., "Quilting." In The Afro-American Tradition in Decorative Arts, pp. 45-75. Cleveland: Cleveland Museum of Art, 1978.

1556. Voegelin, C.F. The Shawnee Female Deity. Yale University Publications in Anthropology, No. 10. New Haven: Yale University Press, 1936.

1557.   Voegelin, Erminie W. "Puberty Rites." In. no. 957, p. 909.

1558.   von Franz, Marie-Louise. Problems of the Feminine in Fairytales. New York: Spring Publications, 1972.

1559.   Vukanovic, T.P. "Monogamic Wives of Orthodox Priests." Folklore 70 (1959): 394-397.

1560.   Wachs, Eleanor. "Query [on narratives concerning mugging of women]." Folklore Women's Communication 26 (1982): 10.

1561.   Wadley, Susan S. "Hindu Women's Family and Household Rites in a North Indian Village." In no. 494, pp. 94-109.

1562.   Waelti-Walters, Jennifer. "On Princesses: Fairy Tales, Sex Roles and Loss of Self." International Journal of Women's Studies 2 (1979): 180-188.

1563.   Wagner, Sally Roesh. "Oral History as a Biographical Tool." Frontiers 2, no. 2 (1977): 87-92.

1564.   Walker, Alice. "In Search of Our Mothers' Gardens." Southern Exposure 4, no. 4 (1977): 60-64.

1565.   Walker, Arda Susan. "The Life and Status of a Genera-tion of French Women, 1150-1200." Ph.D. dissertation, University of North Carolina, 1958.

1566.   Walker, Roslyn A. African Women / African Art. New York: African-American Institute, 1975.

1567.   Walle, Alf H. "Getting Picked Up wtihout Being Put Down: Jokes and the Bar Rush." Journal of the Folklore Institute 13 (1976): 201-217.

1568.   Wallin, Paul. Cultural Contradictions and Sex Roles: A Repeat Study." American Sociological Review 15 (1950): 288-293.

1569.   Walter, Tanis, and Black, Edie. "Hunters and Gather-ers." The Second Wave Winter, 1974: 14-16.

1570.   Warner, Marina. Alone of All Her Sex: The Myth and the Cult of the Virgin Mary. New York: Knopf, 1976.

1571.   ----------. Joan of Arc: The Image of Female Hero-ism, New York: Knopf, 1981.

1572.   Warnick, Florence. "Play-Party Songs in Western Maryland." Journal of American Folklore 54 (1941): 162-166.

1573.   Washington, Ida H., and Tobol, Carol E. Washington. "Kriemhild and Clytemnestra--Sisters in Crime or Independent

Women." In no. 226, pp. 15-21.

1574.   Waters, Ethel, and Samuels, Charles. His Eye Is on the Sparow. New York: Doubleday, 1951.

1575.   Watson, Simone. The Cult of Our Lady of Guadalupe: A Historical Study. Collegeville, Minn.: Liturgical Press, 1964.

1576.   Wax, Rosalie. Doing Fieldwork: Warnings and Advice. Chicago: University of Chicago Press, 1971.

1577.   Weatherford, Elizabeth. "Women's Traditional Architecture." Heresies 2 (1977): 35-39.

1578.   ----------. "Bibliography [of Women's Traditional Arts]." Heresies 4 (1978): 124-125.

1579.   Webster, Sheila K. "Women, Sex, and Marriage in Moroccan Proverbs." International Journal of Middle Eastern Studies 14 (1982): 173-184.

1580.   Weibel, Kathryn. Mirror Mirror: Images of Women Reflected in Popular Culture. Garden City: Anchor, 1977.

1581.   Weideger, Paula. Menstruation and Menopause: The Physiology and Psychology, the Myth and the Reality. New York: Knopf, 1976.

1582.   Weidlich, Lorre M. "Booknotes." Folklore Feminists Communication 3 (1974): 6-7.

1583.   ----------. "'...To See Who had the Longest, Uh, Organ': Hedging One's Way through the Dirty Joke." Folklore Annual 6 (1974): 46-57.

1584.   ----------. "Query [on the public image of a female performer]." Folklore Feminists Communication 8 (1976): 6-7.

1585.   Weidlich, Lorre M., and Roach, Susan. "A New Look at an Old American Tradition--Quilting." Folklore Feminists Communication 3 (1974): 5

1586.   Weigle, Marta. Brothers of Light, Brothers of Blood: Penitentes of the Southwest. Albuquerque: University of New Mexico Press, 1976.

1587.   ----------. "Ghostly Flagellants and Doña Sebastiana: Two Legends of the Penitente Brotherhood." Western Folklore 36 (1977): 135-147.

1588.   ----------. Review of Women and Folklore, ed. Claire R. Farrer. Signs: Journal of Women in Culture and Society 2 (1977): 911-913.

1589. ----------. "Athena (Minerva)." Folklore Women's Communication 16 (1978): inside cover, 25.

1590. ----------. "The 'Curse' and Its Cessation." Folklore Women's Communication 14 (1978): 15-16.

1591. ----------. "Doña Sebastiana in Her Cart." Folklore Women's Communication 15 (1978): inside cover.

1592. ----------. "Hathor Head." Folklore Women's Communication 16 (1978): 25.

1593. ,----------. "Matters Jungian (Jungienne?)." Folklore Women's Communication 14 (1978): 17-20.

1594. ----------. "Nuestra Señora de los Dolores, Our Lady of Sorrows." Folklore Women's Communication 15 (1978): 25.

1595. ----------. "Prostitution May Promote and Preserve Verbal Art." Folklore Women's Communication 15 (1978): 18-19.

1596. ----------. "Salons and Saloons." Folklore Women's Communication 16 (1978): 21-24.

1597. ----------. "Some on Song." Folklore Women's Communication 14 (1978): 16-17.

1598. ----------. "Women as Verbal Artists: Reclaiming the Daughters of Enheduanna." Frontiers 3, no. 3 (1978): 1-9.

1599. ----------. "Girls' Verbal Dueling: Where? When? Whether?" Folklore Women's Communication 18 (1978): 13.

1600. ----------. "Navaho Women on Horseback." Folklore Women's Communication 17 (1979): inside cover.

1601. ----------. "Of Man-to-Man and *Woman-to-Woman Talks." Folklore Women's Communication 17 (1979): 18-19.

1602. ----------. "On Gender and Communication." Folklore Women's Communication 17 (1979): 20.

1603. ----------. "Stela Depicting Goddess and Woman Worshipper." Folklore Women's Communication 19 (1979): inside front cover.

1604. ----------. "Stray Stories." Folklore Women's Communication 17 (1979): 21-22.

1605. ----------. "A Stray Story." Folklore Women's Communication 18 (1979): 14.

1606. ----------. "Tara whakairo: A Tad Private Tattoo." Folklore Women's Communication 17 (1979): 25.

1607. ----------. Spiders and Spinsters: Women and Myth-ology. Albuquerque: University of New Mexico Press, 1982.

1608. Weiner, Annette B. Women of Value, Men of Renown: New Perspectives in Trobriand Exchange. Austin: University of Texas Press, 1976.

1609. Weiner, Nella Fermi. "Lilith: First Woman, First Feminist." International Journal of Women's Studies 2 (1980): 551-559.

1610. Weinstein, Sharon. "Don't Women Have a Sense of Comedy Thay Can Call Their Own?" American Humaor 1, no. 2 (1974): 9-12.

1611. Weisel, George F. "A Flathead Indian Tale." Journal of American Folklore 65 (1952): 359-360.

1612. Weisstein, Naomi. Laugh? I Nearly Died. Pitts-burgh: Know Inc., n.d.

1613. ----------. "Why We Aren't Laughing...Anymore." Ms. November, 1973: 49-51, 88-90.

1614. Weist, Katherine M., ed. The Narrative of a North-ern Cheyenne Woman, Belle Hiwalking. Billings: Montana Council for Indian Education, 1979.

1615. West, John O. "The Weeping Woman: La Llorona." In no. 2, pp. 30-36.

1616. Westermarck, Edward. Marriage Ceremonies in Moroc-co. London: Macmillan, 1914.

1617. Westkott, Marcia. "Dialectics of Fantasy." Fron-tiers 2, no. 3 (1977): 1-7.

1618. White, John I. "'Great Grandma.'" Western Folklore 27 (1968): 27-31.

1619. White, Margaret. Quilts and Counterpanes in the Newark Museum. Newark, N.J.: The Newark Museum, 1948.

1620. Whitehouse, Jeanne. "Of Dusun Women Entertaining." Frontiers 3, no. 3 (1978): 28-30.

1621. Whitten, Jeanne Patten. Fannie Hardy Eckstorm: A Descriptive Bibliography of Her Writings, Published and Unpublished. Northeast Folklore, No. 16. Orono, Me.: Northeast Folklore Society, 1976.

1622. Whyte, Betsy. The Yellow on the Broom. Edinburgh: Chambers, 1979.

1623. Wiggins, Gene. "The Socio-Political Works of Fiddlin' John and Moonshine Kate." Southern Folklore Quarterly 41 (1977): 97-118.

1624. Wigginton, Eliot, ed. The Foxfire Book. Garden City: Anchor Press/Doubleday, 1972.

1625. ----------. Foxfire 2. Garden City: Anchor Press/ Doubleday, 1973.

1626. ----------. Foxfire 3. Garden City: Anchor Press/ Doubleday, 1975.

1627. ----------. Foxfire 4. Garden City: Anchor Press/ Doubleday, 1977.

1628. ----------. Foxfire 5. Garden City: Anchor Press/ Doubleday, 1979.

1629. Wilcox, R. Turner. Folk and Festival Costume of the World. New York: Scribner, 1965.

1630. Wilgus, D.K. "Country-Western Music and the Urban Hillbilly." Journal of American Folklore 83 (1970): 157-179.

1631. Wilks, Carl S. "Cultural Transmission of Exotic Health Practices." Ph.D. dissertation, St. Louis University, 1974.

1632. Williams, Drid. "The Brides of Christ." In no. 64, pp. 105-125.

1633. Williams, Juanita H. Psychology of Women: Behavior in a Biosocial Context. New York: W.W. Norton, 1977.

1634. Williams, Phyllis H. South Italian Folkways in Europe and America: A Handbook for Social Workers, Visiting Nurses, School Teachers and Physicians. New Haven: Yale University Press for the Institute of Human Relations, 1938.

1635. Williamson, Jane, ed. New Feminist Scholarship: A Guide to Bibliographies. Old Westbury, N.Y.: Feminist Press, 1979.

1636. Wilson, Mrs. Davies. "Superstitions Concerning Death-Signs." Journal of American Folklore 2 (1889): 72-73.

1637. Wilson, G. Alick. "'Shelta,' The Tinkers' Talk." Journal of American Folklore 3 (1890): 157-159.

1638. Wiltse, Henry M. "In the Field of Southern Folklore." Journal of American Folklore 14 (1901): 205-208.

1639.   Winslow, David J. "Occupational Superstitions of Negro Prostitutes in an Upstate New York City." New York Folklore Quarterly 24 (1968): 294-301.

1640.   Wisbey, Herbert A. "Jemima Wilkinson: Historical Figure and Folk Character." New York Folklore Quarterly 20 (1964): 4-13.

1641.   Wolf, Eric R. "The Virgin of Guadalupe: A Mexican National Symbol." Journal of American Folklore 71 (1958): 34-39.

1642.   Wolf, John Quincy. "Aunt Caroline Dye: The Gypsy in the 'St. Louis Blues.'" Southern Folklore Quarterly 33 (1969): 339-346.

1643.   Wolf, Margery. Women and the Family in Rural Taiwan. Stanford: Stanford University Press, 1972.

1644.   Wolf, Margery, and Witke, Roxane, eds. Women in Chinese Society. Stanford: Stanford University Press, 1975.

1645.   Wood, Ann Douglas. "'The Fashionable Diseases': Women's Complaints and Their Treatment in Nineteenth Century America." Journal of Interdisciplinary History 3 (1973): 25-52.

1646.   Wood, Edward J. The Wedding Day in All Ages and Countries. New York: Harper and Bros., 1869.

1647.   Wood, Juliette. "The Calumniated Wife: Two Examples of the Foreign Wife in Medieval Welsh Narrative." Folklore Women's Communication 22 (1980): 10-14.

1648.   Wood, Sharon, Emmons, Zette, and Moser, Erika. "Women's Art in Village India." Heresies 4 (1978): 103-107.

1649.   Wooster, Ann-Sargent. Quiltmaking: The Modern Approach to a Traditional Craft. New York: Drake, 1972.

1650.   Wright, A.R. Obituary for Adela Monica Goodrich-Freer Spoer. Folk-Lore 41 (1930): 299-301.

1651.   ----------. Obituary for Eliza Gultch. Folk-Lore 41 (1930): 301.

1652.   Yates, Sybil. "An Investigation of the Psychological Factors in Virginity and Ritual Defloration." International Journal of Psychoanalysis 11 (1930): 167-184.

1653.   Yerkovich, Sally. "Gossiping; or, The Creation of Fictional Lives, Being a Study of the Subject in an Urban American Setting Drawing Upon Vignettes from Upper Middle Class Lives." Ph.D. dissertation, University of Pennsylvania, 1976.

1654.   Yocom, Margaret R. "Women's Oral History." Folklore Feminists Communication 5 (1975): 11.

1655.   ----------. "Woman to Woman: Fieldwork and the Private Sphere." In no. 835.

1656.   Yost, Mrs. Harry. "Quilt Story." Hobbies October, 1953: 43, 60-61.

1657.   Young, Alan R. "Elizabeth Lowys: Witch and Social Victim." History Today December, 1972: 833-842.

1658.   Young, Frank W., and Bacdayan, Albert A. "Menstrual Taboos and Social Rigidity." In Cross-Cultural Approaches: Readings in Comparative Research, ed. Clellan S. Ford, pp. 95-110. New Haven: HRAF Press, 1967.

1659.   Yung, Judy. "'A Bowlful of Tears': Chinese Women Immigrants on Angel Island." Frontiers 2, no. 2 (1977): 52-55.

1660.   Zahler, Leah. "Matriarchy and Myth." Aphra 4, no. 3 (1973): 25-32.

1661.   Zeitlin, Steven, Gross, Sandra, and Cutting-Baker, Holly. "I'd Like to Think They Were Pirates": Stories and Photographs Collected by the Family Folklore Program of the Festival of American Folklife. Washington: Smithsonian Institution and National Park Service, 1975.

1662.   Zelman, Elizabeth Crouch. "Reproduction, Ritual, and Power." American Ethnologist 4 (1977): 714-733.

1663.   Zumwalt, Rosemary. "Plain and Fancy: A Content Analysis of Children's Jokes Dealing with Adult Sexuality." Western Folklore 35 (1976): 258-267.

1664.   Zuntz, Gunther. Persephone: Three Essays on Religion in Magna Graecia. Oxford: Clarendon, 1971.

INDEX

Numbers refer to bibliographic entries except when preceded by p. or pp., which indicate pages in the Essay Guide.

About the Compiler

FRANCIS A. de CARO is Associate Professor of English at Louisiana State University. His earlier books include *American Proverb Literature: A Bibliography* and *Louisiana Traditional Crafts*. He is the author of articles published in *Western Folklore* and *Journal of Popular Culture*.